THE
BANK OF
LIFE

DR. KATJA KRUCKEBERG

THE BANK OF LIFE

A STORY ABOUT THE QUEST FOR HEALTH, LOVE, AND MEANING

Global Leadership Press

Published by Global Leadership Press
London, UK

Distributed by River Grove Books

Design and composition by Greenleaf Book Group, Austin, TX, USA
Cover design by Greenleaf Book Group and Anna Jordan
Cover images used under license from
©Shutterstock.com/letovsegda

Image Credits: Figure 9.1 Icons © O R I M A T, P Thanga Vignesh, Adrien Coquet, ifki, Softscape; Figure 15.1 Icons © Wilson Joseph, RamStu

Publisher's Cataloging-in-Publication data is available.

Print ISBN: 979-8-9875020-0-6

eBook ISBN: 979-8-9875020-1-3

*

For my children

Jolanda and Julien

Love is why we are here.

Every moment is a fresh beginning.

—T.S. Eliot

Author's Note

As this book is mostly a work of fiction and not a classic non-fiction book, it did not seem feasible to cite all the scientific resources that inspired and influenced the writing of *The Bank of Life* in the book itself without disturbing the flow of the reading experience too much. Please find the name of the authors of the books, articles, podcasts, quotes, poems, and other sources consulted during the writing process listed in an alphabetical order in the bibliography at the end of the book. I hope I haven't forgotten to mention anybody or any source that I was inspired by during the writing process! This inspiration was invaluable, and I owe everybody out there a huge thank you indeed. Names, characters, businesses, organizations, places, events, and incidents are either the product of the author's imagination or are used fictitiously.

Contents

✳

CHAPTER 1

Sophia: A Brief Encounter

Chronology: Leonardo and Sophia meet at
San Francisco Airport for the first time.

Would looking back help her to know where she wanted to go? Or did she just have to move forward in order to reach her destination? Sophia tried to tie the many loose strands of her dark brown hair back into the bun at the back of her head, when she caught her reflection in a mirror not far from her. She glanced away quickly. If she had taken a closer look, she would have seen a young woman with a fine-boned face, inquisitive green eyes, a bit of smudged mascara on her cheekbone, and an almost bowlike mouth covered with red lipstick.

But Sophia didn't take a closer look. Instead, she walked a few steps ahead and then stopped again. She felt stuck. After one week in San Francisco, she was in a hurry to catch her flight back to Berlin. Still jet-lagged, her exhaustion was clouding her mind. She stared at the details on the airport departure board without fully taking the information in. *Sydney final call, Buenos Aires boarding, Hong Kong boarding, Amsterdam final call.*

If she did not get her act together quickly, she would miss her flight. She turned around abruptly when she heard a voice. Was there somebody calling her name?

"May I help you, . . . Sophia?"

Surprised, Sophia spotted an old man standing a short distance next to her. Well dressed and wearing a smart beard, he resembled somebody she had seen before.

"Excuse me?"

The man smiled in a charismatic, unimposing way.

"You appeared lost, and I thought I might be of help," said the old man.

"That is very kind," said Sophia with a slight German accent. "I need to catch my flight to Berlin—but I cannot seem to find the gate. I cannot seem to find anything, really." She sighed, smiling apologetically.

"Are you sure this is where you want to go?" asked the old man.

Sophia was too tired to acknowledge the awkwardness of the scene but started reflecting on his question. Was she? She thought about the situation she had left behind in Berlin almost a week ago, but then she came to her senses.

"Yes! My plane leaves in fifty minutes."

She glanced at the old man, who now seemed older than before. His right hand on his chest, he was seemingly gasping for breath.

"Are you okay?"

"Yes. Yes. Listen, you need to go through security over there. Your gate is a hundred meters on the left, right after customs. The airport isn't too busy, which is unusual, and you should catch your flight just in time!"

Sophia felt instantly relieved.

"Thank you so much! That is very kind. I'm sorry . . ."

"You don't have to apologize."

The old man looked at her intensely. He opened his mouth as if he wanted to add something, but then a few seconds passed before he said in a firm voice, "Sophia, I have a letter for you. I know this must sound odd. I have listened to your speech today, but we have never met before, and you don't even know who I am. This letter is also about a book. An important one."

He paused, waiting to see if she would react, and then went on.

"I made a huge mistake and then I left it for too long. Now it is almost too late."

The old man stopped talking and looked exhausted. Sophia noticed how much he had struggled to find the right words. And to her, they had not made a lot of sense either way. She liked him, but she felt slightly uncomfortable at the same time. The old man, who seemed to discern her discomfort, tried to straighten up and smiled at her warmly.

"I know this doesn't sound plausible . . . yet. But if you read the letter, everything will become much clearer."

Sophia didn't know what to say. Time was pressing on, and she had to catch her flight. Would she be an idiot to accept a letter from somebody she didn't even know? At an airport of all places! But then similar things had happened to her before. After giving a speech at a huge event, like she had done at the leadership convention today, she was regularly approached at the airport by people who had been in the audience too, flying home like her, who wanted to compliment her on her performance or tell her how something she had said had moved them. She was not a famous person, not at all, but at these kinds of events she was recognized by people she did not know herself. That came with the territory of being an author and a keynote speaker.

Sophia studied the old man's wrinkly face, which was reminiscent of the figures of classical Greece, with a pair of well-defined cheekbones, full lips, and a strong nose marred by a slight bump that gave it a masculine appeal. He must have been very handsome once, Sophia thought, and she noticed how genuinely kind he appeared. As a coach and psychologist, she was trained to assess people within seconds. And she was sure that this old man was a good person—she could sense it.

"I had intended to give the letter to you at the conference. But after your speech I was told by your Norwegian colleague that you were already on your way to the airport. She offered to call you, but you did not pick up the phone. And I decided to take a small risk and see if I could find you at the Lufthansa gate. And my driver was kind enough to take me here."

He offered the envelope to her in his right hand. "The letter will explain everything! And you won't regret reading it. That, I promise."

For a moment Sophia did not move. She had to catch her plane. But then, almost unconsciously, she stretched her arm forward and took the letter from his hand.

"Follow your heart." The old man smiled enigmatically. "And catch your plane if you must."

With the letter in her hand, Sophia started backing away.

"What is your name?" she asked.

"Leonardo. John Leonardo!"

"My name is Sophia."

"I know!" He smiled again and then added, "Sophia, make the most of your time on this planet. Goodbye. Safe travels. And thank you so very much!"

Her exhaustion forgotten, Sophia started hurrying toward customs.

Around three quarters of an hour later, sitting comfortably in her seat on the plane, she took the envelope from her handbag and began reading the letter that would, slowly but surely, change the course of her entire life.

CHAPTER 2

Leonardo: Against All Odds

All we have to decide is what to do with the time that is given us.

—J.R.R. Tolkien

Dear Sophia,

The idea that you will soon be holding this letter in your hand fills me with a kind of hope and energy that I have not felt since the day my wife Barbara died in a tragic accident more than one year ago. Deep in my heart, I am convinced that reading and taking care of this letter, and the ones to follow, will influence your life in a positive way. I know it sounds presumptuous, but these letters might impact your thoughts, your emotions, and the decisions you will take. And they might even influence who you will spend time with and who you will start or stop seeing in the future. And there is a boyish joy inside of me thinking about one person in particular. For some reason, I believe that the two of you will get along very well. But more about that later!

If all goes well, if my writing is good enough to inspire your curiosity, my biggest hope is that it will not stop with you. In my imagination I see you presenting this message to a wider audience so that many people will benefit from it. However, I don't want to put too much pressure on your shoulders. If only one person will spend their limited time on this planet in a better way, and if this person is you, Sophia, I am content. But if many more people can benefit from the two of us engaging in this project, it'll be a dream come true.

I wonder how you are feeling, reading these bold statements of mine. Maybe you are already sitting on the plane to Berlin, flying over the Atlantic Ocean with some big questions of your own in your mind. How would I perceive this situation if I were in your position? Let me guess. On the one hand, I would be intrigued: What does all this mean? Is this real? Is this nonsense, or is there something more meaningful behind it? On the other hand, I would most likely also be thinking: Who does this old stranger think he is, showing up in my life like this, claiming to be an influential force in the months to come!?

It might even feel spooky holding this letter in your hand, not knowing the person who has written it. My sincere apologies if this is the case. There was no better way I could think of to approach you.

Now, to reduce the awkwardness of the situation, let me introduce myself. I am Leonardo. John Leonardo, to be more precise. I am a half-Italian, half-German American banker originally from New York, who has spent a lifetime accompanying his wife on a quest around the world to find the secret recipe on how to lead a healthy, fulfilling, and meaningful life. I know this sounds like an outrageous endeavor, but I will tell you more about it in the letters to come—for now I hope this is sufficient.

Unfortunately, I am literally running out of time. The clock is ticking on a mountain of debt—emotional debt, I must add—and my body is starting to give in. My wife is dead, and I am now reaching out to the one person who I believe can help me complete her life mission, as I might have neither the energy nor the time to do so on my own. Against all odds, I am hoping this person is you, Sophia.

I have been thinking a lot about how best to write what needs to be written. Many ways lead to Rome, after all. Isn't this a German saying? Or as one of the monks, who Barbara and I met during our travels through Asia, said, "There are hundreds of paths up the mountain, but the view from the top is always the same." So, let me try to put all of this into perspective by giving you some more background information.

When the fire happened that took my wife's life away, and with it our treasured Japanese teahouse and the book that she had spent decades researching, I was full of despair. An overwhelming sense of both grief and sorrow swept me off my feet, and I felt like I was literally losing my mind. And while I knew that my wife Barbara would not have liked me to sit on the couch and cry my eyes out forever, I completely shut down and disconnected from the world around me. I lost all trust in life and myself. I became fearful, paralyzed, confused, you name it—and even chronically ill. Whatever Barbara would have wanted me to do or not, I was in a state of complete shock. And all in all, it took a year until I started slowly waking up again, physically, mentally, and emotionally. And when I did, I realized how much time I had wasted, and the feeling of guilt immediately made me question my self-worth and threatened to drag me down once again.

However, I knew this couldn't go on. It would only be another demonstration of my ego, the very thing that had caused me to make the wrong decisions and create this situation in the first place. And so, with willpower and discipline, I tried to discover what my final task in this life would be. I went through the options:

1. I couldn't get Barbara's life back, and I suspected that she would have said that it had been her destiny to die this way, anyway.

2. I could find an architect to rebuild the Japanese teahouse that Barbara had adored and cherished so much. But I knew intuitively that this was not what would make the biggest difference and that Barbara wouldn't have wanted this either.

3. I could, however, try to rebuild some of our life's work. I could try to find a way to rewrite Barbara's book or at least craft a new version of it.

The moment this last thought crossed my mind, a sense of certainty emerged that had previously been lost to me when Barbara died. All of a sudden, I knew that this would be what Barbara would have wanted me to do more than anything else. And inspired by this newfound clarity, I wanted to get going immediately. Unfortunately, it was then that I noticed a sharp pain in my chest—a pain that had once been familiar to me in my youth but had been forgotten about since. After going to the hospital, a cardiologist told me that, due to an inherited condition that I had been living with surprisingly well for all those many decades, my life was soon to come to an end. Nothing to be done about it. I could go on some life-prolonging medication, but that was that. Difficult news. Redemption was sailing out of sight again, and I was sure I would die feeling guilty.

Nevertheless, life isn't always what it seems, and when I was almost ready to surrender, destiny struck again. Maybe Barbara was right after all, and things were indeed happening for a reason. When studying the website of the pharmaceutical company that produced the medication I was advised to take, I spotted an advertisement for a leadership conference in San Francisco that was open to the general public. My eyes fell upon a picture of a woman who looked surprisingly familiar, and my doomed, old heart started beating a little bit faster. I quickly went to fetch the old pocket watch that I had stumbled upon a few days prior. I lifted my gaze and put my right hand to my chest. I was sure that Barbara had been directing my attention to this website, and a tear ran down my cheek. And believe me, Sophia, I am not someone who cries easily, never have been.

Needless to say that the woman in the photograph was you. After silently praying for some time, I started doing some research on the internet. I found out that you were an executive coach, consultant, and keynote speaker from Berlin. And again, my heart was pounding in sheer joy. Berlin. I couldn't believe it. I touched the old pocket watch that was lying next to me on the desk and repeated its inscription silently in my head: *Lost time is never found again*. And then I read that you had already published a few books and realized you were an author too. I was feeling so optimistic, so hopeful when I copied your address from your website.

Of course, I could not be sure that you were the person I hoped you were, but I knew in that very instant that you would be the person who could help me complete this project. Whether you would want to participate or not, well . . . that's of course up to you. Barbara sometimes accused me of having the empathy of an elephant. I'm not sure if this was meant as an insult for the elephant or for myself, as I'd always thought elephants to be very intelligent, sensitive creatures.

And now, here we are—you hopefully have my letter in front of you and I cannot postpone this question any longer. I sincerely apologize for the peculiarity of the situation I have created for you, but be that as it may, I ask you with all due respect: Are you able to commit yourself to writing a new version of Barbara's book about the essentials of life, as we referred to it, so that those who read it can spend their time more wisely on this planet?

You don't have to answer right away, of course. Time is on your side, Sophia. You are the only person I am asking. I am going "all in," as the gamblers say, even though, as a banker, I would usually advise spreading the risk fairly. Nonetheless, there are occasions in life when you do have to do the opposite in order to succeed.

Marriage is one such example. I have always put all my faith, my strength, and my patience in one person and one person only. And I never had any regrets. Our marriage was a happy one. And this time I feel it is going to be the same. Though the occasion is a very different one, I choose to believe in you. I choose to believe in circles that need to be closed. In stories that need to be written.

You will have complete creative freedom, with no preordained structure to restrict you. You will be able to define the scope of the outcome according to how you see fit. This book can take any shape or form you wish it to. My goal is to provide you with as much content and inspiration as I can in the remaining time I have. And, in addition, I will offer assistance on how you can get the message out into the world, once the writing itself is completed. The rest is then up to forces beyond ourselves.

And now, before I close this first letter, let me ask you another question: How are you investing and spending your time in this life, Sophia? Think about it. In many ways, time is all we have. It cannot be stopped, rewound, fast-forwarded, no matter what happens or does not happen. If we are thriving or suffering, if we are happy or unhappy, if we are moving ahead or feeling stuck, the big clock is always ticking. Time stands still for no one.

Therefore I am asking you, do you have a time investment strategy that is paying off? Is your ROI satisfactory? Are you creating assets or incurring deficits?

I will be in touch again as soon as I can.

Yours sincerely,
J. Leonardo

PS: Sophia is such a beautiful name! As you probably know, Sophia (Σοφία) means wisdom in ancient Greek. Isn't that another perfect sign for us to join forces on this special project?

CHAPTER 3

Sophia: In Transition

Chronology: one hour after Leonardo and
Sophia's brief encounter at San Francisco Airport.

Sophia put the letter down. Was this really happening? She took a deep breath until she could feel her lungs filling with air. Why on earth would she be the one selected to rewrite a book that had vanished in a fire? She tried to remember what the old man had looked like. Picturing him standing in front of her at the gate, she once again felt relieved that he had not appeared to be a weird person in the least—rather the opposite. In fact, there had been an air of sophistication about him. Despite his old age, he had reminded her of a leader of some sort. A man of substance. And Sophia suspected that he had been successful in his career as a banker. He was dressed in an elegant suit—not a formal one, more like an Irish brown tweed suit. He was well groomed, and when he spoke, she got the impression that he was well educated, though he had not said as much. She wasn't sure how old he was—maybe in his eighties or even nineties? There had been a somewhat timeless quality about him. And he had this kind, intelligent expression on his face which had made him appear trustworthy to her.

Had he not looked so agreeable, she probably wouldn't have kept the letter. She must have trusted him enough to do so, and of course her natural curiosity had also pushed her to overcome the initial feeling of discomfort. Sophia adjusted her long legs under the seat in front of her and tried to remind herself of the actual content of the letter again. So, this polished old man wanted her to rewrite a book that would help people make better decisions on how to spend their time on this planet. That did sound presumptuous, indeed!

And still, reflecting on her current situation in Berlin, a part of herself wanted to believe that it was true and that something truly special was about to happen to her. Even though the unexpected intimacy still made her cringe, just as the old man himself had suspected. Raising her thick eyebrows, which she had disliked so much in her youth but had become surprisingly fashionable these days, she looked at the handwritten pages and checked the envelope again, turning it upside down.

Of course, she had already opened the letter when standing in line for customs. Suddenly feeling unsure about the thin envelope, she had quickly searched through its contents. But there had been nothing else inside apart from the three handwritten pages. And after quickly reading through the first lines, she had been so curious that she decided to keep the letter and not to throw it away as she'd admittedly considered for a brief moment. And when listening to the voicemail message that Annicken, her Norwegian colleague who had introduced her on stage earlier that day, had indeed left her, telling her about the polite interaction with a cute old man who had been looking for her at the convention, Sophia had ultimately felt reassured.

And now, gently swiping her little finger over the upward slope of her slender nose as she always did when thinking deeply about something, her mouth twitched with an almost invisible smile. She shook her head. There was obviously nothing suspicious behind all of this, even though a series of questions emerged that remained yet unanswered: Why would this old man ask her to engage in such a personal project? And anyway, if it was a book about the essentials of life that had to be rewritten, why would he pick her? What did *she* know about a life well lived? Sophia had always been known for her self-deprecating sense of humor, and when still living in London, people there had embraced this quality of hers. But these days, there was a bit too much truth behind her humor that stemmed from the sense of disorientation she had been feeling for the past few months.

She closed her eyes and tried to make herself comfortable in the seat when the pilot interrupted her disconnected thoughts to announce that the plane was now flying at a higher altitude. The cabin lights were turned off so that people would be able to sleep and hopefully feel rested when they would arrive in Amsterdam with the rising sun about nine hours later, where she would take a connecting flight to Berlin. Sophia turned around. As this was a long-haul flight, she had intentionally booked a window seat, though it literally made her feel like a prisoner of the people sitting next to her. If she wanted to go to the restroom or simply walk along the aisle to stretch her legs, she would first have to ask for their permission. But on the other hand, restricting her freedom in that way meant the security of not being disturbed herself during the night. All of life was such a trade-off, Sophia concluded, studying the woman sitting beside her. Bent over a small laptop, she appeared to be working on a long document. Maybe she was editing a book? Perhaps not, but this notion triggered a series of other thoughts within Sophia.

The old man had written that he had accidentally come across her profile on the internet when scrolling through the website of the pharmaceutical company that sold the medication he was put on. But why did he recognize her? She could not figure this one out. Maybe he had been looking for a professional ghostwriter to rewrite this book. And maybe, spinning this thought further, he had wanted somebody with her academic and professional background to do so. A doctorate in organizational psychology, a master's degree in international politics and sports medicine and another master's degree in business administration—an odd combination in itself. And in addition, somebody who was an international consultant like her, with a few books under her belt to boot. However, all of this seemed too far-fetched. She peeked at the letter again. This did not sound like a conventional editorial request, and she was not a ghostwriter. There was truly something mystical about this old man approaching her.

But was this not what she had been hoping for when sitting on the plane crossing the Atlantic Ocean in the opposite direction a week earlier?! Leaving Berlin just a few days ago, taking the flight to Amsterdam and then to San Francisco, she had longed for something to happen. Something that would possibly change the direction of her life. As stupid as it sounded, she had wished for a magic wand that would help her sort out her life and feel more grounded again. Adjusting her legs in the limited space in front of her again, careful not to interrupt her neighbor, Sophia wondered if this opportunity was actually the magic wand she needed. A cute little dimple appeared on her right cheek when she smiled and thought that the old man had borne some resemblance to the schoolmaster in Harry Potter. What was his name again? Dumbledore!

After all, she certainly wouldn't be the first person whose life took a turn after something unexpected happened. Winning the lottery, meeting the love of your life, making a bold move professionally that paid off brilliantly. Sometimes, one event could have ripple effects on all subsequent events. She sighed as she remembered the young man who had desperately tried to catch the plane that later had been highjacked by the terrorists on 9/11. He'd had an important job interview in Washington, D.C., that day. But he had missed the plane by a couple of minutes and had been livid about it. One red light instead of a green one at a traffic light had possibly made all the difference and saved his life. Many others had not been that lucky. Sophia knew there were moments in life that could change everything, for the better or for worse, and she wondered if one could recognize them in real time or only in retrospect.

Looking at the letter again, she started reflecting on Leonardo's final set of questions.

What did her "time investment strategy" look like?

Was her ROI satisfactory?

Was she creating assets or incurring deficits?

Bankers seemed to approach everything in life in such a "functional" way. Her thoughts turned to Ruben, her ex-boyfriend, who was one of them. No, she did not have a time investment strategy, and neither did she calculate her ROI in relation to how she spent her time, and so she wasn't sure whether she was creating assets or incurring deficits in that regard. And yes, she was being defensive, but the bankers' jargon used in these questions didn't really appeal to her.

And still, now that those questions had been asked, they somehow lingered and soon started bothering her. After quickly scanning through her memory of how she had spent the past months of her life since moving to Berlin, she uttered in a low, discontent voice, "No, I'm not happy with the way I am spending my time."

The potential editor-in-chief sitting next to her turned her head. "Excuse me?"

Sophia shrugged. "I'm sorry. I was just talking to myself. Out loud. Embarrassingly enough!"

The woman, who was wearing an elegant cream-colored long-sleeved shirt dress, seemed amused. "I do that too. Mostly when I'm frustrated."

"Really? Never happens to me!" Sophia responded with a smile. They both laughed. And then the woman continued typing one character after the other into her document.

Sophia closed her eyes. She wanted to continue her reflection and try to relax a bit. But soon an unexpectedly harsh movement interrupted her stream of thoughts. Sophia had experienced turbulence in the air before, but this was quite unusual. And she could see the anxiety in people's faces around her, which did not soothe her either. Focusing on her breath, she tried to find a rhythm of breathing deeply into her belly, holding her breath for a brief moment, exhaling very slowly, holding her breath for a few more seconds before deeply breathing in again, thereby forcing her system to calm down. This was a technique that she had learned long ago. Even in moments of crisis, Sophia could usually count on being able to discipline herself.

But still, when the plane finally reached a higher altitude and things smoothed out again, she felt exhausted. Looking down at her knees, she noticed the crumpled letter in her hand. And without thinking much about it, she put it back into her bag and started searching for the sleeping pills a doctor at the conference had given her for her flight back. She hadn't intended to take any of them. But, she decided, if ever there was a good time for a chemically induced break, then it was now. Without being fully aware of it, she put both pills into her mouth and swallowed them dry. Glancing at her watch, she leaned back into her seat. Eight hours still to go until they would arrive in Amsterdam, where she would take the connecting flight to Berlin, and Sophia was determined to spend as much of this time fast asleep, not thinking about Ruben, the letter, or anything else.

Fortunately, she did not have to wait long for the sleeping pills to take effect as she slipped into a deep slumber. What a blessing.

CHAPTER 4

Sophia: Blue Sky over Berlin

Chronology: six weeks and two days after Leonardo and Sophia's brief encounter at San Francisco Airport.

The sun was shining brightly the day Sophia finally heard from Leonardo again—a blue sky over Berlin after many weeks of rain. She had slept better than she had in weeks, and her mood was in sync with the change in weather too. After feeling so depleted for so long, she actually looked forward to the day ahead of her. Her plan was to have breakfast in a spacious café in Berlin-Mitte, with the River Spree passing by. It was her day off: no emails, no commitments, no clients for twenty-four hours. Wonderful.

On her way out to the street, Sophia noticed the mailbox on her front door. She had not opened it for several days out of frustration that she had not heard from Leonardo again. But now, on her day off, she could not resist the temptation. Yet, the moment she turned the key in the lock of the mailbox, she regretted it. A stream of invoices and some ads tumbled out—business as usual. It always made her feel down to see this kind of correspondence in her mailbox that only seemed to exist to suck the life out of her. Determinedly she pushed the mail back in, when she suddenly spotted an envelope, and then another, that were different from the rest. There was her name and address handwritten on both of them. One had arrived a few days earlier, one that very day. Sophia felt a shiver of excitement running down her spine. Was this possible?

Since coming back from San Francisco, a lot had happened in Sophia's life. A lot and absolutely nothing, to be more precise. As a consequence of reading Leonardo's first letter, she had made a firm decision to finally let go of Ruben. Reflecting deeply about the pattern of this ill-fated relationship had convinced her that it was about time! They had split up before. A few months ago, it had been the third time that Ruben had applied the same successful strategy with her: instead of apologizing for hurting her deeply, he had turned things around on Sophia, accusing her of pushing him away with her destructive behavior. "Attack is the best defense" seemed to be his motto. Back then, she had to overcome the instinct to hold on to him, no matter what. And since moving to Berlin a month later, she had at least succeeded in not contacting him. But as a matter of fact, she had still followed him on the internet like an addict in disguise and had hoped to hear from him all along.

Nonetheless, after reading Leonardo's letter multiple times, she had decided that this had to stop. She had to make better use of her time and energy. That was obvious. And in the first weeks after coming back from San Francisco, she was acting on her intention, which she had been very proud of. But as time went by and there were no other messages from Leonardo, the uplifting effect of the journey to San Francisco had evaporated. And Sophia realized that she had chosen to believe that the letter from the old man would indeed represent a turning point in her life. Often it took hundreds of impulses for people to move on after a relationship ends, and she had wanted to believe that the brief encounter with the old man had been the final tipping point that would allow her to start anew. After all, she had a lot going for herself, and she wanted to consciously make better decisions to get the rest of her life back into a more attractive shape, including herself. And the first step in this process was to move on. Alone.

But then one week had passed by without any sign of Leonardo, then another one, and then another. No letter, no email, no smoke signals, no nothing from the sophisticated old man, and Sophia had started asking herself whether she would ever hear from him again. She had not found him on the internet yet, and Leonardo had mentioned in his first letter that he had not much time left. Maybe he had already passed away. What a tragedy—a hero coming to her rescue had died on her at the very beginning of the process. She had felt sorry for the hero, but also for herself. And with the ridiculous amount of rain that had been pouring down on Berlin since meeting Leonardo in San Francisco, Sophia's willpower had been gradually washed away in the process.

And when one evening Ruben, who was visiting the German capital on a business trip, turned up on her doorstep unexpectedly, she did not have the motivation to turn him away. After spending one night with him, she had felt like a fool who had fallen into the same trap again. Instead of forgiving herself for this one mistake, the rest of her newly established sense of self somehow collapsed too. She was glad that at least her clients could not see how miserable she was. Who needed a coach who couldn't get their own act together?

And now this! She examined the two letters in her hand in disbelief and was unsure what to do. She hesitantly sat down on the stairs but quickly got up again. She opened the door to her apartment and went inside. In a rush, she searched for her new city guide, closed and locked the door again, and hurried down the stairs and out onto the pavement of the spacious street, looking up into the blue sky over Berlin.

Just like on the day when she met Leonardo for the first time, she started hurrying as if she had to catch a plane. Her strides were long and enthusiastic, and when she arrived at the café, she was not surprised that a window seat was still available for her. How could it not be on such a brilliant day? She quickly ordered breakfast and waited until the croissants, the marmalade, the butter, the cheese, and the scrambled eggs were neatly put on the table in front of her. She did not want to be interrupted later.

When her cappuccino had been served, she took a delicious sip and started reading.

CHAPTER 5

Leonardo: The Big Five

The essentials don't change.

—Adapted from Samuel Beckett

Dear Sophia,

My sincere apologies for making you wait so long for this second letter to arrive. Shortly after waving goodbye to you at the airport, I was taken to the hospital in San Francisco. A security officer had called the ambulance, which I had strongly objected to. But a stabbing pain in my chest, a shortness of breath, and an accompanying dizziness had prevented me from running away, which was a good thing after all. Without the immediate medical care offered at the hospital in San Francisco, I would probably not be in the position to write this second letter to you at all. Even days after the incident, my life was still on the line. But as peculiar as it might sound, Sophia, the prospect of dying didn't frighten me too much. I genuinely cannot wait to be reunited with my wife, however that might be—as unconscious molecules flying through the universe, perhaps, or, if my Buddhist friend was right, in the form of everlasting love.

However, what did seriously worry me instead was the thought of the book project and the possibility that I might not live long enough to see it through. You might suspect that I am overstating the importance of the messages that I want to share, and that might be true. Still, if writing this book would help you to make better decisions on how to invest your time more wisely on this planet, then it would be a valuable pursuit. And if the two of us would succeed in publishing a book that would encourage even more people to accomplish the same, then this is a mission worth fighting for. Wouldn't you agree, Sophia?

Unfortunately, my stay in the hospital was not the only reason for my radio silence. Something else, and almost equally profound, contributed to the delay. Seeing you at the airport had nurtured my hope that you would commit yourself to this project. And even when I was physically at my lowest point, lying in that unfamiliar hospital room, I was mentally still thriving on this optimistic energy. But this changed when returning to our house in Santa Barbara. Whenever I tried to write my next letter to you, I felt incompetent, lost, and confused. For the first time in many weeks, it crossed my mind again that I simply might not have the talent to do what I was striving to accomplish.

Every time I attempted to write something, my mind focused on my lack of *competence*. How on earth should I approach this project? Where should I start? I am not exaggerating when I tell you that I went through another period of utter hopelessness. Sitting again and again in front of another blank page, writing a few sentences, crossing them out, crumpling the paper impatiently, becoming the best friend of my paper bin and an enemy to myself.

And thinking of you and your bright green eyes somehow increased the sense of pressure on me. Leaving you stranded out there without another sign from me, after what must have been one of the strangest encounters of your life, just didn't feel right. I knew my negative thoughts were undermining my possibility for success, and I noticed how I was walling myself in, but I could not stop this downward spiral either.

Despite my best intentions, I had no idea how to extract the meaning out of Barbara's work, how to put her thoughts into simple words without losing the depth of the message I wanted to convey, how to find a structure where there was none. Disentangling our life from our life message was proving to be impossible. I want you to do the work that needs to be done with your own inspiration, but you also need some direction, some sort of clarity to succeed. If a total stranger has the nerve to ask you to engage yourself in a project of such scope, you should at least expect this person to first tell you what the original version of the book was all about. Isn't that true?

As a starting point, it might be helpful to know that for a long time the "book about the essentials of life" served as a working title for a project that constantly changed and emerged over the decades. For many years it was simply a name for a collection of insights gathered over a lifetime that Barbara, and later myself, made use of in our own very different ways to advise and coach people to live better lives. At the beginning, no concrete plans for a book were even specified, but there was a flexible structure to our thinking and a few overarching ideas to organize our thoughts. After decades of exploration, traveling across five continents, always trying to distill the secret recipe of living a healthy, fulfilling, and meaningful life, we began to come to the conclusion that there were five specific areas that human beings had to take care of to create a good existence for themselves—namely their physiology, their psychology, their work, their relationships, and their finances. We spoke about them as the Big Five. The more capable people became in nurturing those five areas of their life skillfully, the higher the chance that they would thrive and succeed in building a *good life* for themselves.

Building on these assumptions, we gradually channeled our attention accordingly. Over decades, we searched for wisdom that would encourage and educate people how to best look after these five areas of their life. We traveled around the world, studied different cultures, had encounters with people whose presence and ideas enriched us beyond measure. Our analog and later our digital database contained an enormous number of anecdotes, facts, and figures, not only from around the world but also from different stages of human history. Thousands of handwritten pages, pictures, graphs, audiotapes, and videotapes. Electronic files saved on different laptops once they had been invented. All of this research formed the basis for the book that Barbara was still in the process of writing in the last months of her life. For her it was like working on a huge, oversized puzzle, and her aspiration for the book was for it to be so scientifically sharp and emotionally compelling that it would not only educate people, but also make them enact their good intentions.

Nonetheless, when I came back from the hospital in San Francisco, eventually sitting down on my desk to write this second letter to you, I suddenly realized that I had no idea how to replicate any of this. The research for the book about the essentials of life was gone. All of it. Of course, I had known this before, but at that moment it hit me on a deeper level. All the thousands of handwritten pages that we had collected and filed over the decades, all the video and audiotapes, photographs, pictures, everything, even the electronic part of our database, which we had not been technologically savvy enough to save in the cloud, had melted away in the burning flames, evaporated into thin air.

So, was there still hope? For weeks I doubted it. I had come home with the very best intentions to make up for my wrongdoing. I had been determined to meticulously take my prescribed medication, to eat and sleep well, to prolong my life as much as possible, to be as disciplined and focused as necessary, to write what needed to be written. But when I again questioned if I had the competence to get anything meaningful on paper and when I started believing that discipline was not enough to retrieve what had been lost, I temporarily reverted back to inaction.

But then one evening, rooting aimlessly around in our bedroom, flipping through the drawer of Barbara's bedside cabinet, I picked up a book, which my wife must have read in the weeks before the accident. The book, *Mindset: The New Psychology of Success* written by Carol Dweck, a well-known psychologist, described how she had set out to investigate why people fail or succeed in life. In one of her experiments, children had been given a series of difficult puzzles to solve. Much to Carol's surprise, some kids had seemed genuinely excited about the process of figuring it out, even when they were

failing in solving the puzzle. This attitude illustrated what Carol later went on to coin as a growth mindset—the belief that abilities, competencies, and even intelligence could be developed through putting in time and effort. On the flipside, I had come to believe that I didn't have the necessary competencies to do what I wanted to do, and I certainly didn't find any joy in figuring it out. This was described as a fixed mindset.

Of course, this was an interesting insight, indeed. But how could developing a growth mindset, believing that I could learn the competence to write well enough by investing time and effort, help me in my current situation when neither of these resources were on my side? Time was clearly running out, and my doctor had encouraged me to take it easy. Doing some additional research on the internet, I soon came across Andrew Huberman, a leading neuroscientist who explained the neurochemical advantage that people were thriving on when succeeding in adopting a growth mindset in relation to any given task. Here is how I understood the matter:

Having a growth mindset basically means that we are rewarding ourselves for small steps in the process instead of attaching our inner sense of reward to achieving a bigger outcome somewhere in the future. And when this is the case, little pulses of dopamine are being released in our brain that make us feel motivated and excited, and we can move forward without the depletion that it would normally bring otherwise. In this state of mind we are neurochemically prepared for enjoying the process rather than relying on the satisfaction of achieving a goal in the future. The big advantage being that we receive energy instead of the effort draining us even if we work toward a big, maybe even a huge goal, as set by athletes, scientists, or other visionary leaders.

So, from the perspective of a banker who has cultivated a rational approach to life much of his career, I instantly understood that the only sensible way forward was to create a neurochemistry in my brain that would support my endeavor. Of course, easier said than done. But based on these insights, I decided to establish a practice for myself: three hours of writing every morning, aiming to relish the process of figuring it out. If enjoyment was what it took to make up for the biggest mistake of my life, I would enjoy the trying! And I really do these days. When I make some notes, even if disconnected, I focus on being content. A precious memory comes back to me, I feel grateful. An idea emerges, I note it down and celebrate inside. And the blockage is indeed gone most of the time. The daily practice, concentrating on the path instead of the outcome, rewarding myself along the way, often just mentally and emotionally—I guess this sums up what has truly helped me to move forward again.

And there was something else that gave me a new direction content-wise. When watching a documentary about the speed of knowledge creation in the twenty-first century one evening, it dawned on me that my contribution could well be of a different nature than I had originally thought. There was no arguing with the fact that new data appeared at a pace we could have only dreamed of in the many decades Barbara and I were looking for new scientific insights like parched travelers in the desert. And much of this information could nowadays be accessed at any time of the day on the internet, without leaving the house or having to pay for it. Barbara used to say in her later years, "Information we have in abundance, wisdom we don't." So maybe rewriting this book was not necessarily about sharing all those scientific details or methods that Barbara and her colleague Sendhil had collected and developed over the decades, which were gone anyway! I knew my memory didn't work well enough to recollect all the necessary bits and pieces of those strategies, nor would I have the time to write them all down.

So, what would I do instead?

That evening, sitting in front of our television, I suddenly knew that I would do what I loved doing. I would share a story. The one story that I still remember very well or at least my version of it. The story of Barbara's and my life and the quest we were on. Not in a linear way—I would most likely jump back and forth in time. I would share big things and small things, odds and ends of our life, whatever seemed to convey meaning. Aiming to reach out not only to people's minds, but also their hearts. Hopefully supporting them to find their inner voice, encouraging them to take full responsibility for their life and eventually gain momentum. Barbara had said it herself before she died—maybe there was another way to convey the essence of all our learnings, one that was equally powerful as all the encyclopedic work we had been trying to get our head around all those years. If she could speak to me now, I know what she would say: "I bet on you!" These four words had a special meaning in our relationship.

And with that in mind, I try to engage with my daily practice. I write small sections each day, mostly with headlines to give you some orientation, careful not to stop the creative parts of my brain from functioning by expecting too much of myself. Not everything might make sense right away, but with your curious mind and your intelligence, you will figure this out, Sophia. I bet on you too.

Fifi, my neighbor, is going to post this letter to you tomorrow. I am glad knowing that you will soon be hearing from me, again. You must have thought that I died on you in the meantime! Not completely out of the question, as you now know, but I am still hanging in there ready to do the work. Are you too?

Take good care of yourself.

Very best wishes,
J. Leonardo

CHAPTER 6

Sophia: Blue Sky over Berlin II

Chronology: six weeks and two days after Leonardo and Sophia's brief encounter at San Francisco Airport. Forty-eight minutes later.

When Sophia had finished reading the first of the two letters, she noticed a series of sensations inside her chest—the most poignant one being relief. Leonardo was still alive, and he still wanted her to engage in this mysterious book project. She had been selected for a special task, and she was more than ready to join the task force. This was the most unusual thing that had ever happened to her. And she had loved everything about this new letter. The idea of the Big Five essential topics in life resonated with her, and she was eager to learn more about Barbara and Leonardo's lifelong quest. Decades of exploration, traveling across five continents, trying to distill the secret recipe of living a healthy, fulfilling, and meaningful life . . . all of this intrigued her. Sophia was fascinated and she could not wait to hear more about it.

Her grandmother, when still alive, had always made her feel as if she was the most gifted little girl that had ever walked the planet, as good grandmothers probably always do. And now sitting here, not that far away from where her grandmother had lived and died shortly after the wall had come down, she promised herself to use this surprising opportunity to her advantage to create a more balanced life for herself. And she had to remind herself that she was not a complete failure. When succeeding in helping a client achieve a breakthrough, for example, she was proud of herself. She loved her profession, and she was good at it. However, the lack of happiness in her relationship with Ruben, the uprootedness that had come with her lifestyle, her low energy levels, among other things, had weighed heavily on her mind of late. Maybe Leonardo's book was a way for Sophia to reclaim some of the things that she had lost on the way to professional success. Not that she was ridiculously successful, but she had sacrificed a lot for her extensive education and her career in the past decade. But in this moment, Sophia was feeling hopeful that the imbalance could be rectified.

Yet, underneath her optimism, there was something that bothered her too. She wondered what would happen if Leonardo died too soon; admittedly, she was more concerned for herself than for the poor old man. Emotionally, she had been at a similar point a few weeks before, after returning from San Francisco and reading Leonardo's first letter. Full of renewed hope, she had aimed to break through the isolation and deep sense of loneliness that had crippled her ever since she had moved to Berlin a few months prior. But when she had not heard from the cultivated old banker for weeks and weeks on end, the reenergizing effects of her journey to San Francisco had started fading away, and she felt herself deflating like a balloon gradually losing air. And she realized that she had relied on something and somebody outside herself to provide her with the motivation to rebuild her life. Sophia intuitively sat up straight with her shoulders back and tried to relax.

Sometimes one had to take a small risk to get to the next level. And was it actually such risk? When she was younger, Sophia had liked to go top rope climbing, a form of climbing where climbers are supported by a rope that runs up and down the rock face. She remembered that when she got stuck, she sometimes had to jump upwards a bit, hoping to find a grip or a hole a few centimeters higher up the wall that she could then step on or put her fingers in. And when that happened, the rest of the climb felt easy and effortless. And when she didn't succeed, there was still the rope that she could fall into with a friend at the bottom taking in the slack rope and providing safety. Unfortunately, there was nobody to take in the slack rope for her at the moment, at least nobody who lived close by. And that was something to reflect about. However, taking in the atmosphere of the light-flooded spacious café so typical of Berlin, Sophia felt reassured that the risk attached to this project was manageable.

Even if Leonardo would disappear before the project came to an end, which was an uncomfortable thought indeed, she would be okay. She would not plunge back into the black hole that she had resided in for too long. Spring was arriving, and she would use the opportunity to invest her time living in this new city in a way that would help her to incur more assets than deficits and generally increase her return on her invested time. She smiled confidently, noticing that she was using the language that she had rejected when reading Leonardo's first letter a few weeks earlier.

Of course, she was still clueless about what her contribution to this book could look like. All her existing books had fallen into the category of specialist volumes on the topics of leadership and organizational development, with her clients as her target audience. And publishing those books had required knowledge, experience, and a good amount of self-discipline. Some creativity as well, maybe, but not too much. Now this project seemed different. And frankly speaking, Sophia had no idea how to craft a book that was based on biographical elements, stories, and anecdotes, if that was indeed what the old man had in mind.

What she had found encouraging, though, was that Leonardo had written about the growth mindset. At least this was an intellectual neighborhood that she was familiar with. All big organizations worldwide were going through major transformation efforts these days, constantly changing their business models and their way of working and operating. And to survive in a world that changed at an unprecedented pace, these companies and their people had to adapt to change as fast as possible, without losing their identity. And within this context, their leaders had to embrace the new reality that they were literally working for two companies at the same time—the one that was making money in the here and now and the other company that would be creating revenues in the future. Embracing lifelong learning was therefore part of the new deal. It wouldn't be the perfectionist but the most agile learner who would take the trophy home in these new times, Sophia had told her audience in San Francisco.

And helping Leonardo publish this book could possibly be another opportunity to practice this mindset and walk the talk, too. Without noticing, Sophia scrunched her eyebrows slightly. She was almost certain that she had to feel her way forward through the fog for quite some time, until an idea would emerge of how to solve this puzzle that Leonardo was presenting her with. And if she could not consider failing as learning during the process, she would probably waste more mental energy than was necessary as she had so often done in the past when tackling a complex problem where the outcome was not quickly visible.

Sophia touched the old oak wood tabletop in front of her. What would help her to relax would be to remind herself to make more conscious use of the word *yet*. If she did not know how to write what needed to be written, to design a chapter, find a publisher, or whatever it was she had to do, she would tell herself she did not know it *yet*. She often recommended this to her clients when they were approaching a difficult task, not knowing what the end product would look like. A growth mindset was all about finding joy in the process of figuring it out and getting motivation from small wins along the way. Sophia had given entire lectures on the growth mindset at different leadership conferences, but reading about Leonardo applying it in his writing process added another layer to her understanding of it.

She was putting the letter back into its envelope when she heard a voice next to her.

Looking up, Sophia glanced into the eyes of the handsome young waiter who had just placed another delicious cappuccino in front of her. What a treat! In a state of joyous anticipation, she reached out to the second envelope lying on the table. This was better than reading a page-turning novel. She couldn't wait to find out what further insights the kind old man had to share with her. Was she falling in love with Leonardo's letters? If she could not succeed in her own age group, then maybe an eighty- or ninety-year-old banker would do just as well!

Sophia was still amused by the thought when she dove into the old banker's world once again.

CHAPTER 7

Leonardo: The Bank of Life

Time isn't the main thing. It's the only thing.

—Miles Davis

Dear Sophia,

What a wonderful morning here in Santa Barbara! Hummingbirds are chirping along happily from the orange trees beside me, the just-risen sun shines softly on the terrace, and the beach is still empty and peaceful. When I let my gaze wander over the ocean, I imagine the islands of Hawaii in the far distance. A picture that always warms my heart and never fails to spark my imagination. Clarity can have such a wonderfully soothing effect on the soul. Now that I have decided on how to proceed, I find it much less daunting to sit in front of a blank page. Sometimes it even seems to fill itself with joy and ease when I begin the journey inside the memories of my past.

So where to start this time? My idea is to tell you about the Bank of Life.

I remember the day when I first shared the essence of this idea with Barbara in a playful conversation one morning over breakfast. I had dreamed about an institution where all human time was being traded. At this institution, everybody alive could invest their time in ways that would maximize their and other people's returns and diminish the fundamental waste of time on the planet. Faced with the shortness of life, everyone, it seemed, could benefit from this endeavor. And at the Academy of the Bank of Life, people could receive training to achieve precisely that.

We had a lot of fun during this conversation, and as it was *my* dream and therefore *my* invention, I jokingly insisted that I would have to be the director of this bank, also legitimized by my background in the banking industry. Of course, Barbara challenged me on this; while she acknowledged my authorship of the idea, she argued that this was a more sophisticated institution where people would invest their time and not their money, so my previous experience wouldn't qualify me for anything. I, on the other hand, pointed out that only the rich and wealthy were in the position to differentiate between time and money. For most people on the planet, making money meant investing time, which made me the ideal candidate for the position of authority. Barbara got confused and said that this was the living proof that bankers had screwed-up personalities. We had a good time together, and after playing pitch and catch for a while, we suddenly looked at each other more intensely.

Was this not a useful metaphor that would help people to move from knowledge to action, from insight to implementation?

"Leonardo, this is it!" Barbara claimed at once, raising her fist into the air as if she was ready to start a revolution, which made both of us laugh and reminded me of the day when Barbara and I first met a decade earlier.

Jumping back and forth in time, like I warned you I would, I am now going to take you to the corner of Haight Street in San Francisco, back then the epicenter of the hippie movement, where this first encounter took place. At the time, I was a young and proud banker from New York visiting his distant cousin from Italy. Being from a working-class immigrant family and having faced severe poverty much of my early life, I was still pursuing the advantages of a solid middle-class existence that these young hippies wanted to free themselves of. Wearing my suit with pride, I could have afforded to book a nice hotel room for my short stay in San Francisco, which would have been my preferred option. But my cousin Lucy, who studied medicine at the university in San Francisco at the time, insisted on me being her guest at her apartment. I naïvely thought that this was the traditional Italian side of her wanting to impress me by being a good host. And so, reluctantly, I agreed.

However, when I arrived at Lucy's place, I immediately regretted this decision. A bunch of people—the number constantly changed—were stuffed in one big room. Not that it was any of my business, but these students did not look like young, aspiring professionals but rather like drug addicts who had lost their minds. My room, I soon found out, was a mattress among a bunch of other old mattresses in the middle of what resembled a dark cave with camouflage blankets hanging from the wall. I liked my cousin Lucy very much, but the moment I stepped into the scene, I realized that her Neapolitan father was right—this girl needed help. I had to literally pull her out of Sodom and Gomorrah to save her. Little did I know what would happen next.

After spending the afternoon with Lucy and her friends in the nearby park with other similar-looking individuals, we returned to the apartment where a woman, who seemed senior to all the others and much more mature, had cooked a big Indian curry. The moment I saw Barbara, I was dumbstruck. I cannot explain it otherwise. My sense of superiority turned into almost full submission to the force of nature that Barbara seemed to exude. She did not look anything like the women I admired in the bank in New York City. Her hair was wild, blonde, and curly. She wore big, colorful clothing, and she had a bohemian look that would usually not appeal to me. But I could not have cared less about what usually appealed to me— maybe this was love at first sight.

As the evening went on, we all sat in a circle around the room, drinking wine and smoking grass. I was never into any kind of drugs. I usually even tried to avoid the occasional drink when clients were around, but when the joint came to me, I did not hesitate to take a few deep puffs. Barbara was sitting to my left; she would be next to take the joint, and I didn't want to be the odd one out. And anyway, by that time, I had forgotten all about my plans to rescue Lucy from Sodom and Gomorrah. In fact, I would have opted to be the king of the two burning cities if that would have meant Barbara would be my queen.

When I passed the joint to Barbara, my vision was already blurred. But to my surprise she did not take it and offered it the young man sitting next to her. I protested silently in my head, dizziness clouding my mind, not feeling well at all. *Stupid me, I didn't have to smoke the joint to impress her* was my last thought before I fast fell asleep at the kitchen table in front of all the people I had wanted to convert into better human beings earlier in the day.

In the subsequent hours, Barbara took care of me. At least, this was her account of the story. My memories of this evening are vague, but in the many years to come, Barbara did not get tired of imitating me lying helplessly under the kitchen table with my suit and my grown-up tie around my neck. My "beautiful neck," she said later, admitting how she had felt immediately attracted to the soft skin on my chest that she had discovered when opening my tie and shirt to give me room to breathe.

For a long time, there was this playfulness between the two of us that we strove to maintain for many decades to come. That is, until we didn't. But more about that later.

From transaction to transformation

Things in life do not always develop in as linear a fashion as one might hope for. And after our first conversation about the Bank of Life, Barbara rejected this concept. She did not want her work to be associated with a metaphor from my world of banking. I think, in some ways, she was still influenced by the vibes of the time, and while my income as a banker provided us with a very comfortable lifestyle in those years, when she reduced her workload or stopped working altogether to develop herself further as a doctor and later as a healer, she often wished the money to support these endeavors came from a different source.

But I did not give up on the idea. First, only in my imagination and then somehow in the real world as well, I started working at this new institution. There was the Bank of America. The Bank of China. The Bank of England. Why not the Bank of Life? Over the years I had worked for so many rich but unfulfilled people that my aspiration to be able to do more for these people than just advise them on their financial assets was appealing indeed.

And so, before the term even existed, I gradually became the number one life coach of my clients in the bank. The topics of our conversations shifted from a purely financial focus to a bigger life perspective. Every so often, I challenged my clients to focus more on an equally, if not more important, currency: their time! And I asked them how they could come up with a better investment strategy for the different pockets in their life overall, instead of exclusively focusing on growing their financial assets.

My clients were intrigued by our interactions, and they started trusting me more. I got an exceptional reputation in the bank, and behind my back I was called the client whisperer, the priest, or the therapist by some of my colleagues. Rumor had it that I didn't even shy away from doing some esoteric work with our clients to attract their devotion—which of course, I didn't.

What I did differently was simply spend more time listening to my clients. Really listening, not just to manipulate them and sell our products. I asked them generic questions to make them think about themselves. And these were not questions that a journalist would ask or a banker or a consultant, but questions that made my clients reflect about their life, the challenges they were facing, and the opportunities they encountered from different perspectives. And without them noticing, we moved from transaction to trans-formation. Insights emerged over time that sometimes depressed them, often motivated them, and eventually impacted them in such ways that they started making changes to their life. These high-achieving businesspeople, who had lived and dreamed with dollar signs in their eyes for decades, opened their minds and hearts to a more holistic approach to life, which back then was not the norm. And the number of personal transformations I witnessed in my clients' lives was deeply satisfying.

Of course, this demand on my attention also affected me emo-tionally. The more confident I became, the more explicitly I told my clients about the Bank of Life—the imagined institution where all human time was being traded. When we sat down in those glamourous rooftop restaurants overlooking Los Angeles, New York, or San Francisco, I asked them to imagine opening five major accounts at our special bank, weaving in Barbara's research on the factors contributing to living a good and healthy life. I then drew a picture of these five accounts on a piece of paper, inviting them to think about how well they did in each of these domains. Could they apply new strategies to create more wealth across these five accounts? What stopped them? What could help them to overcome these obstacles? What genuinely motivated them?

Our Physiology

Our Relationships

BIG FIVE

Our Psychology

Our Finances

Our Work

When I shared this with Barbara, she was pleasantly surprised by how I'd used the idea of the Bank of Life to integrate her research around the five essential topics we had identified as key in creating a healthy, fulfilling, and meaningful life for oneself.

"Maybe not all bankers are useless," she said, grinning mischievously from ear to ear, kissing me on the cheek, which made me laugh too.

"Glad that you have finally figured this out!" I responded drolly.

Wrapping up

Sophia, this was a long, pleasant day. After being challenged so thoroughly at the beginning of this writing project, it now feels like a gift to commit myself to an activity that provides me with so much meaning. Even if some melancholy is always lingering around the corner too, that I can accept. My plan is to send you five more letters in the next weeks and months to come, each of them focusing on one element of the Big Five accounts at the Bank of Life. And in addition, I will work on my final notes, a document summarizing some of the best time investment principles for the Bank of Life that I have collected over the years.

Today I have extended my three-hour writing practice by far. I somehow must have gotten into the flow of writing and remembering. The beach is almost empty again and the temperature has dropped quite a bit. What a wonderful country this is. Warm and sunny during the day, cool and fresh at night—a true paradise from the perspective of one from the south of Italy. My bed is calling me. I am tired now, but I promise to be in touch again.

Yours sincerely,
J. Leonardo

PS: Have you thought about how you choose to invest your time on a daily basis?

CHAPTER 8

Sophia: Blue Sky over Berlin III

Chronology: six weeks and two days after Leonardo and
Sophia's brief encounter at San Francisco Airport.
Another fifty-five minutes later.

Sophia's gaze wandered over the River Spree that was flowing softly underneath the high windows of the café as she pondered the words she had just read.

The Bank of Life, an institution where all human time was being traded, and everybody alive could invest their time in ways that would maximize their and other people's returns and diminish the fundamental waste of time on the planet.

That was a worthwhile mission indeed. The human species was, as a matter of fact, highly creative when it came to wasting time. She thought about the sheer volume of emails capturing the world's attention around the globe, day in and day out. . . . Was this a tragedy, a comedy, or a blend of the two? And not to mention the quality of those emails. She often thought about a quote of Mark

Twain when responding to some lengthy messages: *If I had more time, I would have written you a shorter letter.* Unfortunately, many people felt that they did not have enough time to first think things through more thoroughly, and as a consequence, people were frequently dumping irrelevant or incomplete information onto each other, usually copying in more people than necessary.

Or what about attending meetings literally from dawn to dusk? Most of her clients complained both about the quantity and the quality of the meetings they were attending at some point in their coaching conversations. Sophia continuously challenged them to regularly review the meeting culture in their teams and the entire organization. Which meetings made sense? Who should really attend those meetings? Which meetings could be canceled? How could meetings be conducted in a way that justified their existence and also created a pleasurable experience for their attendees?

And these were just two examples. There were many more, with people engaging in activities that were neither effective nor enjoyable. Would that qualify as a good definition of how to waste one's time?

Sophia moved around uncomfortably on her chair, trying to put some of the loose strands of her dark brown hair back into the bun on the back of her head as she did many times each day. She too had unintentionally polished her skill set in that regard, letting her electronic devices hijack far too much of her attention recently. Instead of connecting with herself and the world around her, she had most definitely wasted too much of her time in the past months unsuccessfully trying to fill an inner void by distracting herself in the virtual world, too. And one usually had to bear the cost immediately for such behavior: X hours of screen time usually resulted in X% less happiness afterwards. How bizarre!

But interestingly, there was something else going on simultaneously in our societies these days. While time was wasted so generously on the one hand, people on the other hand were constantly in a hurry to save time, which was of course necessary when an overload of often disconnected tasks came one's way every day.

One of the most popular ways of saving time was multitasking, trying to do two or more tasks at the same time. Even though research clearly showed that multitasking was mostly an illusion, Sophia knew that people still did it in attempt to save time. In reality, one's brain was madly switching from one thing to the next, often losing data in the process, resulting in lower quality work and many unnecessary mistakes made along the way. Many of Sophia's clients suspected that their way of operating was ineffective, but in a world in which organizations set out to generate more profit using fewer resources, less manpower and incurring fewer costs they could not help it. And the scientific explanation for this irrational behavior was that the more people multitasked, the more their brain got addicted to it as it created the good feeling of making progress—independent of the actual results produced.

In her coaching work, Sophia had seen it time and time again. When her clients had to choose between efficiency and effectiveness, they often went for the first category, as it resonated more with their inner state of being. After all, it took awareness, self-discipline, and even courage to stop and reflect about the bigger outcome to be achieved when everybody around was trying to work faster but, unfortunately, not always smarter. And so, with billions of people around the globe being in a hurry day in and day out, the saved-up time mostly disappeared and was never seen again.

Sophia shook her head quietly. What madness was that! Time is all we have. Leonardo was right about that. Time stopped for no one. The big clock was ticking away, whether we made good use of our time or not. But how often did people stop to think about what really mattered?

Earlier that day, when walking around the corner of an old residential building, a small store specializing in high-quality notebooks and pens had caught Sophia's attention. Without much hesitation, she had gone inside to choose a handmade journal with a soft leather cover. And now she smiled at the thought that she could put it to use so soon. If she really was about to make a contribution to Leonardo's book, it might make sense to scribble down some of the thoughts that were crossing her mind along the way and maybe make some drawings. She was a visual person, and she liked to draw. When she was young, she had even taken classes—apparently this was an interest that she shared with this wise old man.

Excited about applying this new concept of the Bank of Life to herself, she started by copying the five major accounts that she was opening for herself into her notebook, just as Leonardo had suggested, slightly adjusting the language to fit her own sense of self. Doing some reflection and a brief, intuitive assessment, she quickly noticed that more than one of the accounts was in the red.

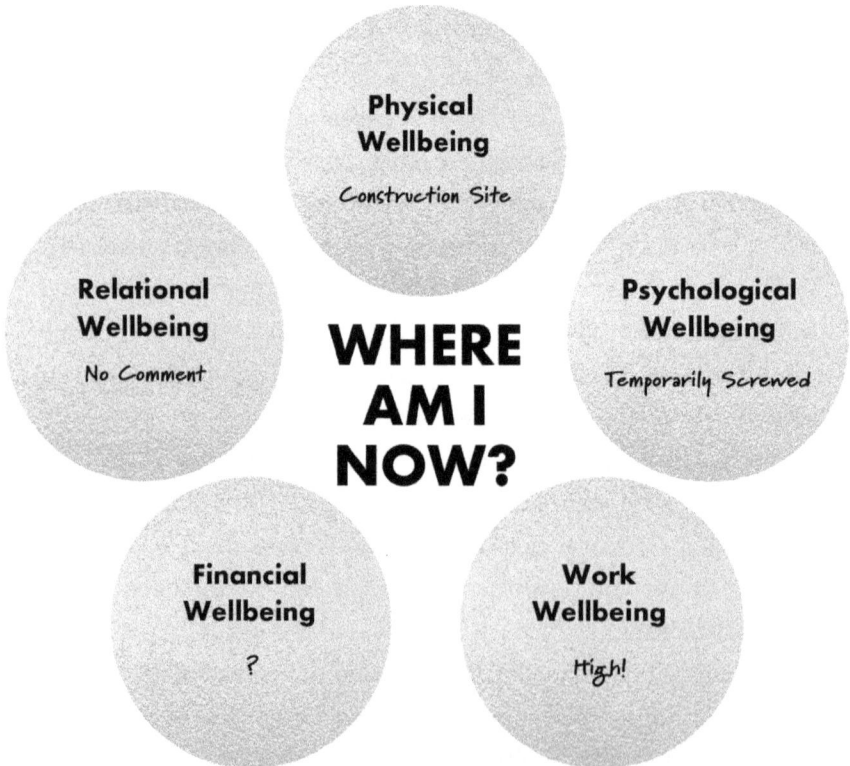

Physical Wellbeing

Construction Site

Relational Wellbeing

No Comment

Psychological Wellbeing

Temporarily Screwed

WHERE AM I NOW?

Financial Wellbeing

?

Work Wellbeing

High!

In fact, three or even four out of five areas of her life needed more attention. What a mess she was! The most promising girl from her college year—good grades, best in sports, popular among her friends—had come very far indeed but had so little to show for it. Why could she not make better use of all this potential?! Many of her school friends also had careers like herself but at the same time were married with children, had solid homes, circles of friends in the area they lived in, both feet on the ground, and were presumably happy and healthy, or so it seemed.

"Hope dies last!" she said aloud, trying to encourage herself with a good old German proverb. And then she looked at Leonardo's letter again.

How had she been investing her time and making her deposits across these different areas of her life to get these results in the past years?

The account that she was the happiest with was unsurprisingly the one that had probably received her most dedicated attention—her work account. She had established herself as an international consultant, executive coach, book author, and keynote speaker. Her work was intellectually stimulating, and it provided her with endless opportunities to grow, most likely for decades to come. Her clients were extremely loyal, and she never invested any time marketing her services, as there was always enough demand building up organically. And while she had never really looked after her finances—being successful at her work also meant that there was nothing to worry about in that area of her life. But she suspected that it was high time to start planning her financial future. So, there were two accounts with a positive balance, even though one needed more of her time going forward. Maybe not as bad as she had initially thought.

Next, she focused on the less positive areas of her life. The accounts most in the red were probably that of relational and emotional wellbeing. Despite being such a well-connected, even popular girl throughout her childhood, her youth, and later in university, as an adult Sophia had come to a point where she felt stranded socially. While she possessed many qualities that would draw people to her, she was very much on her own at the moment. She had a handful of close friends and a bunch of inspiring colleagues spread across the world but no community situated in one place. Following her academic and then professional interests, she had moved from one place to the next, just as her parents had done throughout her childhood. And while she had always been quick to adapt, now well into adulthood she had no place where she was truly at home. No local community that she belonged to. And to compensate for that, she had probably always done more of the same. Whenever her need for love and connection was not met, she had leaned toward work. And instead of facing and addressing the underlying issue of her discomfort, she had invested more of her time into working and studying and then more and more. And when the Ruben situation had worsened, instead of reaching out to others, she had cocooned herself away and turned toward an unhealthy lifestyle.

Sophia looked down on her notebook, striking her fingers softly across the gentle leather cover. If all of her time was being represented by a circle—let's imagine a big German cake, like the one her grandmother used to bake for her with red cherries on top of it—the question was, who had eaten her cake? She thought about her ex-lover: Ruben, his name synonymous with heartbreak and sorrow. Ruben, the man with the deep voice and the most delicious body she ever touched. The man who had obviously not loved her, even if it had so often felt like it. Ruben had received a lot of her attention and had eaten a huge portion of her cake for years. Even when he wasn't around, her thoughts and her emotions had been hijacked by his absence. Which probably meant that it wasn't him eating her cake, but rather her throwing it after him. This was even more pathetic. Sophia frowned and then continued to reflect.

The next piece of the cake had gone straight to work, and at least this seemed to have been a successful way of investing her time. She felt relieved and went on. And what else?

If she was honest to herself, she knew that the remaining two big pieces of her cake had gone to screen and bedtime in the past months. A well-balanced time investment strategy would probably not only look different but would hopefully create different results.

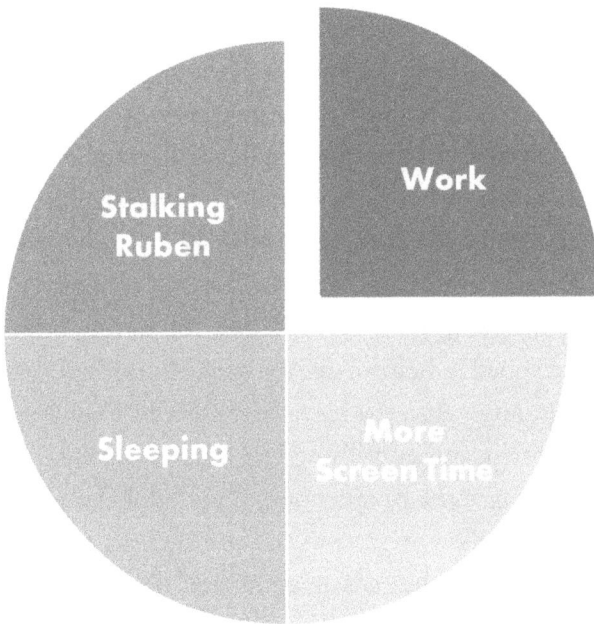

Sophia sighed. Again. But she knew that regret for "having wasted time" would only result in more wasted time. So, how could she invest her time more sensibly at the Bank of Life going forward? She scratched her neck and looked up at the ceiling. Every time Leonardo got in touch with her, more questions than answers arose in her mind. "This is a good thing when you want to create a new path that has not existed before," she would tell her clients in such situations, suddenly recognizing with a smile what a smart person she sometimes was.

Determined, Sophia got up. She had done enough reflection for the day, and she knew what she wanted to do next. After paying for her breakfast and chitchatting with Liam, the young waiter who happened to be an exchange student from London, she stepped outside the café and turned right. A few months ago, she had bought a city guide of Berlin and its surroundings, which she had ignored ever since. And now she finally wanted to put it to good use, starting with a walk around the inner boroughs of Berlin.

But sauntering along the famous boulevard, which was named after the lime trees that lined the grassy pedestrian mall, she soon sensed how out of shape she was. Exploring London and riding her bike had been one of her favorite hobbies when living in the UK, and today she could not understand why she had not made more of an effort to move around Berlin too. The city's energy was contagious, if one was receptive to it. And after still having been down in the dumps, trapped in her isolated existence in this city only yesterday, she could now sense the elevating effect of Leonardo's letters, the sunny weather, and everything else around her too.

When arriving at the Brandenburg Gate, Sophia watched groups of tourists from different parts of the world passing by. It was difficult to imagine now, but she remembered how the Brandenburg Gate had once been situated in East Germany, inaccessible for both East and West Germans alike when Berlin was still divided by the wall. She had vague memories of visiting this place as a child, well before the wall had come down. Her parents had wanted to spend the day with her grandmother in East Berlin. But things had not worked out at the border checkpoint, as often happened back then, and Sophia remembered following her parents as they walked along the sinister-looking wall in a subdued mood for what seemed like hours on end.

And now, all those decades later, she was standing here facing the Brandenburg Gate again, and people from all over the world were cheerfully walking right through it, as if this was the most normal thing ever. Despite the brutality of the war, the division of the wall, and the challenges of reunification, Berlin was continuing to look forward.

If this city could reinvent itself again and again, could she not do the same? At least once, for heaven's sake! Sophia looked up into the blue sky over Berlin and smiled in anticipation of receiving Leonardo's next letters and the difference they would make to her life.

CHAPTER 9

Leonardo: Our Health

Health is the first wealth.

—Adapted from Ralph Waldo Emerson

Dear Sophia,

It is another wonderfully sunny morning here in Santa Barbara. The blue sky is dotted with fluffy white clouds that drift lazily in the gentle breeze, and my gaze is wandering over the ocean with grace and gratitude. You might have déjà vu reading these first lines. And the truth is, these days I could start every letter telling you about the stunning view. After two years, during which I was not able to appreciate this beauty, I now breathe in the fresh, salty air and enjoy this fabulous spot of the earth. This little house by the sea has been a source of such joy and happiness over a lifetime. Two lifetimes, to be more precise! And I would love to be present when you first set eyes on it, even though this might not be part of the greater scheme of things.

Yesterday I had an appointment in the cardiology unit in the hospital in Santa Barbara. And to my great relief, the doctor had good news for me. My heart is beating more steadily again, and I am feeling strong enough to do what I have set out to accomplish.

So let us dive right into it and let me introduce you to the first element of the Big Five at the Bank of Life: our physiology! Our physical health! Our physical wellbeing! Our energy levels! There are many names for it. In essence, it concerns how well we take care of our body, as this is the vehicle that takes us through life as we know it. Every second of the day is being influenced by the state our physiology is in. Like when we are tired or worn down, our body might feel like a prison, and our thoughts and emotions can become negative as a result of it—a cause-and-effect relationship that often stays undetected by our conscious mind. When we don't feel well physically, the world around us is often tainted with darker colors, and while we might assume that this is how it is, it is more often than not our physiology playing a trick on us, clouding our perception of ourselves and everything else around us too. And of course, there is also the opposite effect: When we are feeling physically strong and full of energy, every thought might be bathed in brighter colors, too. Optimism, joy, and happiness emerge out of nowhere, and everything seems more joyful.

Therefore, as the secret director of the Bank of Life—you know by now how much I love this metaphor—I strongly advise all my clients to manage this account first and foremost. The first wealth is health. If this account closes down, everything else stops as well. Of course, we all know that. It is rather obvious. And yet many of us seem not to care and live a suboptimal life because of it.

The beginning of a quest

For my wife, supporting others' health and helping them avoid unnecessary maladies was the key theme of her life. And being the educated person you are, Sophia, you might ask yourself why Barbara was so extraordinarily driven as she was. I have been thinking a lot about this too. In our lives, there are often defining moments in which we experience either intense happiness or intense suffering, which then has a lasting impact on the person we become. Under the waterline of our consciousness, these moments gradually influence what we choose to believe in, the emotions that we habitually feel, and the decisions we take in life.

For Barbara, it was a time of suffering—a long valley—that had the biggest impact on how she led her life. When she turned fifteen, she lost both her parents within one year. She had not even finished high school when she suddenly became an orphan. Her father, who had been overweight all his life, had died from side effects of diabetes, while her mother—equally overweight—had had a heart attack when climbing up the stairs to their home.

This, as you can imagine, had left Barbara heartbroken. She was traumatized but soon also determined to dedicate her life to studying medicine so that other families wouldn't have to endure what she did. Despite, and because of, her grief, she finished high school and college with honors and fought herself into a scholarship for one of the most prestigious medical schools in California. Being from a lower-middle-class family, her parents would have never been able to finance such an elite education. Nonetheless, when she later got offered a post at one of the leading pharmaceutical companies in the world, she declined the offer. The pay was appealing and the prospects excellent, but Barbara was not interested in such a career. She wanted to use her education to work with real people, treating real problems.

And this was what she was up to around the time when we first met in Lucy's apartment in San Francisco. Having just finished medical school, Barbara's intention was to gain some experience as a doctor. A professor from medical school had recommended her to Tom, the owner of a practice in Santa Barbara who had offered her a position as an assistant practitioner. And as uncomfortable as I was about the prospect of leaving New York, I was soon ready to give it a try to move our relationship to the next level.

Smashed up against the ocean by the mountains, Santa Barbara was not called the American Riviera for nothing, and I told myself that this was an opportunity to reconnect with my Italian roots. It was a quiet location back then, but LA was not far away and every drive starting from Santa Barbara was breathtakingly beautiful, no matter what direction one would take. There were some fancy houses here and there, and there was always a rumor that somebody famous had been spotted in this restaurant or that, but without investing a fortune, we were able to buy a small house by the sea with my savings. We loved it. On the outside, we probably still looked like an unlikely entity in those early years. I had consciously tried to loosen up, which at the beginning meant that I didn't wear a tie on Sundays, while Barbara looked more like a bohemian artist at the time. But we were young, in love, working hard for our respective jobs, and both truly content about where we were with each other.

However, nothing in life is set in stone. After these initial years of bliss and happiness, things started shifting slowly but surely, and Barbara began talking about the winds of change. It soon became apparent that there was something more substantial behind these comments. One day when we were walking along the beach, she shared what was on her mind. She had studied at one of the most prestigious medical schools in the world, she explained, but all she did nowadays was prescribe drugs for her patients.

"In a way, I am nothing but a drug dealer. A legal drug dealer at least!" she uttered in a melodramatic tone that made both of us laugh. But she really meant it and added on a more serious note that she felt totally unequipped to really help her patients.

"I have no idea how to find the root causes of all this suffering that I encounter on a daily basis. I do what I was trained to do, and I guess I do it well, but it doesn't feel right, Leonardo."

The sun was setting now, the beach was almost empty, and we were holding hands strolling along the shore. But Barbara's mind was troubled with questions she could not answer: Had her parents' deaths been preventable by taking better drugs, more drugs, or other drugs? Or would it not have been wiser to look at ways to treat their diseases, focusing on the root causes that had triggered them?

As always, I admired Barbara's sincerity, and I told her right away that if she wanted to go back to university, I would be fully supportive in whatever she would choose to do. But Barbara surprised me again.

"Isn't the definition of madness to always do the same thing and expect different results?"

She stopped walking and stared at the ocean so that I could hardly hear her.

"Some of the smartest people teach at medical schools, people who are much smarter than I am, and still, I don't think that it would help me to find the answers that I am looking for. Not that I even know what questions to ask."

She sighed, and we continued walking along the beach in silence.

Searching for a new direction

A few months after this conversation, Barbara finally decided to speak to Tom, who, to our great surprise, generously granted Barbara time for an extended sabbatical to do some exploration, maybe some traveling, to reflect and further educate herself. A Swiss friend from medical school had told Barbara about an international medical conference that would take place in the city of Prague the following summer, which she and her husband were going to attend. And Barbara was interested in joining them, and I was too.

I had been to Prague many years before. And while I won't go into the details of this trip, as it is not relevant to our mission, it was there that I had met a young girl with dark hair, bright green eyes, and an Eastern European accent whom I had become fascinated by. At the time I was reading Dostoevsky, an author who explored the depths of the human psyche, which I then saw reflected in this smart girl from the Czech Republic. I soon found out that she was from Berlin, with no Eastern European relatives at all, but I did not question my earlier judgment about her unique character traits. She was residing in the house next door to my mother's cousin, whom I was visiting at the time, and we soon befriended each other.

The memory of this brief encounter in this foreign country never entirely left me. And over the years I sometimes looked at the watch she gave me as a farewell present on my last day in Prague in silent contemplation. I never doubted for one second that Barbara was the woman that I was meant to spend my life with, but I still had questions that persevered. Sometimes I forgot about this brief encounter for many years, but then those questions reappeared. Why could I not let go of this memory?

When I saw your picture on the internet, I suddenly knew.

However, I am getting sidetracked now. And you might legitimately wonder why I brought up this episode at all. I promise to shed more light on the matter in time. For now, I ought to hold on to some structure in my storytelling so that you don't get lost! Let's therefore move our attention back to the summer of Barbara's sabbatical.

In the end, we decided not to travel to Prague. Barbara was afraid that it would be more of the same content-wise, and while she did not know exactly what she was looking for, she sensed that it would have to be something that took place outside the world of conventional medicine. To figure out what to do, she studied many different journals and magazines, visited the library, and talked to a variety of people across the medical community. And she ultimately found the answer where she least expected it, during a formal dinner in Los Angeles to celebrate the success of a nationwide project at my bank that I had participated in.

I was by far the most junior person invited at the dinner, and much of the time I politely made conversation with a member of the board sitting next to us, whose wife did not even bother to speak to us at all. Thus, when the CEO of our bank came to join Barbara and me later in the evening, I was really delighted. But unfortunately, my wife was not in a mood to please my CEO just for the sake of it, and when asked about her interests, she started sharing her criticisms of the medical establishment quite bluntly. Maybe because he was part of the establishment, too. I guess this happens to all of us some of the time. We apply certain established ways of thinking, even if they don't fit the occasion. Anyway, sipping too much from my glass of wine, I was relieved when our CEO responded graciously, not taking offense at my wife's attitude in the least.

"Barbara, you should meet Aaron. I went to college with him. He is a renowned professor at the faculty of health sciences in Jerusalem. Not exactly around the corner. But you seem to have much in common, the two of you."

He paused and then continued, "Aaron will be in New York in two weeks' time, visiting his parents. I will be out of the country, but maybe I can connect the two of you."

Our CEO smiled, looking at Barbara. "But I must warn you: Aaron is a bit left-wing." I giggled rather too loudly in response, as I knew how little that would worry Barbara.

When we left the dinner, my wife's mood had changed. I loved the way she looked in that moment. Her blue eyes were beaming with joy, her long curly blonde hair was slightly out of control, as was often the case, and her curvy figure made me fall in love with her all over again. A feeling that was possibly magnified by my relief about the fact that the evening had turned out better than anticipated.

And sure enough, two weeks later, Sophia was indeed contacted by Professor Aaron Antonovsky himself. And after talking with him on the phone for quite a while, he made her an offer that seemed too good to be true. There was a convention on holistic medicine taking place at the University of Jerusalem, and if Barbara was interested, she would be invited to share her story around the challenges she faced working as a general practitioner in the US. A friend of Aaron, another doctor from Brooklyn, and his wife, who had originally been invited to speak at the convention, had had to cancel their commitment that very morning due to unforeseen personal circumstances.

Barbara and I grinned at each other. We knew we could count on each other to be spontaneous enough to seize an opportunity with courage when it occurred. And a week later, with visas organized by Aaron's team, and a little bit of help from my CEO, we sat in a plane flying across the Atlantic Ocean, not knowing what to expect.

The Convention for Holistic Health

Our stay in Israel was surreal, and never could we have anticipated how liberating it could be to follow the footsteps of others when these footsteps led to exciting new places that one would not have dreamed of exploring otherwise. With the acceptance of Barbara's speaking assignment came a sightseeing adventure, getting to know Aaron's institution for holistic health, and attending the convention itself.

We enjoyed these days like a huge, unforeseen treat that was miraculously tailor-made to our needs. And we soon learned what a stunningly gorgeous country Israel was. Walking through the streets of the ancient city of Jerusalem, marveling at the Western Wall, and then exploring astonishing museums, we felt like we were traveling back and forth in time. And we also loved the countryside. Floating in the Dead Sea, rubbing ourselves down with mud, we experienced the softest skin we'd ever had. And eventually, wandering around charming streets of Tel Aviv and eating the world's most amazing falafel and a huge variety of exotic snacks, it was as if we had arrived in culinary heaven. So much so that we often reminisced about this fine cuisine when back in Santa Barbara.

"That was food to die for!" Barbara once said, sitting on the terrace of a fast-food chain back home. "This, however, is food to die of," she said, and we both started laughing, enjoying our French fries anyway.

And that was only the beginning of our trip to Israel. The conference that started a few days later took place at the university, where Aaron and his team were indeed approaching the subject of health in a completely new way. Barbara was impressed by this new environment, the values people held on to, and the importance being placed on asking questions. "There is nothing more practical and effective than asking the right question," she would hear Aaron say various times. "Questions can change everything! Answers, as valuable as they are, can blind us from taking on a wider view." He even opened the conference itself with a series of questions that, in his view, had not received enough attention from the traditional medical community yet.

"What generates health? Do we know that? Why are only some of us sick, although all of us are facing difficulties? Do we study that in depth? What are the factors that keep people in good condition, in sometimes chaotic inner and outer circumstances?"

What a mind he had and what a presence. There were people

from all over the world sitting in the audience with different backgrounds and different views. But they all seemed to be fascinated by Aaron's expertise and genuine curiosity. And Barbara was too. Over the years, she had channeled a lot of the trauma of losing her parents into her work. Understanding what had caused their deaths to help other people not to experience the same had become her life mission. In medical school, she had come to understand the name and nature of countless diseases, the biochemical reality of these conditions, and their destructive power. She had learned about what drugs to prescribe in order to better manage these conditions and keep them in check. However, what she had not understood yet was why her parents and many of her patients had gotten so chronically unwell in the first place and how this could have possibly been prevented. Was it their predisposition alone that led to their suffering? She doubted that. Could better drugs have saved them in the long run? She questioned that too. There must be more to learn, Barbara thought, and inspired by this new environment, she did.

During the conference, she felt as if blindfolds that had shielded her sight for years were taken away from her, and she was introduced to a new salutogenic model of health. Learning about this new approach, she could suddenly see the limits of her previous interactions with her patients until then. The term "salutogenesis" stemmed from Latin (*salus*, meaning health and wellbeing) and Greek (*genesis*, origin, meaning originating from health). This was the opposite of "pathogenesis," which meant originating from disease. Unlike the traditional school of medicine that focused on understanding the anatomy of disease, Aaron and his team encouraged researchers around the world to explore the factors that could help people to move toward more wellbeing.

To explain his vision more vividly, Aaron used the metaphor of a *river of life* to explain the process of health creation.

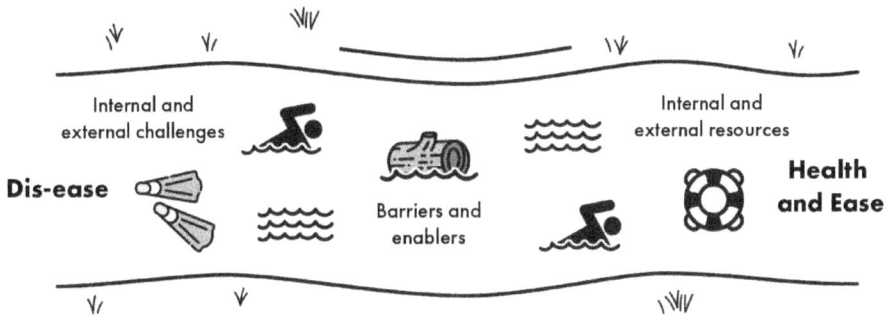

What he meant with that was that every person was in the *river of life* all of the time, either moving toward ease or dis-ease, depending on the internal and external resources they were activating and the circumstances they were facing. For some the river was rough, or even poisoned, and for others it was more like a whirlpool in a five-star hotel. Some people had inherited difficult genetic predispositions, while others had been luckier in that regard. But fortunately, it was neither the quality of people's life conditions nor their genetic make-up alone that affected the outcome of health for each person. The swimmer in the river came along with certain personal characteristics too. And while some people had been dealt a challenging hand, those who took responsibility for their fate and who were willing to learn were often able to identify the resources necessary to improve their health.

And that was Aaron's main philosophy. To empower themselves, people had to realize that they were not just at the receiving end of health or disease, but active participants in the process of creating one or the other. Of course, one's genetic make-up did matter, and Barbara knew that the zip code of a person had a bigger influence on people's health than some might expect. Still, what she had never liked about the traditional approach to medicine was that patients were treated almost like children. The doctors were the experts, and the patients were neither challenged to think about how they might have contributed to their problems, nor were they seen as part of the solution. All that was usually asked of them was to take their drugs as prescribed.

Adopting a new paradigm

I am not sure, Sophia, if it is obvious how revolutionary this new perspective was—for my wife, it changed everything. Following our trip to Israel, Barbara radically shifted gears in her approach to medicine, hoping to add more value to her patients by helping them to create physical stamina instead of simply treating their illnesses when they had already occurred. It might sound subtle, but it made all the difference. After studying and practicing disease control for so long, she now set out to learn more about the biology of health creation, which to her felt like moving from the dark to the light side of her profession.

And with her background as a traditional doctor, she used the remaining months of her sabbatical to study and learn about concrete practices that her patients could engage in to strengthen their physical health. Inspired by a series of conversations with doctors from around the world during the conference, she started with the most obvious path: nutrition, exercise, sleep, and relaxation.

She read everything out there, and we set about trying it all as well.

We switched to a diet that consisted of lots of vegetables, our protein mainly coming from fish but also beans and lentils, and high-quality fats like olive oils and avocado. We cut out all soft drinks and replaced them with water, herbal teas, and in the evening the occasional glass of red wine. Barbara had grown up with the Standard American Diet, today known as the SAD diet, which contains high amounts of saturated fats, lots of meat and fast-burning carbohydrates like sugar, white bread, French fries, and sodas. Coming off the SAD diet was like going through a process of detoxification. It got worse before it got better.

However, we both felt the energizing effects of our new way of eating on our body and mind within a matter of a few weeks. We also started going for walks along the beach more regularly, and we blocked out more time to recharge our batteries. Before our trip to Israel, we had often worked very long hours in the evening. This was the time before the internet, and while the temptation to continue working in the evening was not as strong as it is today, I was often trying to get my head around certain investment decisions until late at night while Barbara was studying new scientific data in her fields of interest. And we noticed how much better we slept when we consciously decided to not work after a certain point in the evening. But despite these positive developments, Barbara also faced some setbacks along the way.

The new way of treating her patients meant that they had to assume more responsibility for their own health. That was the new deal. And indeed, some of Barbara's patients, who changed their nutrition and way of life as much as we had done, experienced miracle healings. No exaggeration. Barbara was impressed beyond words what those dietary changes could do for her patients that the world of medicine with its high-tech approaches was not capable of: bettering or even healing chronic conditions that were known to be irreversible by addressing the root cause of the issue.

I remember her account of one overweight couple in particular, Donald and Hilary, who averted an impressive list of chronic conditions—like diabetes and cardiovascular problems—that they had both suffered from for decades, within a period of a few months. Their family life improved, and Donald even got promoted at work, which allowed them to move house and have their children go to the schools that seemed to better support their development. Barbara was ecstatic—this was one hundred percent why she had gotten into studying medicine in the first place.

But truth be told, it was only a minority of Barbara's patients who fully bought into this new paradigm—the majority did not. Many patients felt disturbed by her unwanted interventions. They could not relate to the metaphor of the river of life and did not want to be treated as swimmers but as normal patients. They felt criticized and not well taken care of, despite the extra time Barbara was dedicating to them. More and more complaints came in until one day even Tom asked Barbara to return to the more traditional way of treating her patients. Tom liked and respected her ambition, but he too was silently questioning if she was doing what was expected of a doctor.

This did not come as a complete surprise for Barbara. Nevertheless, when the feedback was brought to her, she didn't handle it well. The enthusiasm that had kept her going since our trip to Israel temporarily collapsed. She had invested so much of herself, so much of her time and energy to help these people, and now she felt criticized and treated unfairly. There were days when she had difficulty in motivating herself to go back to work.

Connect first, consult second

But come rain or shine, Barbara would not have been Barbara if she let this get on top of her for too long. After withdrawing and licking her wounds for a while, she got her act together and made a serious attempt to analyze the situation from different angles.

From her youth onwards, whenever she had felt stuck, her way of coping had been to study more, learn more, acquire more knowledge. However, this time she realized that acquiring more knowledge wouldn't make a difference. This time, it was about her becoming more skilled, reaching out not only to people's minds but also to their hearts. She could not force her way of thinking on other people.

Paradoxically, when acting like a traditional doctor, this was somehow different. She would prescribe drugs and people usually just went along with it. Nobody really questioned her advice. Maybe the big advantage of the traditional approach was that her patients experienced it as more efficient. Making a doctor's appointment, taking a certain drug did not require that much time or effort and did not interfere much with one's daily life. This was in stark contrast to the new approach that Barbara suggested, which required a considerable amount of time, particularly at the beginning, and in addition some substantial motivation to change one's attitudes and behavior. This was a lot to ask of her patients. And for this approach to work, she had to communicate in smarter ways.

"You do not bust into a person's house and tell them that the furniture is all wrong!" she said to me one day, pointing her finger at me as if I had been the one receiving the feedback. I shook my head in amusement and told Barbara that I would consider that in the future.

But we both knew there was a lot of truth in this statement. With all of her good intentions, Barbara had too often preached at her patients, trying to educate them about all the mistakes they were making, thereby triggering a level of defensiveness which was not a state of mind conducive to learning and insight.

It was not as straightforward as giving her patients information and expecting them to run with it. Her role was to communicate in a way that would truly resonate. They had to start imagining themselves leading a different life, a life filled with energy and health that would allow them to do what they would want to do and feel like they would want to feel. Many people wanted to make the change. And she needed to figure out how she could help them achieve this in a subtler way. Connect first and consult and educate second was a new mantra that she had learned from a British medical doctor, Rangan Chatterjee, that she now wanted to live up to more skillfully. And she also understood that some people would probably always prefer taking a pill instead of changing their way of living. Every person had a right to own a different truth. And she learned to accept that too.

In hindsight, these setbacks were the biggest accelerator in her becoming the doctor she wanted to be. She was still convinced that health, for most people, did not have to be complicated, and she developed the concept of the "four lifestyle doctors" who, when engaged regularly, could work in one's favor often without even being paid for. Their names were Dr. Nutrition, Dr. Sleep, Dr. Exercise, and Dr. Relaxation. According to Barbara, and much research out there, they were the most effective doctors in the world and the least expensive ones. Barbara was certain that people were needlessly suffering, and after decades of being a doctor, she had come to the realization that the vast majority of her patients could feel so much better than they did already just by making a few different lifestyle choices. And this belief was later scientifically supported by global twin studies. Only 10% to 20% of the participants' health could be explained by genetic predispositions, while up to 80% to 90% was determined by how they lived their lives on a daily basis.

Making deposits

As the secret director of the Bank of Life, I always imagined our health as a bank account, where we are continually making deposits and withdrawals by using our time in a way that either nourishes or taxes our physiology. If we make too many withdrawals and not enough deposits, our body budget becomes unbalanced and we may experience negative outcomes such as low energy, fatigue, stress, lower resilience, pain, and ultimately disease. For some that happens quickly, whereas others seem to live just fine on an accumulated mountain of debt in this area of their life. But, usually sooner or later, one has to pay the bill. And you do not need to be a medical doctor to notice that in yourself. A chronic imbalance in this account over a long period of time leads to unwanted capital depreciation.

However, Barbara realized that the very idea of making deposits seemed to have something satisfying about it. It motivated people to continue with their efforts, do something to support themselves even when the results of their actions were not immediately visible, as it is so often the case when doing something that is beneficial for our health. The good feeling of making a deposit seemed to inspire people to move on and do the right thing.

And so, in the spirit of the Bank of Life, where humans can invest their time in ways that would maximize their returns and diminish their wasted time, Barbara started inviting her patients to think about growing their wealth in this account by making regular appointments with the four lifestyle doctors that she had identified.

Spending quality time with Dr. Nutrition seemed particularly valuable. There was not one single chronic disease that Barbara could think of that was not powerfully influenced by what people eat. And research these days shows very clearly that cancer, cardiovascular problems, diabetes, dementia—the ugly four of the twenty-first century—all have strong relations to our diet. Whatever we eat affects literally every cell in our system, every second of the day. Whatever we choose to put in our body has a direct bearing on our daily energy levels and long-term health, and it even drives our mental and emotional well-being too.

However, in the richest countries of the world, people are eating the poorest diets of all time. And the effects of these diets are devastating. Only yesterday I saw an article in a well-respected medical journal claiming that, in the US, there are more obese and chronically ill people than ever before in human history. And other developed countries around the world are heading in the same direction while spending more on health care than was ever the case. Whatever we do as a society, it does not seem to be working.

Barbara herself advocated a Mediterranean diet mostly based on plants; vegetables; some fruits; high-quality protein from fish, beans, lentils, and nuts; and healthy oils, like extra-virgin olive oil or avocado oil for many decades. Later in life, she turned to a fully plant-based diet, and I did to. Drinking lots of water while reducing sugar, refined carbohydrates, alcohol, excess red meat, and any highly processed food from the supermarket led to many of her patients healing from chronic conditions and creating a new level of health for themselves that they could not have anticipated. "Eat the rainbow," she would tell her patients, and today more and more scientific data is backing up the importance of the variety and the amount of vegetables we have in our diet.

But to be crystal clear, this is by no means nutritional advice for anybody. Today you can be vegan, you can be paleo, you can be "pegan" as our friend Mark Hyman—who leads a clinic for functional medicine in Cleveland, and who uses food as medicine— would point out. People differ greatly in the way they respond to food, and I am not a medical doctor who ought to give out any kind of information in relation to this topic. I can only tell you what worked for us.

Barbara and I were also big fans of a time-restricted eating schedule. Twelve hours a day of not eating was the minimum that we adhered to. But we usually tried to eat in an eight-hour window, to have sixteen hours of not eating in which our bodies could recuperate and make use of the mechanism of autophagy, a process which helps the cells clean themselves by recycling old tissues. Today this is known as the unrivalled number one intervention to increase one's lifespan.

Another great way of making deposits into one's health account is spending quality time with Dr. Exercise, which also generates high returns on one's investment. Our bodies are designed to move, but many people don't move at all these days or, at least, not enough to maintain one's health. Instead, they spend a large amount of their waking time seated, continuously making withdrawals at the Bank of Life, often without even being aware of it. Seated at the breakfast table, seated in their car or on public transport, seated behind an office desk, seated when attending various meetings, seated when eating lunch, seated when heading home again, seated at the dinner table, and then seated on the couch when looking at various screens. Spending too much time seated, however, not only reduces any measures of fitness, but also increases appetite and curbs the desire to participate in any physical activities. It's well known that a sedentary lifestyle is a risk factor for a wide range of chronic diseases, including the Ugly Four.

The good news is it is not so difficult to counteract on this ongoing imbalance. Research shows that moderate exercise already makes a big difference. People who walk for half an hour to an hour each day, and maybe do some additional exercise and stretching at home, can already make all the difference. Until recently, I loved using a health app on my mobile phone with a goal of walking 10,000 steps a day. Now I am not in a position to follow this any longer, but I still do the best I can, moving around the house and the terrace with my walker to stay fit enough to finish what I have set out to do.

Another particularly joyful way of making deposits into this account is to spend more time with Dr. Relaxation—a doctor who protects people from what the World Health Organization has claimed to be among the greatest threats to our health in this century: stress. For short-term situations, stress can be beneficial to our health. It can help us cope with potentially serious situations, and it can motivate us toward achieving our goals. Yet if the stress response doesn't stop firing and these stress levels stay elevated far longer than is necessary, then this takes a huge toll on people's health. And this is where Dr. Relaxation comes into play, working in the opposite direction and encouraging the body to release chemicals that relax the system, support immune function, and increase blood flow to the brain.

The health benefits of spending time with Dr. Relaxation are amazing, and fortunately the methods in his portfolio are many-fold. Yes, there are breathing techniques, prayer, meditation, tai chi, qi gong, and yoga and so on and so forth that can help people relax deeply and effectively, improving brain functioning, the immune response, and overall health of a person. However, enjoying the company of good friends, pursuing one's hobbies, laughing and having fun, and integrating more playfulness into one's life are powerful options too. The ways to invite Dr. Relaxation into our life are numerous, and not all of them ask us to sit down and meditate in silence.

And finally, without making a fuss, comes Dr. Sleep. The most time-consuming of the four lifestyle doctors, this doctor Barbara admired for the high return on one's investment. Good sleep leads to increased energy levels, better mood, improved memory, better decision-making, and improved physical health overall. However, knowing about all these amazing benefits of a good night's sleep might not be particularly comforting for those to whom sleep does not come easily. And I can only encourage those people to do some deeper exploration on this topic, if this is the case. In general, one might say that Dr. Sleep depends on the other three lifestyle doctors making their contributions first. Because when Dr. Relaxation is not set up to do his job properly, if Dr. Exercise is lying on the couch, and Dr. Nutrition is not put to work either, Dr. Sleep can't come to fruition.

Barbara did several things to improve her own quality of sleep. Number one was to get daylight within an hour of waking up to set her circadian rhythm for the day. Number two was to engage in ten minutes of exercise in the morning to boost her cortisol level at the right point in time. Number three was to walk 10,000 steps a day. Number four was to reduce bright light in the evening. And number five was to avoid food, work, and too much screen time after the sun set. For her this worked, but sleep is a delicate topic, and everybody needs to find their own recipe.

But having said all that, it is important to highlight that this is not about striving for perfection. Not at all. While we largely tried to walk the talk, we still liked our glass of red wine in the evening, and I really did not want to live like an ascetic. And we really didn't.

The table below is the last version of our daily appointments with these four lifestyle doctors. It is still pinned to our refrigerator. And since recovering from my stay in the hospital, I try to engage with it as much as I can. I have a mission to accomplish, and without putting too much pressure onto myself, I try to do what I can to stay happy and healthy.

Wrapping up

Now Sophia, before you engage with the endeavor of planning and writing the book itself, I wonder if you might want to take some time to see how all of this relates to you personally. I know you are

Doctor Nutrition	Doctor Sleep
• Drink water regularly! • Eat the rainbow! • Eat less often! • Enjoy! Healthy Fats High-Quality Proteins Healthy Carbs	• Daylight early in the morning after waking up to set our circadian rhythms • 10 minutes exercise in the morning to boost cortisol • Physical activity during the day • Reduce bright light in the evening • No food, work, or screen time if possible after sunset
Dr. Relaxation	**Dr. Exercise**
• Morning routine • Pursuing hobbies & having fun & play • Spending time with friends and family • Practicing the Golden Habit 	• 10,000 steps • Stretching each day • Weight lifting 2x per week

an expert in your own area. However, embracing some of these ideas in practice might not only put you in a much better position to write a more compelling version of this book, but could also help you to reconnect with a stronger version of yourself.

So, think about it!

How well do you feel in this area of your life on a scale from 1–10?

How are you investing your time into this area of your life?

Are you making some daily deposits that outweigh your withdrawals?

And remember, the time to fix the roof is when the sun is shining. So even if you are already happy about where you are in relation to this account at the Bank of Life, you might want to consider new and joyful ways of making your deposits.

In the envelope you will find a template with five questions that Barbara had used with her patients as a starting point for them to take more responsibility for their health and their daily energy levels. I hope you enjoy looking at it, and please make amendments as you see fit. Barbara always said that we were basically the architects of our physiology. And the good news is that by investing one's time wisely into this account, one can make a difference in a relatively short period of time. In three months' time, by engaging Dr. Nutrition, Dr. Exercise, Dr. Relaxation, and Dr. Sleep—eating healthy, sleeping better, restoring our energy reserves more effectively, and exercising enough—we can literally impact every cell of our body and feel much better.

Ecco qui! Here you go! I hope this was enough food for thought to think about the importance of this first account at the Bank of Life, and maybe you and others will feel inspired to invest your time smartly into this part of your life.

In my next letter, I am going to focus on the next account at the Bank of Life: our psychology. The more experienced Barbara became as doctor, the more she realized that there were often psychological factors at play when supporting her patients in the process of creating physical health for themselves, and she wanted to understand these factors at a deeper level. And it was this new angle of her quest that opened the door to the next chapter of our life, which included traveling to India and deep into a forest in Florida where we found more peace of mind.

Yours with warmest regards,
J. Leonardo

CHAPTER 10

Sophia: Building Up Energy

Chronology: two months and twelve days after Leonardo and Sophia's brief encounter at San Francisco Airport.

"Would you like another tea?"

Sophia raised her head, distracted.

"Yes please."

So absorbed was she by Leonardo's writing, it took a while for her to slide back into the reality of sitting in an English teahouse in the middle of Berlin, which was confusing enough in itself. Even more so, as the waitress had addressed her in crystal-clear received pronunciation. Maybe she had seen the letter and assumed that Sophia was a native English speaker too. Sophia leaned back into the comfort of the cozy velvet chair. Not even many Berliners knew about this enchanting reed-thatched cottage tucked away in the northwestern corner of the parkland of the Tiergarten, far from the hustle and bustle of the city. And the only thing missing to make this place feel even more British was a fireplace, she thought. But then she noticed a traditional fireplace right there at the other end of the room. Sophia smiled—she liked it here.

When the tea was served, Sophia sat up straight as befit the occasion. She marveled at the tea flower enfolding itself inside the glass vessel like a small masterpiece of its own. For the first time she could see the outline of an idea emerging of how these letters could be turned into an actual book. Leonardo's writing was very different from anything she had ever engaged with before, but it appeared almost complete on its own. So, all she might have to do was to provide a context, a framework in which his letters would make sense. How she would specifically go about this was still beyond her, but she was determined to enjoy the process of figuring it out, just as Leonardo had suggested.

For now, she wanted to focus on the theme of the letter, and her physical wellbeing. And she was reminded of Leonardo's question: whether she was making deposits into this account at the Bank of Life that outweighed her withdrawals. Sophia put the teacup carefully back on the saucer. The answer was obvious. She was not making enough deposits and far too many daily withdrawals! She looked at the energy audit that had been attached to Leonardo's letter. Thinking about each question carefully, she started filling it out as best as she could.

| How much energy did you have on a scale from 1 to 10 in the past 3 months on average?

1 = totally exhausted
10 = maximum energy available | 

1 2 3 4 5 6 7 8 9 10

• Low energy. Feeling tired most of the time. Lots of headaches. Gained weight. Not even fit enough to explore the city walking on my own feet. How pathetic! |

Assuming that you can influence this, where would you like to be in 3 months' time?	 • Back to where I was two years ago. Maybe unrealistic. But overall direction: more energy, much fitter and slimmer. • Need to think more about that!
How can Dr. Nutrition, Dr. Exercise, Dr. Relaxation, and Dr. Sleep help you to move closer to this goal?	• Eat differently, like I used to. • Have already started walking and biking more regularly!!! Do some exercises in the morning? • Go to bed earlier. Reduce screen time. • Relax . . . HOW?
What is the "story" that you tell yourself that is holding you back from investing more smartly into this account . . . and how can you change this story?	• Story: "Am too tired to exercise or eat better. The bad weather. I will start tomorrow. It does not matter anyway. It is all because of Ruben." • How can I change this? • Have to think about this more in depth!
What exactly are you feeling and thinking in those moments when you are engaging in lifestyle choices that harm your physical wellbeing? Keep a journal for ten consecutive days, and write down what you observe.	• Good question! • ~~Start making notes next week.~~ • I start today and write down my observations each and every day. Promise!

Sophia studied the results of her reflection. Health was the first wealth—wisely put! It reminded her of a friend of Ruben's, a successful investment banker from Manhattan who had had a stroke before his hair had turned gray that had left him disabled. Of course, she had no idea if it had been entirely preventable, but it underlined the importance of Leonardo's words. Ruining one's health was not a sensible thing to do.

And still, Sophia had been doing precisely that: engaging in a massive form of asset devaluation over the past two years and particularly over the past few months. And as a result, her body budget had become unbalanced, and, yes, she was experiencing all sorts of negative outcomes already: low energy, increased stress, lower resilience, back pain. She ticked all the boxes. In her youth she had been the fastest girl on her track team. And later she had loved climbing, kayaking, and hiking. With her narrow hips and her athletic legs and shoulders, her clients still assumed that she was a sporty person. But this was currently not the case at all.

Sophia moved a little bit closer toward the window and let her eyes wander out over a small lake where a number of baby ducks were following their mother, making joyful sounds. It was time to change things for the better, and improving her physiological wellbeing was a good starting point. When she noticed a group of people doing some outdoor exercises in the distance, she could suddenly feel a new sense of determination emerging.

No longer would she contribute mindlessly to the mountain of debt in this area of her life. She would reduce the daily withdrawals and make more deposits. The idea of taking responsibility for her health and being a player, rather than a passive spectator in the process, appealed to her too and suited her personality much better. She picked up the letter again and searched for the one sentence that had attracted her attention the most.

"In three months' time, by engaging Dr. Nutrition, Dr. Exercise, Dr. Relaxation, and Dr. Sleep—eating healthy, sleeping better, restoring our energy reserves more effectively, and exercising enough—we can literally impact every cell of our body and feel much better."

Sophia liked the sense of optimism that this sentence evoked in her. And she had indeed already started being more active again, walking and biking through Berlin over the past few weeks. Now it was time to change her diet. Of course, it was easier said than done. As a coach, she knew that it was relatively easy to come up with a good plan, but it was more difficult to stick to it. Without an understanding of the deeper underlying needs that one had been trying to satisfy with the old destructive behavior, a plan was often dead before it was put on paper.

Reflecting about the question of why she often ate all the wrong things, Sophia noticed that she was hungry. Funny enough, this always happened when she thought about wanting to adjust her diet. Amused about herself, she walked to the other side of the café and soon stood in front of a massive, beautifully decorated buffet. Homemade bread, croissants and pastries freshly baked throughout the day, cheese, marmalade, fruit salad, and more made Sophia's mouth water in anticipation.

So much abundance! Always available!

For most of human existence, people had lived in a world of scarcity and ever-present danger, and to survive in such conditions, humans—just like animals—had been designed as eternal seekers, always motivated to move on, do more, and find more. Sophia flirted with a delicious chocolate muffin sitting right in front of her. The neurological trick behind this ever-seeking behavior worked like this: If she ate a piece of the muffin, she would experience a moment of pleasure, triggered by dopamine released in her brain. However, this joy would not last very long. As her dopamine level would quickly fall again below baseline, she would tip back toward pain, thereby experiencing a craving for more, which, if she followed this craving and ate another piece of the muffin, would lead to another release of dopamine and a short moment of pleasure. And so on and so forth. Long-lasting satisfaction was not the aim of the genetic game. And it was these fluctuations of dopamine levels that drove the actions of organisms for thousands of years to secure their survival. What a genius way to make humans do what they had to do!

Sophia examined the impressive buffet. Yes, what a great system if one was living in a world of scarcity, but wasn't it a terrible system in a world in which food and other pleasures were available without pursuit!?

With everything at people's fingertips literally all the time, the brain ended up working so hard that one could not enjoy much anymore and definitely not one's broccoli or going out for a walk, as these things could not compete with the elevated dopamine responses of the more potent stimuli of the modern world. And Sophia had experienced this to be true ever since arriving in Berlin.

The initial dopamine surge that she had gotten regularly from easy pleasures like Netflix, her smartphone, pizza, chocolate, potato chips, and the like was at first *comforting*. And she had convinced herself that she had needed that. She had been new to the city; she had been on her own, and it had been raining literally every day. But before long, these aggressive dopamine surges had gotten weaker and shorter, and the aftereffect—the dopamine deficit—and the feelings of emptiness, discomfort, and diminished self-worth had gotten stronger and longer. And so, without intending to, Sophia had dug the hole for herself deeper and increased her feeling of misery and loneliness, applying a set of coping mechanisms that had quickly turned their back on her. This was just as Anna Lembke, a neuroscientist and an expert on this subject matter, had described in her book, *Dopamine Nation*, which she had read recently.

Two gregarious young women standing next to Sophia started laughing, and the sweet aroma of freshly baked bread, cakes, and pastries caught her attention again. Yes, she would enjoy eating this delicious chocolate muffin now. Very much so. And it was also true that she had enjoyed binge-watching Netflix and eating comfort food on all those evenings and weekends after first arriving in Berlin. But to get out of this downward spiral, she had to break the cycle and go about a different way of getting her dopamine *indirectly* at some point in time . . . by eating healthily, exercising, writing, taking a cold shower, getting off that stupid coach, working toward something, etcetera. While these activities would at first tip her balance toward pain and a feeling of discomfort, after a while, her body would start creating a healthier, more sustainable, homemade source of dopamine. And that would lead to longer-lasting joy and a feeling of increased self-worth and confidence.

Sophia returned to her table and sat down on the cozy velvet chair, feeling proud of herself. She had withstood the temptation! Instead of the muffin, she had opted for plain yogurt, some berries, and a bowl of nuts and seeds, which she now ate carefully. And she knew if she would continue having this as breakfast, she would even start craving it, maybe even more than the toast or sugary cereals with which she had started the day within the past months. Sophia put one of the last strawberries into her mouth and closed her eyes. The taste was fruity and juicy with a little bit of acidity. She felt the sun peeking through the window, warming her cheeks and shining light on the table in front of her.

When she opened her eyes again, she spotted a beautiful antique English wall clock at the other side of the room. She searched her bag for her mobile phone. She had indeed been sitting in the teahouse for almost three hours now. And her back was hurting slightly. Putting her journal into her city bag, postponing further reflection on what she could do about the other lifestyle doctors, Sophia got up. Maybe it was time to get some fresh air and move on.

Back on her bike, cruising through the park, breathing in the fresh air, she was struck by how green this city really was. It reminded her of London with its unexpected swaths of open parkland, tree-lined avenues, and lakes. She still missed that city. But

London was also the place where her relationship with Ruben had unfolded like a rollercoaster ride, with ups and downs that made no discernible sense and came at an unprecedented pace. And until today, she still felt exhausted by it all. Ruben hadn't been treating her well, she was sure about that. But then, every good story needs a villain, doesn't it?

Sophia now passed a monument for Goethe, a famous German poet, and she intuitively looked across the street to the Holocaust Memorial just a few hundred meters away. The best and the worst of Germany's history closely situated together. It was impossible to be in Berlin without being drawn into its history. She spontaneously decided to visit the Holocaust Memorial, which consisted of a field of more than two thousand rectangular blocks of concrete laid out in a grid formation, resembling tombstones. As was intended by the designer of this memorial, Sophia sat down on one of the blocks and opened her travel book.

She was now sitting in the former Soviet sector of Berlin, she learned. And when she would cross the street again to continue her bike ride in the park, she would reenter the former British sector, which also explained the existence of the English garden that she had visited earlier. How peculiar that she had not known this before.

But there were so many things that Sophia did not know. About Berlin, about the subject of health and wellbeing, and about life in general. And today this felt like a good thing. There was so much out there still to learn, do, and experience. She was curious to find out more about the Big Five at the Bank of Life. She wanted to read about how Leonardo and Barbara's life had further unfolded around their quest. And she could not wait for his next letter to arrive. Her eyes lit up. Leonardo's letters were indeed starting to have a positive impact on her, and they were even influencing her decision-making. She could already see that. Things were moving again. And even if there were more ups and downs along the way, as was probably always the case in life, the period of stagnation was over. Decision made.

And now she had a date with Dr. Relaxation. A cheeky smile flickered across her face. She did not want him to wait on her. She put her journal back into her bag. Enough reflection for the day!

CHAPTER 11

Leonardo: Our Finances

You will die, but were you ever alive?

—Iain McGilchrist

Dear Sophia,

Stormy weather today in Santa Barbara, an unusual experience during summertime. Usually, I love sitting on our terrace. It makes me feel being close to Barbara when I look across the beach, observe the many different people walking by, and let my gaze wander over the ocean. But today is different. My view is rather restricted, and the usual sound cocktail I enjoy here has been reduced to the noise of the rain pouring down on the roof. Don't get me wrong, I certainly don't mind that it is raining. If you live in a place where the sun is shining on most days, a bit of rain is a welcome distraction for good old Mother Nature and myself alike. And mind me, my life has become surprisingly meaningful again, in a way I could not have anticipated a few months ago. I am sitting at our kitchen table in front of a fresh mint tea and a lot of blank pages that are my friends now most of the time. My paper bin is still jealous, but it is slowly adapting to the new reality. Things are changing, as they always do. And with this I need to tell you that I might have a surprise for you, too.

My original idea for this letter had been to focus on the second element of the Big Five at the Bank of Life—our psychology! My aim was to share with you how our life enfolded around this new angle of our quest. But this is now not going to happen. I had to switch to a new medication which takes a while for my body to adjust to. In a couple of weeks, I can expect to have more energy again—at least that is what the cardiologist tells me. To still use this time in the best possible way, I have decided to first focus on another element at the Bank of Life—our finances, the foundation for our material wellbeing. After all, finance has been the subject I've spent my life studying, which makes it somehow easier for me to tackle this task first.

But to manage expectations: I personally liked being a financial adviser both to the average middle-class person earlier in my career and to my wealthier clients later in my professional life. But that job is done and dusted. So just for you to know, I am not aiming to use this letter to offer any kind of financial advice. That would be ridiculous without knowing your personal circumstances. However, what I am striving to do instead is to create awareness around this account at the Bank of Life so that you and others might feel motivated to invest your time accordingly. If you ask me, and I am still a banker at heart, this is in many ways not the most important subject of all. When you look at the whole picture, other elements like our physical and psychological wellbeing are more influential. And yet, for reasons I will put forth later in this letter, I am deeply convinced that our finances deserve a front row seat in our attention at least some of the time. And as my biography is so tightly entwined with how my thinking in this area has evolved over the years, I will take the chance to reflect on myself too. A good thing to do when the end is near!

My roots and why I became a banker

So what were the early influential forces in *my* life?

Maybe it all began with my parents' argument about my name: John Leonardo. A strange combination of names, driven by a rather stubborn struggle between my mother and father that eventually concluded when the administrative bodies of America had to put a name into their registration files at some point in time. This is how my life started, and in many ways, it probably says a lot about how it later unfolded. But let's not rush too much.

My parents had emigrated from Italy to New York in the first decades of the last century. My mother would have never dreamed of engaging in such an endeavor so soon after leaving Germany after the First World War only a few years prior, but extreme poverty in the south of Italy drove them to desperate measures. And when I was born in New York City, all my mother hoped for was for me to adapt to the American culture as quickly as possible. For her America was still a foreign country, and feeling lost and uprooted herself, she wanted me to be at home somewhere. Anywhere really. And in her view, a boy named John was more likely to achieve that. My father was different. For him, being in New York was an adventure. And a son named after the greatest artist and polymath of all time resonated with my father's sense of optimism, despite the difficult circumstances my parents were living in. And as both of them were strong-willed, John Leonardo I eventually became. My mother was first relieved and later disappointed when she noticed that the

Italian community started calling me by my second name, but in retrospect, she understood that she too got what she had hoped for.

My childhood was a happy one in many ways. We did not live a big city life. The nickname of our neighborhood, Little Italy, very much described the atmosphere of the place. We were living in a Neapolitan village with its own language, customs, and cultural institutions. And even though it was the poorest neighborhood in the city back then and many residents began moving to Brooklyn and other more spacious locations soon after they arrived, I loved it. That time of my life was full of love, friendship, excitement, and awe. That being said, when I grew older, I hated to see my parents having to work as hard as they did. Sometimes, my mother took on three different cleaning jobs at a time. She seemed constantly exhausted, and I remember thinking that all her beauty and talent were being wasted away, without her ever having had a chance to showcase it. And the same was true for my father. While never giving up on his gregarious nature, he worked his butt off to make ends meet. And the money he earned usually did not even bring us to the end of the month.

And as money was what was truly missing in our life, I oriented myself toward it. I loathed the idea of my beautiful, strong mother cleaning the toilets of total strangers, and all I could think of was getting her out of that position. Nevertheless, I did not blame my father for the situation we were in. His mission had been completed by taking us to a new continent and building a provisional nest in which we could all survive. The responsibility to reach the next level of our family's financial wellbeing was on my shoulders. That is how I saw it. And there were no words that could describe the deep sense of satisfaction I felt when I was finally able to take care of my parents financially. We never spoke about it explicitly, but I think my mother, who had felt uprooted for most of her life, eventually found some inner peace in her later years, which still warms my heart to this day.

Happy money and unhappy money

There are many ways to be a banker. And now that you know why I was attracted to this profession in the first place, let me tell you about a brief encounter that had a huge influence on what kind of banker I chose to become. It happened in the early years of my banking career in New York City when I was privileged enough to listen to a speech given by Mr. Ken Honda, one of the most successful investors of our time. My boss had dragged me along to take some notes for him. And already the opening line of Mr. Honda's speech impressed me so much that I wrote it down word for word, which my boss later commented on with a dismissive shaking of the head.

"Of all the idiots I have met in my life, and Lord knows there have been many, I think that I have been the biggest."

What a man, I remember thinking in that moment, and I asked myself if I would ever have the courage to be that open in front of such an elite group of people. But looking at my boss's facial expression and checking in on the rest of the audience, I wondered if this was actually a good idea. While the wise old man had definitely caught everybody's attention, it seemed likely that the presentation would become more of an uphill battle from then onward.

But Mr. Honda did not seem to care and continued regardless, now telling us about his childhood.

His parents had been poor immigrants from Japan and through study and hard work, his father had successfully established himself as a well-regarded accountant in Manhattan. As a boy, Mr. Honda had often served tea to his father's clients when they visited him in his office—an activity that had led to surprising insights for him. One thing he noticed was that some of his father's clients were in a constant state of agitation and worry over their finances. Independent of their financial situation, they did not appear to be happy, and they often lost a lot of money in the process. In contrast, Mr. Honda's father's more peaceful, Zen-oriented clients would mount up wealth in a more sustainable manner, and they became wealthier over the years—and not just financially. Money for them was not simply a score to keep but a positive tool for supporting the things that mattered.

"And you would perhaps assume that this wisdom then stayed with me," Mr. Honda said, addressing the audience of senior bankers. "But it did not!"

He shook his head to support his message before he continued.

"The truth is, spending all those decades in the banking industry, I could think of one thing only, and that was: MORE. I was blinded to what life had to offer and what it expected of us in return. Today I can tell you that only if you think of money as ENERGY . . ." he paused, "you will be able to free yourselves."

There was the sound of murmuring and muttering in the audience. I saw the skeptical faces of the elite bankers in their expensive suits sitting there on the most glamorous floor of our building with a view over Manhattan, regretting wasting their precious time instead of working on some major deals. "What has he been smoking?" I heard a very senior colleague next to me whispering and my boss laughing quietly as a response. But Mr. Honda went on with a calm gravitas and recommended that we should all take a different approach to money, an approach he would later go on to explain in his book *Happy Money*.

"Consider that you can 'charge' your money with positive energy," he said. "There is happy money which you produce when investing in a business with a positive purpose or a community project. Donating some of our hard-earned dollars toward a charitable cause. Receiving remuneration for work or services from satisfied clients or employers."

He stopped for a moment.

"Conversely . . ." Mr. Honda was now pointing his index fingers into our direction, "there are numerous examples of unhappy money gained by unfortunate or even unethical means. Like investing in stocks that bring suffering into the world. Or receiving a salary from an employer for a job you don't like."

He paused again, before he continued.

"The same currency, the same dollar bills exchanged, but a completely different outcome. If you circulate money in frustration, anger, sadness, or despair, it is unhappy money. Contrarily, money put toward people and matters of perceived value is Happy Money."

I remember the facial expression of the senior bankers in the audience, who back then embraced the idea of capitalism like a religion. And while I found Mr. Honda's words quite surprising too, thinking about them today, these were the words of a pioneer. Today, there is a growing interest in new ways of sustainable investing. Through the combination of traditional and more innovative approaches, investors ranging from global institutions to individuals are taking a sustainable approach to pursuing their investment goals, taking economic but also social and environmental concerns into consideration and striving to make money the happy way. But back then, this was still unheard of. And when Mr. Honda talked about the School of Hope for underprivileged children in Africa as one example of how investing part of our money back into society could make a difference, the audience seemed to be hardly listening at all. For me it was different, and it was particularly the last sentences of his presentation that stayed with me forever.

"Some people are so poor, all they have is money!"

Mr. Honda paused one last time to let this message sink in before he finished with a question that reached my core: "You certainly do not want to belong to that category of people, do you?"

The audience started applauding politely. Had Mr. Honda not been such a legendary investor, the senior bankers in the room would not have bothered to react to him at all. Mr. Honda might have gone nuts, in their eyes, but given his financial resources, power, and status in the industry, he was still too influential to be ignored.

For me it was different. And despite my junior status, I approached Mr. Honda respectfully when he came out of the CEO's office later that day. Squeezing myself in the same elevator, I bombarded him with questions. And Mr. Honda, who did not respond to my questions at all, asked me if I wanted to accompany him walking the streets of SoHo, where his parents had first lived after immigrating from Japan.

"Leonardo, when I left the bank, I was poor, and I really mean it. I had drowned the possibility of living a meaningful life in the pursuit of financial wealth only. I got lucky, had some talent, worked hard, and finally over-succeeded. But my heart was empty. Today I am convinced that there are better ways of becoming wealthy."

There were long pauses in our conversations. And when we eventually came to a cinema that was advertising a movie called *Out of Africa*, Mr. Honda stopped walking for a moment to contemplate the poster in silence. Apparently being reminded of Africa again, he went on to tell me more about his charitable ambitions in Kenya and about the safaris he undertook.

"Go and visit the School of Hope. It will teach you more about life and wealth than any financial institution in the world ever could. When you get married, and if your bride is of an adventurous nature, take her to Kenya, go on a safari in the Maasai Mara before it all changes, visit the School of Hope. If you do, give me a call and I'll put you in contact with a bunch of people whose acquaintance will make you richer than any amount of money ever could."

Well, I would love to say that I immediately adopted a different approach toward my career after this encounter. The truth is, I did not for a while. And despite my best intentions, I did not even go and watch *Out of Africa*. The wise old man and his ideas about happy and unhappy money, the School of Hope, the bright and colorful pictures of Africa, were still in my head. But as weeks and then months went by, other things happened in my young life, and this brief encounter somehow receded to the back of my consciousness.

And yet, this changed years later, on the very day I asked Barbara to be my wife. I had not planned for this to happen, but in the hours following my proposal, I told Barbara everything I remembered about Mr. Honda, and I broke the news that I would take her to Kenya as my wedding gift, which came as a surprise to both of us. I wanted us to have an extraordinarily rich life with extraordinary things happening. And while Barbara was skeptical about the destination, she was enchanted by my enthusiasm and accepted both proposals.

Under the African sun

On our flight to Africa, we both slept surprisingly well, and when we woke up, we instantly fell in love with the epic landscape and its warm, beautiful colors through the windows of our airplane. However, going through a long corridor at the airport, we were reminded that the word transit actually meant moving from one place to the other—in our case from one continent to the next. You might think that the plane had already done this job, but on the plane we had still belonged to the protected Western world. Now we were trading the known for the unknown—a deal that Barbara had doubts about.

The hallway was packed with unfamiliar people and unfamiliar things. We saw chickens in small baskets and little piglets running around freely. And what stood out the most were four towers that looked like gigantic cages about ten meters high, packed from top to bottom with suitcases.

"When you consider the percentage of suitcases that get lost every year," a fellow American backpacker said to Barbara, "it is

surprising that there are not more towers like these in other airports. Maybe there are towers for lost socks, too. So funny."

"Very funny indeed," Barbara responded, looking at me, ignoring the backpacker. "Before we explore this further, can we pick up
our suitcases first?"

As it turned out, we could not. Barbara's suitcase was, unfortunately, among the missing. This was not a good start to our journey,
to say the least. And while the nice lady behind the lost luggage
counter assured us that they would do everything to find it, I could
see that Barbara was not convinced.

In the situation, I felt encouraged to remind my wife of the
words of our travel agent: "When anyone goes on a trip to Africa,
you expect the unexpected and just roll with it." I mimicked the
words of the travel agent with a sense of reignited optimism and
added, "Put on your African robe and enjoy the ride." I smiled at
Barbara. But my words did not have the intended effect.

"How wonderful, Leonardo. You have adapted *so* quickly, you
almost act like a native already," she whispered so that the lady
behind the counter could not hear us. "My suitcase is already gone!
What is the next thing I lose and just *roooolllll* with? My life?!"

This was a bit dramatic, but I wisely decided to take her into my
arms against her protest. And, when our prebooked driver did not
show up in the following hour either, I remembered another piece
of advice provided by our travel agent that I kept to myself: "Never,
and I really mean never ever, go anywhere in Africa without a prebooked driver or you might never return." Now, left stranded at
Nairobi Airport with my unhappy wife at my side, I started resent-
ing the travel agent almost as much as Barbara did. And when we
finally saw a friendly man holding up a board with our names, I
could have kissed him. It was time to leave the airport behind,
with or without Barbara's suitcase, and start the pleasant part of
our journey.

The land of dreams

Sitting in the taxi driving through the concrete urban jungle of Nairobi, we finally started to relax. Nairobi was known to be the beating heart of Kenya at the time and one of Africa's most cosmopolitan cities. In the short span of a hundred years, it had risen from uninhabited swampland into a bustling modern metropolis. But after the stressful moments at the airport, we both felt relieved that the small cottage I had booked as our first accommodation was located in a beautiful, peaceful suburb of the city. In the midst of a formal old garden with hundred-year-old trees, huge jacarandas, cacti, bottlebrushes, and a large population of birds, it seemed like an oasis. The cottage itself was lovely too. It had high-beam ceilings with a fireplace, a beautiful stone floor, and a wooden veranda that invited us to relax while enjoying the birds, butterflies, and flowers of the garden. And the best was yet to come. What Barbara did not know was that this place had an intriguing history. When sitting on the colonial-style bed in our cottage, she noticed a brochure lying on the bedside table.

"This place is called the Karen Blixen Cottages. Is this where she lived?"

I nodded and beamed at her. A month prior to our departure, I had organized an evening for the two of us to watch *Out of Africa*, the movie that Mr. Honda had recommended to me years prior. And now here we were in the original place, where the real Karen Blixen, the real-life protagonist of the movie, had had her farm.

I looked at Barbara with anticipation. She smiled brightly.

"This is the kind of surprise that suits me. Tell me about her story. Everything you know."

Barbara loved listening to me sharing stories. I often did that at home too. And with my wife lying on the cozy bed, I started telling her about Karen Blixen, the daughter of a Danish aristocratic family who had felt stuck in what felt like too restrictive a life for her.

She was from a wealthy family indeed, but she was in pursuit of a different kind of wealth, something that her luxurious upbringing could not offer her. And when she had not found anyone to marry in her late twenties, she and her Swedish aristocrat cousin decided to become partners in crime. The following year, the two of them moved to Kenya, which at the time was a part of colonial British East Africa. They were wed on the day after their arrival, and Karen assumed the title of Baroness Blixen. While the marriage was not a happy one, Karen still fell in love with Africa, experiencing a kind of wealth that money could not manifest.

After a while, I noticed that Barbara was already asleep, and I joined her in the bed. For the next few days, I had to tell Barbara everything I knew about Karen's life. The reality of modern Kenya was, of course, at odds with the cinematic image that we were fantasizing about. And Barbara pointed out all the problems that most African countries faced at the time: the breakdown of tradition and tribal culture, poverty, political crisis, corruption, the shifting of basic values, plus the decimation of the legendary herds that roamed the precincts of the tented camp that once was Nairobi. And of course, I knew she was right. But we were on our honeymoon, and for once I pleaded with Barbara to take a break and just focus on the beauty of life instead.

For the romantic travelers like us, there was still some of the old Africa to be explored. And looking back, I am glad that we did precisely that. Sometimes the land of dreams is closer than it seems.

Going on safari

The second leg of our African honeymoon took us to the Maasai Mara Park, which is situated in a huge valley surrounded by a series of glorious mountains. Mr. Honda had described his own experience on this safari as one of the most enriching experiences of his life. But once again, things didn't get off to a good start. After a very challenging, long, and bumpy ride in a safari vehicle that kept breaking down, the first night in our tented lodge was not entirely relaxing either. It was surprisingly cold, and a whimpering noise kept us awake for ages. It took a long time to fall asleep, and soon after a strange human, almost-crying sound emerged, and I felt disoriented when I woke up. Not knowing where I was, I took the flashlight and shone it to the other side of the bed, where Barbara was sleeping under the mosquito net. She had somehow gotten her leg out and it hung down alongside the bed. She was stirring and moving restlessly, whimpering in her sleep.

It was awful. We slept fitfully throughout the night, with one nightmare following the other. And when we arose before dawn, I felt guilty that I had organized this safari despite my wife's concerns. She hardly spoke a word, but after swallowing a couple of headache pills with a sip of water, we left the tent together and were instantly greeted by our guide, Badu, who was preparing a cup of locally grown coffee for us.

And as the sun rose, our mood seemed to brighten as well. Soon feeling so much better, we started seeing the world around us. And this world had nothing to do with the fearful images that had tormented us throughout the night. The lodges were a replication of the permanent tented camps of the last century and much nicer than we had realized upon our arrival. And the picturesque views over the Sand River and the neighboring grassy hills and plains were exhilarating.

Sitting around a wooden table, Badu told us that the camp was right on the migration route for millions of wildebeests, zebras, and Thomson's gazelles that moved between Serengeti and the Maasai Mara. If we were lucky, we would have the privilege of exclusive views of the plains and hills dotted with thousands of animals, all from the comfort of our camp. And then he went on to tell us about the Big Five that he seemed to love with a passion. "The elephants and the lions." He opened his mouth and made a realistic lion-like sound, and we shrieked and laughed. "The leopard, the buffalo, and the rhinoceros. Without the Big Five, Africa would not be the same," he claimed, and he went on to describe those animals vividly. Listening to Badu's passionate account of his homeland and its inhabitants was fascinating, but experiencing it later ourselves was truly priceless.

I had thought that I would be prepared for this African safari. I had bought the recommended clothes for us, plus field glasses and a good camera, and I was ready to take it all in. But what I was not prepared for was the actual feeling of being on safari. It is difficult to describe, Sophia, but when you are sitting in your safari vehicle, mere feet away from these wild animals out in the African savanna, one feels both tremendously excited and calm. Time seemed to slow down, and we were acquiring a deep sense of connection to the natural world around us that felt truly unique. The sheer size of this landscape was breathtaking, and it made us feel like a tiny grain of sand in a big universe.

In the following days, we started most of our mornings watching an epic African sunrise, spotting different animals feeding nearby. After breakfast, we would pack our things and start our journey through the bush. One day, we came across a herd of fifteen elephants sitting quietly in the shade, fanning themselves with their ears to keep cool. Badu had told us that that this was the season that elephants gave birth to their young and that we should keep an eye out for newborns. Sure enough, we spotted two baby elephants. One was huddling close to its mother, while the other smaller one was enjoying running through the tall grasses with a look on its face that can only be described as pure joy. On another day, our destination was Lake Naru. Arriving at the lake was the most beautiful experience one could imagine. Flamingos everywhere! Long legged, long necked, and well dressed in pink feathery coats, these beautiful creatures must be top models in the bird world, I whispered into Barbara's ear and kissed her neck. It was almost too much to take in.

In the evenings, when the sun had gone behind the hill and there were shadows all across the plain, Barbara enjoyed spending time on the terrace of our lodge, where she watched the small animals feeding close to our camp, dropping their heads and switching tails. The nights out there in the bush were magical. And I usually went to the campfire with Badu to have a gin and tonic or two, and this is where I got to know Leboo and Mingati, two local Maasai men who came by to support the camp during the night.

On our last evening out there, it was only me and the two Maasai men. And I could not stop myself bombarding them with questions about their way of living. And Leboo, who was half Maasai and half English, kindly acted as my translator. The Maasai were extraordinary people. Originating from ancient lands and simpler times, they had lived in East Africa for hundreds of years. And while several of their customs were controversial, I was fascinated by their attitude. And when Leboo shared with me that Mingati was known to be the fastest hunter of their community, I was wondering how he could possibly hunt animals barefoot with just a stick in his hand. Mingati was silent for a while before he responded that a courageous heart and silent feet were the most important qualities for a hunter. And with that, he started walking around the campfire, his feet barely touching the ground, making gestures to follow him, which of course I did, carefully trying to imitate his elegant moves, with Leboo at my back correcting me. What I didn't know was that Barbara was watching us from our terrace. Back home this was the incident that she would make fun of.

"Please Leonardo, walk like a Maasai around the dinner table, it looks so real," she would tease me. It makes me smile to think about what a rich life we lived.

The School of Hope

After finishing our safari, we returned to Nairobi to take a flight
to Kisumu, a town set at the shore of the Victoria Lake, where
we would visit the School of Hope. I remember vividly when we
first approached the yellow school building that I had already seen
pictures of during Mr. Honda's presentation many years before.
It seemed as if music was coming from everywhere. Loud, joyful African music captured our souls before we even entered the
building, seemingly inviting us in. It was Inauguration Day. The
new building for the secondary school classes had been finished a
month prior, and that day the many helpers and donors were being
thanked with a special event. Going through the big doorway, we
came into the courtyard, which was decorated like an outdoor
theater. There were children everywhere welcoming the visitors,
dancing with such rhythm that Barbara and I stared at them in
fascination. These children seemed so happy that it was contagious.

After lunch, the new building was officially inaugurated and for
the first time we met Natalie, the director of the School of Hope.
A warm-hearted, strong lady, who fought every day to make things
work. And we found out that she had fond memories of Mr. Honda,
who had died a few years before. Enjoying a cup of coffee together,
we talked about his ideas of happy and unhappy money. And while
she was open enough to admit that she had initially questioned the
value of this concept in a country like Africa as well, she shared
with us how his thinking still inspired her to that day. One could
see that this was more than a job for Natalie, and it was easy to
understand why people thought of her as the soul of the school,
even though she emphasized that the children were at the center of
this small universe.

At the end of the day, Natalie accompanied us to the big doorway that we had entered in the morning. And it was there that we
saw a boy standing outside in a corner. We had noticed him before,

as he had stood out amongst all the other happy children, seeming somewhat more present, somewhat more unique. But now he was crying, secretly wiping his tears away. Natalie talked to him in a soothing voice while we waited politely a few feet away.

The boy's name, we learned, was Duncan. Duncan Sundays. And we soon understood that, unfortunately, Duncan's happiest day in the School of Hope was also his last. His father's brother had died a couple of weeks before, and as his father had taken on the responsibility of supporting his brother's family after his death too, there was no money left to finance his son's schooling. And with that, Duncan's dream to one day study medicine and become a doctor who could support the people in his community had died as well. Our heart sank when we heard this story. We had consciously decided to take a break from reality to restore our batteries. But in this moment, it was difficult to just leave this place without any form of intervention as we had originally intended.

What Africa taught us about wealth creation

Sitting in the huge airplane that took us back to California, we could not believe that it had only been three weeks since we had first set foot on the African continent. When had three weeks ever made such an impression on us?

Mr. Honda had claimed that this journey would teach me more about wealth creation than the finance industry ever would. He was certainly right about that, even though not all these insights were as obvious at first glance. But in the following decades of being a banker, I reflected a lot about the role money played in people's lives. There is a saying that money cannot buy happiness, and while I tend to agree with this statement, there is an arrogance to it, too.

For Duncan Sundays and his family, our monthly transfer of money to cover his school fees and later university tuition did buy a great deal of happiness and meaning over the decades. And from Natalie, the head of the School of Hope, we knew that Duncan's family was tremendously grateful for that.

So, depending on the context, a certain amount of money could make somebody feel tremendously rich, whereas in another context the same amount could make other human beings feel poor as a church mouse. This statement might not sweep you off your feet intellectually, Sophia, but it was this insight that triggered a deeper thought process that formed the basis for my thinking around money for the rest of my life. I realized that to be successful in the money arena being good at handling one's financial resources or having a great adviser was not enough, not even for my wealthy clients. To master the area of personal finance, we had to get our head around our relationship toward money first. Of course, I could help my clients make better investment choices, but if they were not ready to engage with the topic on a deeper level, their struggle for *more* could easily become a never-ending one.

If this sounds nebulous, I ought to admit that I initially failed to communicate these thoughts more clearly to my clients as well. What helped to get my messages across more effectively was to rely on Mr. Honda's distinction between Money IQ on the one side and Money EQ on the other side, which he also described in his book *Happy Money*. According to Mr. Honda, Money IQ relates to the skills and expertise obtained from areas such as money management or investing. This is the kind of financial literacy that my clients expected me to share and apply for them. Reading the market, knowing about different investment strategies, asset allocation, understanding the tax structure of certain investments, risk protection, and so on and so forth. Money EQ, on the other hand, is a different ball game altogether. It taps into our emotional intelligence and reflects our personal beliefs, thoughts, and emotions around money and our personal finances.

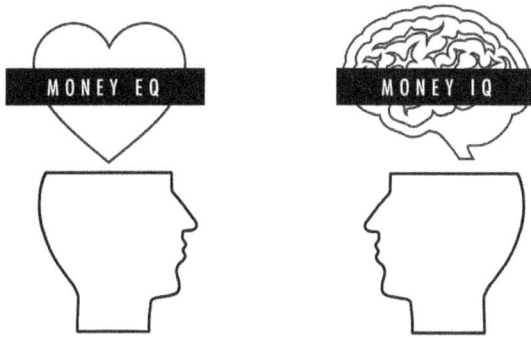

Of course, this latter concept was more difficult to grasp and sell. And despite being a banker for many years, I could not answer what money meant to me emotionally either. I was so focused on the mechanics of making money that I found it difficult to bring the concept of emotional financial intelligence to full fruition. My mind was spinning from the symmetry of this equation I suddenly faced: rational and logical on the one side, and emotional and somewhat irrational on the other side.

But over the years I understood that these were two sides of the same coin, and the side that I favored revealed something essential about the person I was back then. Prior to meeting Mr. Honda and traveling through Kenya with little hesitation, I would have believed exclusively in the side that was logical, rational, and exact. But now, much to my own surprise, like a man who suddenly realized he was developing into a more mature version of himself, that other emotional side was providing the breakthrough that I was unconsciously looking for.

And while Barbara was still searching for the recipe for a healthy life, I was silently working on distilling the essence to creating financial wisdom for people to make peace with money.

Making deposits

Today I am more convinced than ever that having a high Money EQ is a cornerstone of subjective financial wellbeing. And the good thing is, it is a skill anyone can learn. So, for you to invest your time smartly at the Bank of Life and make deposits into the account of your personal finances, I would like to share a few questions that might help you and others to raise your emotional intelligence around this topic and make sense of this underexposed side of the subject at hand.

1. What does your money mindset look like?

After returning from Kenya, I started reflecting on Mr. Honda's question about what my money mindset looked like. As a young banker from New York, whose parents had lived through the Great Depression and endured poverty in three different countries so that their thoughts had mainly circled around survival, I never forgot the sleepless nights hearing my parents roaming around the house, discussing our perilous financial situation. And it was during these nights that I had promised myself to one day get us out of poverty. While this pain had been a helpful driving force, it now took me in the opposite direction. I realized that I had become stuck in a scarcity mindset—a sure way to make withdrawals from this account at the Bank of Life, as it often leads to people spending their time worrying and never feeling financially secure no matter how comfortable their circumstances. And this often happens without us even noticing.

So, what about you, Sophia? Does your money mindset allow you to find peace of mind, or is it creeping in, making undue withdrawals from this account at the Bank of Life without you even being aware of it?

2. What do you usually focus on?

If I learned one thing over the course of my banking career, then it is this: Whether people feel they have enough is not decided by the bottom line of their bank account. I remember a time when I was the financial adviser for a well-known celebrity, who herself was from a wealthy family that had already made a fortune in the hotel business over generations. Despite all the accumulated financial wealth in the background, this woman was restless and never felt safe. In her mind she had to earn one billion with her brand herself before she could settle down and feel at peace. A true story! So even having all the money in the world doesn't prevent people from worrying about money, if you focus on what you don't have.

Research overwhelmingly shows that people's happiness does not grow proportionally with their financial resources beyond a certain amount that covers the expenses of a normal middle-class existence. Feeling rich is, in these cases, much more a mental game, as it is a reflection of what you objectively have. If you are a multimillionaire jealously watching the superyachts of the billionaires, and I have met a few of those, what is the point of it all? So, ask yourself, what do you usually focus on?

If you focus on what you don't have, happiness will always remain elusive. If, however, you feel *grateful* for what you have and focus on what you can contribute to the lives of others, chances are that you will always find a way to be resourceful and feel rich in life, creating millions of opportunities along the way.

3. What does wealth mean to you?

Before investing too much of one's time exclusively focusing on making money, I would suggest you first explore what wealth really means to you. Recently, I learned that the United States scored in the top ten of the most stressed-out citizens in the world despite

being the wealthiest nation in the world. This is even more puz-
zling when you consider that the other countries in the top ten
were countries like Rwanda, Uganda, Sri Lanka, Iran, Albania, and
Tanzania—countries in which people fear for their primary safety,
survival, or even basic human rights.

At the bank, I was helping my clients to become richer. And for
most of them, that meant having an abundance of financial resources
and valuable material possessions. But what Africa taught us was
that there were many other forms of wealth that could make a human
being feel rich, like being close to nature, nourishing one's spirituality,
forming relationships in one's community, feeling strong physically and mentally, living in the here and now. So, distributing your
resources wisely at the Bank of Life includes reflecting deeply about
what wealth really means to you before you start investing your time
in ways that do not get you what you really want on a deeper level.

4. Are you assuming full responsibility for this area of your life?

While there is no linear relationship between the amount of money
in one's bank account and one's level of happiness, health, and fulfillment, research shows that a troublesome financial existence is
pushing people straight into the opposite direction. Did you know,
for example, that financial stress is known to be one of the main
causes of divorce? Or that people even commit suicide if they don't
see a way out of their financial worries? While having money is
not the magic key to a great life per se, the absence of money can
truly make life hell. It can absorb all of people's attention, just like a
toothache. You can have a great life, but if your tooth is constantly
aching, you have a problem that you cannot ignore. All it matters
then is to get rid of the toothache. And the same is true for serious
financial problems.

For the majority, there is a lot that revolves around money in some form or fashion, and in combination with the other qualities of the Big Five at the Bank of Life, having our financial house in order provides the basis for a good life and helps us to avoid chaos and misfortune. So, if you are a teacher, a rocket scientist, or a business owner, from my perspective everybody is well advised to assume full responsibility for this area of their lives. Even if the cards are stacked against you, ignoring this subject usually only makes things worse.

So, the question is: Are you assuming full responsibility for your personal finances, Sophia?

The other side of the coin

Now, after looking at the emotional side of this subject, we ought to admit that the equation itself is not symmetrical without shining some light on the rational side too. As a financial adviser, I was trained early in my career to help people do exactly that: save money for retirement, minimize tax burdens, make wise investment choices. However, the rules of money constantly change. Tax laws change. Investment strategies, buyer trends, and trade dynamics change. And so, just as I didn't provide you with specific health advice in my previous letter, I won't push you toward investing in a certain asset class, buying into a certain retirement option, exploring certain cryptocurrencies, or hiding gold ingots under your mattress. What I will do instead is to share five basic thoughts for you to think on when making deposits into this account at the Bank of Life going forward.

1. Educate yourself

Given the same other conditions, people with a higher Money IQ are more likely to make small and large financial decisions that work in their favor. From my point of view, this is a skill so essential that it should be taught in school, which is of course true for all of the Big Five elements at the Bank of Life. How come we leave school without the basic knowledge in these areas of our life that would help us go through it more smoothly? So if you feel, like many people do, that you are lacking the necessary insights to master this area of your life, my recommendation would be to approach somebody knowledgeable, whose income is not attached to the sale of certain financial products itself—as this person might be biased, despite their best intentions. In addition, you might read a couple of introductory books on this topic too. I will provide you with a few recommendations on where to start. Once you have done that, you are in a better position to fine-tune your financial planning activities.

2. Personal financial planning

Personal financial planning is a systematic approach whereby a person maximizes the existing financial resources through proper management of one's finances to best achieve his or her financial goals in the future. While we cannot predict the future, we can certainly be better prepared for it. Whether you have just left university or are nearing the end of your career, whether it's having enough for short-term financial needs or saving for your child's education, you can always create and move toward a stronger financial future. And the first step is to evaluate where you are now. To make sure your number is correct, you must get an overview of your current financial situation. First, figure out what you need to be financially secure. How much money do you spend each month for the essentials (1. Your home / 2. Food / 3. Utilities / 4. Transportation / 5. Insurances / 6. Other necessary items)? For the majority of us, these six categories make up about 65 to 75%

of our expenses. If you add these numbers up and multiply that sum by twelve, you will find out what you need to earn in a year to achieve financial security based on your current standard of living. The following step is to figure out what you spend on leisure time activities, eating out, clothing, traveling, and the like. Multiply that by twelve too and add to your essentials. Equipped with these insights, do the math. What do you earn? How do these figures go together? If they don't, what will you do?

3. Set goals that suit you

If you ever visit a financial planner, they are highly likely to begin your financial planning activity by asking you what your financial goals are. But while it's sometimes helpful to look for examples or guidelines, don't just adopt someone else's plan. This is about how you want to live *your* life! So, think about what suits you and your needs. And do not try to build a financial strategy that prevents any investments into the playful side of life for too long! For instance, if investing into a certain hobby or extensive travel is who you are, take that into consideration. So, with this in mind, ask yourself: How much money do you need to be safe and financially secure? What does it take to be financially independent? What are your dreams and ambitions for your financial future? Trust your intuition. It is going to be very helpful to have clarity around this number, as it will guide your actions in a miraculous way. So, write that number down and let it sink in. For many people that figure might feel daunting at first. But go ahead. Some solid analysis will provide you with the financial planning insights you need to turn your financial expectations into reality. Most people spend more time planning their vacation than identifying their financial goals. But having this kind of clarity can bring peace of mind to your life and shape your decision making in a constructive way.

4. Live within your means and stretch the boundaries smartly

If you want to live like the proverbial Zen Millionaire, one way to approach this is to live within your means and stretch the boundaries smartly by borrowing money only for the right reasons. Like investing in your personal development, buying your own property, or building your business. Borrowing money just to finance consumption is an absolute no-go from the perspective of an old-school banker like me. You might consider this old-fashioned, but I know that many of my younger colleagues out there still agree with me on this principle. So my advice is: spend less than you earn, invest a proportion of what you earn smartly, and learn skills for making a good income!

This approach will allow you to progress while still enabling you to live a balanced life. Of course, some entrepreneurs might reject these ideas. Always striving for more is what has made them succeed. And I am sure there is some truth in it, too. But doing this over a lifetime is a risky game to play if you work around the clock toward some future financial goals that might never manifest themselves.

However, if you choose to do exactly that, make sure you pursue something that is of meaning to you and others.

5. Tap into the power of the eighth wonder of the world

As mentioned earlier, I do not want to interfere in finding the right strategies to pursue your goals. However, if you want to make your money work effectively for you, you need to tap into what Albert Einstein allegedly called the eighth wonder of the world: compound interest. Compound interest occurs when the interest you earn on a balance in a savings account is reinvested, earning you more interest. As Benjamin Franklin once said, "Money makes money. And the money that money makes, makes more money." And the earlier you start using this magical principle, the better.

To illustrate this, suppose we're looking at two brothers, William and James, with two different approaches to saving money for retirement, an example taken from Burton Gordon Malkiel, a Princeton University economist and author of the all-time classic finance book *A Random Walk Down Wall Street*.

- William saves $4,000 annually starting at age 20. He stops investing at age 40. Thus, over a period of 20 years, William's total investment adds up to $80,000.

- His brother James saves $4,000 annually starting at age 40. He stops saving at age 65. Thus, over a period of 25 years, James's total investment adds up to $100,000.

The question is: Which brother has more money in his account at the age of retirement when they compare their returns? William, who invested $80,000 over 20 years, or James, who invested $100,000 over 25 years?

The answer is (drumroll please!): William! He won the race hands down! William, who invested a smaller amount overall, ends up with roundabout $2.5 million. James has less than $400,000. That's a gap of over $2 million. By starting to make use of the power of the eighth wonder of the world early in life, William had earned 600% more than his brother even though he invested the exact same amount per year for less time.

Remember, the two brothers were not earning interest on just the $4,000 they saved each year—but they were also earning on all the interest payments their account accrued over the decades. And while the interest rates used in this example were arbitrarily high from my perspective, the same principles apply regardless of the rate. And that is why the power of compounding is the most important principle to ensure a healthy retirement from a financial perspective, even if you are not in your twenties or thirties. It is never too late to make the eighth wonder of the world work for you.

Wrapping up

Now if taking care of this element at the Bank of Life sounds like work, Sophia, I can assure you it is. However, once you have acquired some basic knowledge, engaged properly in your financial planning activities, and implemented your strategies, the time investment needed to keep this going in the years to come is limited. Unlike some of the other elements at the Bank of Life that need daily attention, this one is happy on its own much of the time. We often can get away with checking in with our strategies and seeing how they work as little as once or twice a year. Time-wise, there is a substantial investment in the beginning, but then it pays off in the years to come.

And remember, success is what you see in it. And here we come back to the emotional part of the matter. Over the years, I've met many people who were living their best life on average or high incomes or even below-average incomes. And the longer I live, the more I realize what a great psychologist Mr. Honda had been when he had claimed that in many ways people only have one relationship in their life. Whether we think of our material wealth, our family, our work, or our health, we are always in a relationship with ourselves first and foremost. And this relationship determines how we perceive and interpret the world around us.

Many people who strive for more and more money and material possessions unconsciously aim to fill a deeper void inside, like a fundamental lack of certainty, connection, or recognition. But these holes in their souls cannot be plugged with financial resources.

So, whatever you choose to strive for, Sophia, make sure that you do not miss out on life altogether. Delaying gratification is, without question, a huge part of most financial success, but remember you only get one life. And if you would ask me today if I would rather be young and poor or rich and old, I would choose young and poor.

Because, at the end, we all realize that time is all we ever had.

Many best wishes,
J. Leonardo
Still a banker at heart.

CHAPTER 12

Sophia: Finding Abundance

Chronology: three months and eight days after Leonardo and Sophia's brief encounter at San Francisco Airport.

It was a cloudy day in May, and Sophia was sitting in the Five Elephant in too-cool-for-school Kreuzberg. Once the city's poorest area, it now boasted countless museums, galleries, as well as many of the trendiest cafés and restaurants in Berlin. The Five Elephant claimed to serve the best African coffee in town, and when Sophia had finished reading Leonardo's last letter, she was intrigued once again. His account of his journey to Kenya prompted warm memories of watching endless documentaries about African wildlife that had been so in vogue in her childhood. Leonardo had a way of writing that pulled her in almost instantly, and she found it fascinating to read about his upbringing, his travels with Barbara, and everything else too. How much this man trusted her! It warmed her heart.

Though admittedly sometimes it was exactly this seemingly unfounded trust that still bothered her. On such days, she had the impression Leonardo's attitude toward her was overly familiar, and their relationship felt static as their communication only went one way. Then she'd wondered why Leonardo had chosen to contact her in particular. From a certain point of view, it definitely made sense. She was an author, a coach, and a keynote speaker and thus had many avenues to get Leonardo's message out into the world. But why had seeing her picture made such a difference for him?

A couple of weeks ago, she had even contacted her Norwegian colleague Annicken to shed more light on the matter. Under the pretense of discussing some work-related issue, she had casually brought up the brief encounter with Leonardo again. After all, Annicken was the only other person she knew who had met Leonardo in person as well. Sophia had been beating around the bush, as she wanted the letters to remain her secret. And so, without going into any kind of depth, Annicken had just confirmed what she had already shared with her in her initial voicemail message.

Sophia scanned the café with its minimalist décor and huge windows—so typical for Berlin—with her eyes wide open.

How was it possible that there were now two bankers touching her life in this peculiar way? One was presumably in his nineties, wise and kind; the other, a man in his prime, smart and bold. Both present and absent when they chose to be.

She took another sip of the hot drink made of Ethiopian coffee beans, freshly grated ginger, spiced with cardamon and a tiny bit of cinnamon, blended with frothed milk. She relished the exotic taste when it suddenly occurred to her that she had met both men through air travel. How very strange indeed! But while the encounter with Leonardo seemed to have been planned for reasons that were still beyond her, meeting Ruben had been a pure coincidence.

Back then, she had lived on the outskirts of London, in a small, beautiful town. She remembered how moving there had felt like moving back in time. Sophia had loved living in Britain; for her it had been liberating to leave Germany behind for a few years, particularly career-wise. In the country where she grew up, one had to have a specific degree in management to get the position she had been offered in the internationally renowned business school situated right on the River Thames. Sophia, however, had preferred to study everything that had interested her before applying for her first job.

In England, this diverse approach to learning had been appreciated and not looked down upon. And after a few years there, the CEO of a Scandinavian management consultancy had asked Sophia to join their newly established office in London, a challenge that Sophia happily accepted. From then onward, she worked as an international consultant, commuting regularly either to the city of London or flying all over the world. And on one of these flights, when returning from a business trip to Copenhagen, Ruben—with his straight, light-blond hair, his striking blue eyes, and fine nose and lips—had sat next to her on the plane. Sophia had been genuinely surprised that he, sharp witted, successful, and handsome, had asked her for her phone number. He was a Danish investment banker based in London, who was working for a leading global investment manager as Head of International Advisory Services for the EMEA region. And while Sophia had not expected to hear from him again, he did indeed call her, and they met for a shopping trip at Harrods. They both needed Christmas presents for their families back home, and from then onward they had been an item—or so Sophia thought.

She looked at the finger where she had once worn the expensive ring that he had given her for their first anniversary. Ruben was a force of nature—charismatic, funny, and sometimes bossy. He seemingly had no problem with upsetting people when somebody did not deserve his kindness or got in the way of him achieving his goals. And while Sophia could be quite assertive as well, her high level of empathy was often at odds with her own well-being. Being that sensitive was a double-edged sword—it was the aspect of her personality type that made her so successful in her profession but at the same time undermined an energy-efficient operation, as Ruben had put it. Maybe it was not such a surprise that the two of them had not been a good match after all. A more contained, cultivated, and more agreeable man like Leonardo would possibly suit her better. However, Leonardo was on his way out, and her relationship with Ruben was over and had been over for a very long time. Everybody but Sophia had known that. She had been riding a dead horse for too long; the absurdity of this image made her giggle. Ruben was very much alive, but the relationship wasn't. She sighed.

And now there was Leonardo, another banker, pushing her to take more responsibility for her personal finances. Ruben had done so too when she was still working in London and even more so when she decided to set up her own business and become self-employed. But Ruben was gone. And independent of his presence or his absence in her life, she had not been taking care of this account at the Bank of Life yet.

Sophia looked out of the window dreamily. In the past few weeks, she had been able to establish a series of routines to raise her energy levels again, which already showed some positive effects. Of course, getting her head around the topics of health, nutrition, and fitness had been much easier for her than engaging with the topic at hand. But reading Leonardo's letter made approaching this new task seem less daunting, and it gave her the satisfying feeling that she was already better at it than she thought. Financial wellbeing could be achieved in different ways. And it was as much a mental game as it was about accumulating assets. That resonated with what Sophia had observed over the years in her coaching practice too.

No matter what people achieved—hitting the jackpot, receiving a huge bonus, reaching retirement—long-lasting happiness was apparently not part of the evolutionary design. Even when financial or other goals accomplished were enormous, moments of pleasure were usually short-lived, and the emotional backswing was already on its way. And responsible for this dilemma was again the tiny neurotransmitter in the brain called dopamine, which was swinging back and forth like a seesaw. Feelings of pleasure induced by a dopamine hit would forever be followed by moments of pain induced by a dopamine deficit to make human beings go and seek it again. Sophia made a drawing in her notebook.

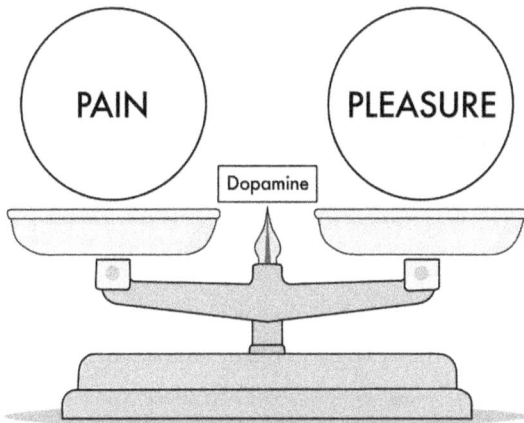

Arriving at a happiness plateau to then rest on one's laurels happily ever after was never about to happen. Humans were built to want and to strive. Without striving toward something, they felt empty, often lacking energy, no matter the bank account. And the only sensible solution to the problem presented was to attach one's feeling of contentment around that: a pursuit that balanced out pain and pleasure. There was no escaping this law of nature. This tiny neurotransmitter was relentlessly swinging back and forth, and even winning an Oscar or becoming a multimillionaire could not make this ancient actor behave otherwise.

Sophia's eyes sparkled. These were fascinating, and incredibly useful, insights. Gaining a deeper understanding of dopamine explained so much about the struggles and disappointments people were experiencing these days, and it even supported Leonardo's message about the importance of raising one's Money EQ first too.

But of course, there was also the other side of the equation, which Leonardo referred to as Money IQ, or her financial literacy. This was definitely an area where she could make more deposits in. She could certainly give herself credit for the fact that she was on a respectable day rate, and there was an impressive stream of income coming her way across the year. However, while she was fairly good at making money, she had neither taken care of her financial future nor taken time to invest her money in smart ways at all.

Sophia examined the hand-carved wooden giraffe statue standing close to her. She loved learning, and maybe by digging into this subject, she could generate some curiosity for it along the way too. For her, finance had always represented the boring side of life that she had shied away from. But she was determined to plan in some time to make her initial deposits into this account. And she would start by reading a book on personal finance that Ruben had given her a couple of years ago and then make a plan on how to proceed. She smiled thinking again about Mr. Honda and his ideas around happy and unhappy money. Did such thoughts ever cross Ruben's mind when advising his clients to make this or that investment? Whether she liked it or not, the answer was probably yes. She had to admit that the truth was usually not as one-sided as the heart of a disappointed lover wanted it to be.

Following a sudden impulse, Sophia finished her coffee, biting on the spicy ginger. After paying her bill, she stepped out of the

Five Elephant and went back on her bike. Riding alongside a picturesque canal that ran through Kreuzberg, she noticed the canal's leafy banks bustling with people in cafés, shops, and restaurants. She liked this neighborhood. There was a different energy to it compared to the fully gentrified streets of Berlin-Mitte, where she usually spent most of her time. Following her intuition, she soon came across Victoria Park, which she had read about earlier in her city guide and now reminded her of the Victoria Lake in Africa that Barbara and Leonardo had visited. This was how selective attention worked. From her brain's perspective, Africa—that much was obvious—was the theme of the day.

When she parked her bike next to the artificial waterfall on top of the hill overlooking the city, she thought about how she herself had visited Karen Blixen's home in Denmark a few years prior. Following Ruben's recommendation, she had taken a train from Copenhagen to the center of Rungsted, a small place by the sea, and then walked about a mile through the woods to discover more about the life of this truly original character. Sophia remembered examining Karen Blixen's study, in which she had written her internationally renowned stories about Africa that had formed the basis for the famous movie that Leonardo and Barbara had watched together.

Back then, Sophia had asked herself if she would also one day engage in a more creative form of writing. As a child, she had dreamed of becoming an artist, a musician, a painter, or a writer. But she had doubted that she had the talents to do so. And now here she was, in the middle of Berlin, ruminating on a letter from an old investment banker who had once visited the African home of an author whose Danish home Sophia had visited a few decades later, and who was now asking her to engage in a project that might offer her the opportunity she had been dreaming about all that time ago.

Everything seemed so interconnected to Sophia in this moment. Life was truly a mystery.

CHAPTER 13

Leonardo: Our Psychology

What you think, you become. What you feel, you attract.
What you imagine, you create.

—Buddha

Dear Sophia,

Good morning from Santa Barbara. Do you like palm trees? I
have asked a gardener to plant two small palm trees at the spot
where the Japanese teahouse once stood. For me, it is a soothing
thought that these trees will be growing strong here while I am
in the process of disappearing, following Barbara into the vastness
of the universe. Jokingly, I have named the one standing closer to
our house Leonardo and the other closer to the beach Barbara. Can
you promise me to look after both of us, Sophia? I have always been
more of an introvert, I guess, but my wife needed to talk to feel
alive. So if you direct most of your attention to her, that's okay, but
we both need water and sunshine to thrive!

You might wonder how an old man can have such an immature sense of humor, and the truth is, while my body ages, there are pieces in my identity that seem to survive all passage of time. Barbara and I discussed this a lot. As children we believe that everything *inside* will feel completely different when we grow up, and this is true, but also not true at all.

So let me transition to the main topic of this letter. As you know, Sophia, this is not the first time that I set out to write about one of the possibly most complex accounts at the Bank of Life: our psychology. Our mind. Our soul. Again, there are many names for it. And while for some it might be all the same, others might use a whole different language to describe what is happening inside of us.

Nonetheless, for our mission, conceptual perfection is not the highest goal. Let's just assume our psychology encompasses a number of aspects, such as imagination, perception, belief, identity, personality. And that it includes the study of conscious and unconscious phenomena, as well as feeling and thought, and maybe more. Whatever way you look at it, this account at the Bank of Life is all about these invisible dynamics that determine the filter through which we experience our life and the world around us. And I can tell you that it was not easy to settle on a way to address a topic of such an immense scope. Faced with the vagueness of this endeavor, I was arguing with myself for days—first not being able to decide which pieces of our life I should put under the spotlight in order to tell this part of our story well. But then something happened that helped me to get unstuck.

One evening, when I was sitting on the couch ruminating on some unhelpful thoughts, the doorbell rang. Hesitantly pushing my rollator in front of me, I walked toward the intercom system to see who was there. It was Fifi, my new neighbor. I hesitated to open the door for a few seconds, but the moment I did, a sparkle of inspiration swept into the house. Fifi, with some delicious food in her arms, asked me to have dinner with her.

After chitchatting for a while about this and that, enjoying our food, I carefully started sharing some of my concerns around my writing with her. On the one hand, I did not want to disclose too much about our joint mission, as this is a secret that the two of us share exclusively. On the other hand, I knew that I could use some inspiration. But Fifi seemed to understand. And after listening to me attentively, she asked whether I thought it might be of help to start the next day by drawing a mind map on a piece of paper, focusing on the question on how it all began. I nodded. This sounded like a plan.

For the rest of the evening, we sat together sharing a bottle of red wine, looking out of the window into the sunset. We didn't mention my writing again. Care dressed in the gown of unobtrusiveness is surely a gift that human beings can pass on to each other, and I wondered if this was a skill that could be taught in school too.

Interestingly, this was all it took to get an old engine started again. The next morning, I made a few notes in my book, and now three days later, I am actually writing this part of our story using the mind map to organize my thoughts. By the way, I will meet with Fifi again over the weekend. As a behavioral neuroscientist working at a private institution in Malibu, she kindly offered to be of help with some of the information that I want to share with you in this letter. But for now, let's focus on the question of how Barbara and my interest in this new subject matter was ignited in the first place.

A phony cure

The truth is that both of us had always been fascinated with the question of how our mind worked. And Barbara had frequently asked herself why the link between a person's thoughts, attitudes, feelings, and behavior and their physical health had received so little attention in her medical education. However, it really hit home when she ran into Alex one day, an old acquaintance from medical school who had been visiting one of his customers in the Santa Barbara area.

Alex was still working at the same pharmaceutical company that had offered a job to both of them right after finishing medical school. And all those years ago, Alex had accepted the offer, while Barbara had decided against it. The idea that all of life could take on a different direction by making one single alternative decision at a specific moment in time had always intrigued Barbara.

And when the two of them sat down at a seaside restaurant, they both filled each other in about how their careers had developed since leaving university. And with her typical enthusiasm, Barbara told Alex all about the possibilities and limitations of being a general practitioner, the trip to Israel, and how that had inspired her to move toward a more holistic approach of treating her patients. Alex listened with interest, but based on his comments, she was not sure if he could make sense of it all. And when Barbara described the river of life and how she was now trying to equip her patients to become better swimmers, instead of rescuing them when they were already drowning, it seemed as if she had lost him. However, she did not feel offended. Alex's interest had always been in scientific data and generic evidence and not on treating people as such. And he was still such an engaging communicator that Barbara could have listened to him for hours on end about his work at the pharmaceutical company. Sharing some news about his latest research projects he was overseeing, Alex joked about how Mr. Placebo might be ruining his plans for this year.

"He is doing it again! I hate this guy. I really do!"

Barbara looked puzzled. "Who?" She was not quite sure if she had understood him correctly.

Alex looked at her in exaggerated disbelief. "We used to call you Speedy Babs. You read the textbooks at the speed of light. Don't disappoint me now."

Barbara, who had never heard this nickname before, started laughing so much that she choked on her drink. When she had calmed herself down, she exclaimed, "AH! You mean the placebo effect."

"Correct, my dear. You need to look after yourself!" Alex mimicked concern and touched her on her shoulder. It was just like in the old days, she thought, when Alex continued.

"Believe it or not, in our clinical research, the placebo effect is one of the most annoying problems of all. It is no secret that we earn good money in our industry, and I would be lying if I said I did not enjoy my work. However, we are under immense pressure to be profitable and satisfy our stakeholders. Of course, we want to help our patients, but as in any other business, we have targets that need to be achieved. And if I look at this year, it is going to be tough for us. We have three promising drugs in the pipeline, and now our good old friend 'Placebo' seems to want to fight for our bonus too."

In medical school Barbara had been fascinated by the idea that something as harmless as a sugar pill could relieve a person's pain or hasten their recovery just by the expectation that it would. But Alex interrupted her thoughts.

"Did you know that the word placebo comes from Latin and means 'I shall please'?" Alex paused and continued. "It does not please me, I can tell you that!"

He laughed again and made a boxing gesture, as if fighting against an invisible force in front of him. Barbara smiled, as was expected of her. Her former colleague was indeed very entertaining, but she was hooked on the topic now and wanted to understand the deeper meaning behind what Alex described from a medical perspective.

"I see. I see. But how do you explain the placebo effect as a researcher?"

"As a researcher?" Alex looked dismissively. "Basically, there is nothing to explain. It is just in people's heads!"

And then he continued, adopting for the first time the tone of the senior scientist he truly was. "Our hypothesis is that the placebo effect is produced by the self-fulfilling effects of response expectancies, in which the belief that one will feel different leads a person to actually feel different. The belief that one has received an active treatment then produces the changes thought to be produced by the real treatment."

Alex paused.

"So in a way it is all just psychological nonsense, and yet it still ruins my deadlines!"

Barbara shook her head and they both laughed. In some ways, Alex was not the most profound human being she had ever come across, but she truly appreciated him. He was a researcher and a very good one indeed, considering all his achievements over the years. And his work really mattered, even if not all the drugs produced were put to good use and many people would be better off if they were advised to make different lifestyle choices so they wouldn't even need those drugs to start with. Barbara, on the other hand, was working with real patients and was interested in every single one of them. And maybe for the time being, it was her job to find a deeper meaning behind this conversation and not his.

The power within

In the weeks to come, Barbara tried to do precisely that. And she soon found out that the placebo effect was not exclusively in people's heads as Alex had claimed but happening on a physiological level measurable with conservative clinical diagnostics. People who took placebos showed positive changes in blood pressure, heart rate, brain chemistry, blood test results, and so on and so forth. And interestingly enough, it also worked the other way around. The naughty brother of the placebo, the nocebo effect (in Latin, I shall harm—Barbara smiled when she looked this up in the dictionary) seemed equally influential.

The impact these two volatile relatives could have on one's physical health was simply amazing. In one study by Irving Kirsch, participants suffering from severe depression were given pills labeled as either fast-acting antidepressants or placebos. Participants who took the placebo reported decreased depressive symptoms and even showed increased brain activity in areas of the brain linked to stress regulation. Another study by Walter Brown centered on a group of people who had thought they were being exposed to poison ivy. The expectation of a reaction alone was enough for a visible rash and boils under their skin to break out, as well as itching and other symptoms. And when the experiment was reversed, and a group of people who were allergic to the substance were indeed exposed to poison ivy but told that it was a completely harmless plant, less than one in six reacted to it.

One evening, when Barbara had just finished sharing another one of these stories that she had come across that day, she leaned back in her chair.

"But now what, Leonardo? What do we do with these insights?"

We had just enjoyed our dinner with some fresh salad, baked salmon, and a glass of red wine from Napa Valley a few hundred kilometers north of Santa Barbara. I was feeling content, and I looked at Barbara in anticipation. After weeks of zooming out, collecting data, stories, and insights, this was Barbara's moment of synthesis.

"If so many patients can improve with a harmless sugar pill or distilled water, getting the desired result without actually taking the pharmacologically active substance, should we not feel compelled to explore this further? These studies clearly indicate that we all have all the biological and even neurological machinery to activate healing in ourselves by ourselves by THOUGHT ALONE! A belief can change the physiological reality of a person. This is revolutionary and yet nobody seems to care!"

I nodded in agreement and Barbara continued.

"Think how much more doctors could accomplish if they strove to activate this effect."

She only stopped for a second.

"And the next question that we should ask ourselves is: Do people really need a sugar pill or an injection to change their state of being? Or could we teach people to accomplish the same thing without needing a doctor to trick them into it?"

Barbara took a sip from her glass and looked at the ocean. This was not a dialogue in any sense of the word, but I knew that my presence was important for her thinking process.

"What if people began to believe in themselves, instead of experts outside of themselves? What if they learned how to move themselves to the same state of being as someone who's taking a placebo?"

In those moments, Barbara reminded me of a waterfall with thoughts cascading from her brain, like water from the top of a cliff. One thought after the other, one question leading to the next. I sometimes wondered what would happen if she did not have me to listen to her in these moments. She needed these one-way exchanges like the rest of us needed to breathe. But the good thing was I loved those moments too. I genuinely respected Barbara for her capacity to question things, and it made both of us feel more alive in our relationship too.

Cleaning up the kitchen a little later, still reflecting about our conversation, I asked Barbara if she thought that the placebo effect would shed a different kind of light on Aaron Antonovsky's work as well. Just then I heard a shattering sound, and looking around I saw that my favorite wine glass had broken.

"What a wonderful husband God has granted me," Barbara uttered in my direction. And with a theatrical gesture she took my hand and kissed it over the pieces of my broken glass.

"Look, we need to think this through. Really think this through. From the bottom upward and backward and sideward. If you know what I mean. Why don't we go for a walk on the beach to take this further?"

She hugged me while I was trying to get hold of the vacuum cleaner to take care of the mess on the floor that Barbara had already forgotten about.

And when walking along the shore some twenty minutes later, we both reminded each other of our trip to Israel and how attending the conference had impacted Barbara's work with her patients but also our daily life in the subsequent years. But what Barbara then realized was that, as a conventionally trained doctor, she had still been predominantly absorbed by the physiological aspects of creating health. Aaron, on the other hand, had very much emphasized psychological and sociological factors intervening with people's overall wellbeing. And while he had always pointed out that the context people lived in was also very influential in this process, his research had overwhelmingly demonstrated that the inner strength of a person was capable of overruling both genetic and socioeconomic conditions when well developed.

For a long time, Barbara could not stop thinking about this topic. If the human psyche was so powerful, then why did conventional medicine not attempt to make more intentional use of it? With the help of a few consistent lifestyle choices, human beings could affect each cell of their physical existence in a positive way within a matter of weeks or months. Could people also become the architects of their psychology, thereby positively influencing their health and wellbeing overall? And if so, how could one use one's mental strength to implement new lifestyle choices more sustainably?

A whole array of new questions emerged, and while it seemed obvious that Barbara would not possibly be able to explore all of them in depth within one lifetime, she wanted to start somewhere. The power of the mind could not just be ignored when attempting to be a good healer—that much was unambiguous.

Looking on the bright side

This time Barbara did go back to university. After substantially cutting down on her workload, she signed up for an academic program in psychology. And back on campus, she truly enjoyed being in education again. Her brain absorbed every piece of information it came across. And even though she was often mistaken as the professor of the class she attended, she did not mind at all. One day when sitting in the library, still feeling grateful about all the learning opportunities coming her way, she studied the book of a famous psychologist. In one of the last chapters of *Motivation and Personality*, Abraham Maslow addressed the scientific community with an urgent claim to return to the earlier mission of psychology—focusing on improving normal life instead of exclusively concentrating on psychological dysfunction. This, for Barbara, was like a lightning bolt.

She suddenly realized that all of the classes she had been attending so far had been directed toward the downside of psychological functioning. One psychological disease after the other had been put under the microscope, and she was surprised how little she had thought about that before. Apparently, she had enjoyed the process of learning so much that she hadn't noticed that she hadn't found what she had originally been looking for. She would not become a psychotherapist or psychiatrist, that was for sure. She was a doctor who wanted to help her patients activate the power within, nurture their psychology, and support them to act on their positive intentions. However, these kinds of questions had not been remotely touched upon at all.

Enlightened by this sense of clarity, she shared her observations with some of her professors and raised the question around how the positive side of human potential could get more attention. Nonetheless, the professors she talked to were not only *not* interested in her ideas but almost hostile toward this way of thinking. And even those who had respected her professional experience before changed their attitude toward Barbara.

But my wife was not a young undergraduate who could easily be intimidated. While these reactions surprised, confused, and even offended her, she did not give in. Clinical psychology as it was taught at university served a purpose, Barbara was sure about that, but there was a side of psychology that seemed to be largely neglected. Feeling somehow frustrated, she wondered if her time on campus would come to an end earlier than anticipated—but then something changed her views.

On a sunny autumn day, a few days before the start of the new semester, Barbara overheard a conversation of two students walking in front of her, talking about a new visiting lecturer. His name was Daniel Goleman. He had done his dissertation at Harvard, and rumor had it that he had already worked as a journalist at the *New York Times*. When Barbara saw Daniel driving around the campus in a fire engine–red VW later that day, she sensed that this guy was going to offer something different from what she had been exposed to during the first years of her studies. Smiling at the unusual sight of the car, she spontaneously decided to sign up for Daniel's new course, which proved to be easier said than done. Forbidden fruit usually does not miss its audience, and as the offer seemed to be so far outside the conventional map of psychology back then, hundreds of students gravitated toward it.

The course itself was a surprise package. Daniel's lectures mainly focused on ancient Asian psychology, which—honed over centuries—represented a theory of how mental and spiritual training could lead to a series of sustainable positive outcomes, unheard of in the field of clinical psychology at that time. He spoke about the Buddhist psychological system, his travels to India, different meditation practices and highlighted the possibility of altered personality traits as a consequence of consistent mental and spiritual exercises. Clinical psychology was, in his view, too focused on scrutinizing specific problems, like high anxiety, and then trying to fix that one thing. The Asian psychologies offered a completely different way of looking at people, aiming to enhance the positive side of the human potential.

Barbara was intrigued by this fresh, new perspective. And what fascinated her most was how Daniel combined biographical insights with psychological content, real-life stories with psychological theories. What a powerful teaching method and so unlike her other professors at that time. The students were in awe and literally hanging on his every word. And we discussed much of the content of his lectures and his stories at home too. I even accompanied Barbara to one of Daniel's classes to be able to listen to him in person as well.

Attending Daniel's lecture was truly eye-opening. And Barbara suddenly understood that there were already familiar dynamics at play. While the science of disease was well established both in Western medicine and psychology, the science of health was still lagging behind in both fields. Hence, when the unconventional guest lecturer was gone, Barbara felt that it was time for her to move on as well. She wanted to continue the study of the mind elsewhere, shedding more light on the bright side of the mind's potential too. Her years at the university had been extremely valuable. She felt much more qualified than before to notice mental problems in her patients and refer them to experts in the field. But listening to Daniel's stories and discussing them at home had triggered an appetite for adventure in both of us.

We read Daniel's book *The Science of Meditation*, and we wondered if we could experience some of what he had talked about firsthand.

Traveling inside

And indeed, a few months later, we sat on a plane pursuing this new angle of our quest. This time our destination was India. Following Daniel's recommendations, our trip took us to Dalhousie, a beautiful small village located in the branch of the Himalayas. But it was not the magnificent setting that had brought us there, but a ten-day meditation retreat that Daniel had suggested. We had already engaged in a daily meditation practice at home, but Daniel had argued that this deep dive would allow us to experience the power of meditation on a whole new level. And while I was open to the enterprise itself as well, really looking forward to our journey to India, the long duration of the retreat somehow concerned me. A feeling that was reinforced when we were informed about the peculiar sleeping arrangements upon arrival. I was asked to sleep in a tent for men and Barbara in one for women.

This was not my idea of a getaway. We were still quite young at the time, and I had hoped for a bit of intimacy with my wife along the way too. Not content with the situation, I wanted to convince Barbara that this arrangement would not work for us. But before I came to it, the next thing that we were introduced to was the principle of "noble silence," which meant that we were not allowed to talk to anyone about anything! No nothing to nobody. I was frustrated but realized that this had a comical side to it too. And Barbara and I had been anticipating this trip for such a long time that I tried to accept the situation as it was. Easier said than done.

Every morning, I went to the meditation hall where we would sit down on a cushion that would be our residence through the twelve unnerving hours of meditation that the daily schedule called for. Sitting in the usual half lotus position, our mental task for the first days was to tune into the sensation of breathing through our nostrils. However, all I could think of was the growing muscle pain that started in my legs and soon extended to my back and my whole torso. Sometimes, I had to occasionally stop myself from giggling desperately, as the situation was getting more ridiculous by the minute. We had invested so much energy, time, and money to sit here at the other end of the world, to experience muscle cramps that I had not known before. I was glad that my colleagues from the bank could not see me. The cost benefit analysis would not run in my favor.

But then, after a few days, things started shifting. While my muscle cramps were still troublesome at times, I started getting glimpses into a new sense of well-being here and there. And a couple of days later, I found myself entering a state of total absorption. The frustration was gone and without realizing it, I became fully present. So present that I was not even aware of it. My thoughts and my ego were resting, finally. And at the end of the retreat, this presence allowed me to sit for hours on end. Time itself had seemingly changed its characteristics. And both Barbara and I were convinced that there were methods out there that could deeply transform our minds in order to produce a greater sense of wellbeing. Happiness was maybe not as much a function of circumstances as we often thought in our Western societies.

After the retreat had ended, we still had almost a week left to explore the countryside. We soon found out that Dalhousie was a haven for people like us who simply liked spending whole days walking in nature. Surrounded by hills and valleys covered in snow, this place looked no less than magical. Sometimes we caught glimpses of the majestic Mount Everest, which back then had only been hiked by the most adventurous human beings on earth. One day we came across a temple that was crowded by the people of the village who had come together to celebrate the goddess of the mountain. Another day, we walked to one of the most amazing waterfalls that we had ever seen. Perched at a height of more than two thousand meters above sea level amid tall pine trees, it offered spectacular views of the snow-capped peaks surrounding it. We felt blessed but, at the same time, deeply centered—a state of being that we had not known in such intensity before.

And only when traveling back to the US, stuck in various airports, did the high begin to disappear. When meditating again at home, we still experienced the healing effects of meditation on our body and our mind. Though to tell the truth, it was not easy to reach this state of total bliss again. Sometimes, we compared it to traveling to a foreign country. While we knew that this country existed, the transportation system to get us there was not functioning as well, or as quickly, as we expected.

The voice inside our head

After our trip to Dalhousie, we wrote a long thank you letter to Daniel, describing our retreat and our subsequent holiday worshipping nature, the culture, and the people of Dalhousie in great detail. After all, without Barbara attending Daniel's course and listening to his stories, we would not have experienced any of this.

We also admitted to him that we did not find it easy to integrate this meditation practice into our daily life, being back in the US. But speaking to Daniel on the phone a couple of weeks later, he was completely nonjudgmental about it and recommended trying out a different form of meditation called mindfulness in addition, which would possibly fit more easily into the Californian way of living. He suggested we visit Michael Singer, a spiritual teacher who lived in a meditation center in Florida, where people of all belief systems could gather together to find more inner peace. And that is what we did. Following in Daniel's footsteps once again, we attended a three-day mindfulness retreat as the final peak activity of Barbara's study and education time. And it was worth it.

Arriving at the "Temple of the Universe" in the middle of a huge forest in Florida, we quickly realized that this retreat was indeed going to be different from the first one in Dalhousie. It was much shorter, with less travel time and no separate tents for men and women to start with. And while the principle of noble silence applied there as well, some of the time our mindfulness meditation involved walking and moving as part of the practice, which was good news. What reminded us of our first retreat in India, however, was that the set of instructions provided were not complex—rather the opposite. The task for day one was to simply watch our mind all day long. We did not have to sit still or try to empty our mind; our task was just to watch. And what we soon noticed was that our mind was active all the time. There was a voice inside our head that never stopped talking. Sometimes it said nice things, and sometimes it said not-so-nice things. But it never stopped chattering away.

"This voice isn't everything who you are," said Michael when he joined us in the evening. "It is just a voice, but you have the capacity to observe it. You are the one who hears the voice. You are the one who is aware there is a voice. And when you are, you will see what it does to you."

We found this confusing at first. But the second set of instructions came the next day. We were again encouraged to listen to the voice inside our head, but this time we were asked to also watch how our thoughts corresponded with our emotions and how our body responded too.

This was an interesting experience, indeed. Barbara and I both noticed that when our voices said negative things, our emotions were right behind the corner, reinforcing those negative thoughts, or the other way around. And this was accompanied by a series of sensations going through our bodies too—a tightening of the chest, a tingling notion here and there, a change in our breathing pattern. All sorts of things were happening inside our body depending on the quality of our thoughts and emotions that we had not been aware of to that extent before.

On day three, we were then introduced to the Golden Habit, which invited us to watch our thoughts, our emotions, and our bodily sensations and consciously relax into it whenever our voice was talking to us in a way that was not helpful. The task was to surrender to whatever came our way, focusing on relaxing our bodies, slowing down our breath, and repeating a mantra that we could choose ourselves. Something like, "I can cope with this, I can relax into this." The task was to stick to the same mantra throughout the retreat and use it whenever our voice was disturbing us or identified something inside or outside of ourselves that we did not like, which it frequently did.

That evening, sitting around a fireside outside the meditation center, Michael spoke to us again. "If you want to live in a more peaceful state of mind, you have to let go of the part inside yourself that wants to create melodrama. Your mind will tell you that you can't do this, but you can. You can think negative thoughts, feel uncomfortable feelings, and that will most likely always be part of your life, but instead of getting lost in those thoughts and feelings, try to consciously breathe and relax into them."

This really spoke to us, and we listened in fascination.

"A wandering mind is an unhappy mind. When you stop getting hijacked by the voice inside your head day in, day out, when you learn to relax into it, you will awaken to the sights, the sounds, the smell, the touch, and the taste of the present moment. Life is too precious to drown in an endless stream of thoughts. Think about that." And then Michael laughed in such a contagious way that we all joined in.

For Barbara and me, this final three-day retreat was another true awakening. We did not feel the intense bliss that we felt after our time in Dalhousie. But it was a revelation to get a deeper understanding of how our minds operated and affected our emotions and our bodily responses too. We had been blinded to the truth that there was a place inside of us that allowed us to simply watch what the mind did instead of helplessly becoming entangled with the voice inside our head that was often distracting us from what life had to offer.

Transitioning back to normal working life

You cannot step into the same river twice, or so a two-thousand-year-old saying goes. This also describes Barbara's experience returning to full-time work after almost three years of studying, traveling, and part-time work. Fresh water was flowing down the riverbed of our life, and inside of us things had changed too, mostly for the better.

The medical practice was attracting more and more patients and Tom, Barbara, and the new guy on the block, Sendhil—who had joined the team during Barbara's study years—were always busy. The good thing about having an extended team now was that they could each establish themselves according to the unique strengths and interests they brought to the table. Tom was mainly into traditional medicine, which was of course still needed, while Sendhil offered additional nutritional and practical advice around applying the new lifestyle medicine.

Born in California with Indian heritage, he expressed an interest in studying Ayurvedic medicine and nutrition on the side, and Barbara loved the new spirit that he brought into the team. We often called him the wise guy. He had the physical appearance of somebody ten years younger than his age, but he had a way of interpreting the world that somehow seemed to reflect the wisdom of more than one person. Barbara herself was moving into the direction of functional medicine with a focus on creating health, looking at the person in a holistic way while integrating the best of what conventional, high-tech medicine had to offer.

The memories of our trip to Dalhousie and Florida motivated us to stay on track too. We organized a series of events on Friday evenings to share stories from our journeys and encourage people to seek out yoga classes, mindfulness practices, and meditation retreats to fully engage with the deeper healing power of Dr. Relaxation. These evenings were well attended, and many of Barbara's patients started signing up for such classes. Like us, those who engaged with these activities regularly saw great improvements in their overall health and happiness.

However, within a few months, Barbara and Sendhil noticed that they still faced one particular challenge that they could not get their head around. They differentiated between three types of patients. The first category was composed of those who wanted a diagnosis, the right drug or conventional treatment prescribed, but were not interested in any kind of lifestyle changes. The second category was made up of those who wanted to take ownership for their health, became friends with Dr. Nutrition, Dr. Exercise, Dr. Sleep, and Dr. Relaxation, and then without further ado, or so it seemed, implemented the necessary lifestyle changes accordingly, often achieving quite amazing results. The third and final category was those who also wanted to take ownership of their health and had the intention to follow up on these new instructions but again and again fell off the wagon. Despite their very best intentions, they did not succeed in changing their behavior to match their goals in the long run.

And it was this third category of people Barbara and Sendhil wanted to now focus on. How could they help those people who wanted to change, who knew enough about the strategies to apply them but were still not able to see them through? What stopped them, and how could they be helped?

After discussing this with Sendhil and later myself, Barbara designed an "observation task" that was inspired by the mindfulness practice that we had gotten acquainted with in Florida. For this purpose, she asked her patients to consciously observe their thoughts, their emotions, and their actions throughout the day—particularly during those moments when they acted in favor or in violation of their positive intentions. When reading through the results, Barbara realized that people were usually in one of two states of being.

In a powerful state of being, people usually had positive thoughts, would experience some uplifting emotions, and were often able to implement those behaviors that led to the outcomes they desired—like sticking to their exercise routine, their new food options, or other positive things. However, a reverse pattern was detectable when being in a weakened state of being. In this state, people would have negative thoughts mostly about themselves, other people, or the situation they were in, which then triggered negative emotions which would often be followed by destructive behavior, like emotional eating, that did not support the goals people were pursuing and led to even more frustration.

THOUGHTS

I will make a mess of things

I will lose control

They will think I'm weak or stupid

I am lonely, I am not good enough, etc.

BEHAVIORS

Emotional Eating

More Screen Time

Skipping Exercise

Avoiding People

Over-checking, etc.

EMOTIONS

Irritable

Sad

Anxious

Embarrassed

Guilt

PHYSICAL SENSATIONS

Tense

Shaky

Nausea

Weak

Butterflies

Hot and Sweating

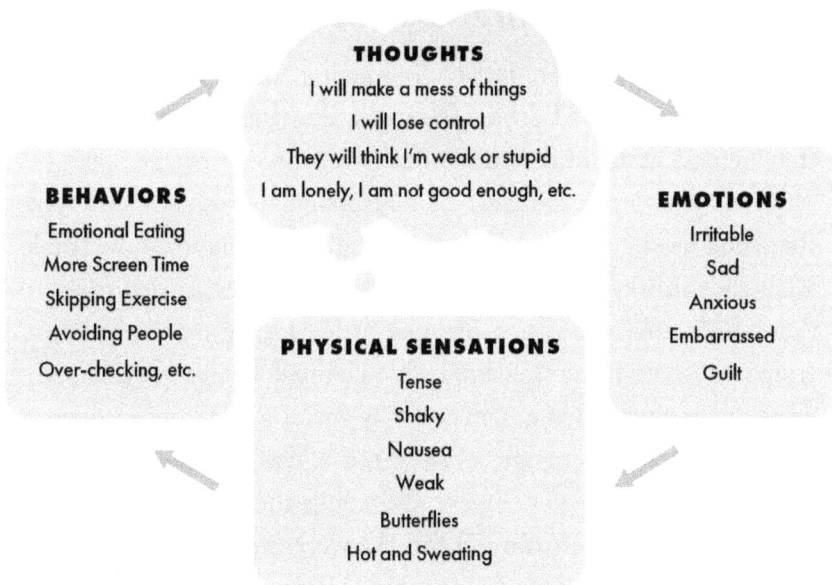

Reading through the protocols, Barbara and Sendhil realized that the majority of their patients seemed to spend most of their time in such a state of mild suffering. There was always something small to worry about, to stress about, to be upset about. The inner dialogue that many people had with themselves on an ongoing basis was so undermining that it was almost tragic. We sometimes joked about this. If our thoughts were broadcast on the radio, the channel would be sued in no time at all for its negative propaganda.

And of course, Barbara sometimes felt exhausted and frustrated about this too. She wasn't finding a solution for the problem she tried to tackle. The question was how they could help their patients to break through this cycle of inner thought when they were not sticking to the mindfulness practice that could possibly show them a way out in the first place.

Revolutionary findings in neuroscience

For a while things were not really moving forward in relation to these questions. And Barbara felt stuck. But then things developed that helped us to understand the issue from a new perspective. New insights from the field of neuroscience gradually emerged that shed more light on why human beings do what they do, think what they think, and feel what they feel. It was explained to us in depth and detail, and then little by little, the big puzzle we were trying to solve became clearer. We claimed before that knowledge on its own does not necessarily make a difference when it comes to personal change. However, this was different. This was knowledge about *how* people could equip themselves to stick to the changes they were aiming for. We were literally given the key to the boardroom of our inner radio station, which was exciting, even for an even-tempered banker like myself.

And now, to tell you what I need to tell you next, I have asked Fifi to lead the way. I want to be sure that I am getting it right. And I have chosen to write this next part of the letter as a dialogue between Fifi and myself. There is quite a lot of information to be taken in, and I feel that this is a better format to deliver the necessary content in a digestible way.

So, let the curtain rise on Fifi, a dedicated behavioral neuroscientist, and myself, who together endeavor to unpack the mystery of how human beings can embark on personal change more sustainably.

A drama in three acts . . .

Act 1: Living in a loop

"Fifi, can you explain the anatomy of thoughts, emotions, and behavior from a neuroscientific point of view, in simple terms?"

Fifi laughed. "This is a complex question, Leonardo! But let's see how far we get."

She sat up straight and then started explaining things as clearly as she could.

"Our brain consists of billions of nerve cells. We call them *neurons*. For human beings to think, feel, or do anything, these neurons need to communicate with each other."

Fifi paused while I was scribbling in my notebook.

"Communication in this context means one nerve cell releases a chemical—a so-called neurotransmitter—that the next nerve cell then absorbs, and so on and so forth. When the same nerve cells communicate frequently—for example when we think the same thought again and again—the *synaptic connections* between those cells strengthen and form a *neural pathway*."

Fifi waited to give me some time to finish my notes.

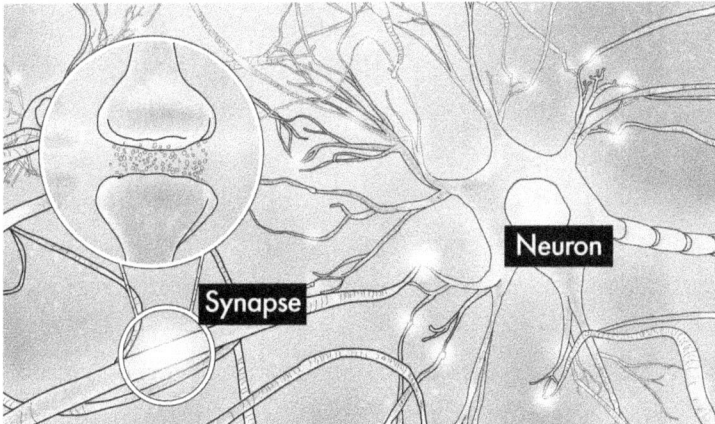

"Just think of your brain as a dynamic, connected power grid with billions of neural pathways lighting up every time you think, feel, or do something. Some of these neural pathways are well traveled. These are your habits, your established ways of thinking, feeling, and doing. Every time you think in a certain way, feel a specific emotion, or practice a particular task, you strengthen this neural pathway, and it becomes easier for your brain to travel this pathway through the 'habit loops.' These well-traveled neural pathways are the highways of our brain, and the brain always wants to use them first. Efficiency rules."

I took a deep breath, trying to digest the information.

"So when somebody has adopted a negative belief as a child, something like, 'I am not good enough, I am not lovable, I am not competent,' as many people have, this belief is such a road well traveled."

I again scribbled into my notebook when Fifi continued.

"And it works the other way around too. If you have built a high level of confidence, it will most likely stay with you even in difficult circumstances, as you have strengthened the neural pathways accordingly."

"How interesting, Fifi. Another question: During our mindfulness practice, Barbara and I noticed that emotions and thoughts seem to constantly influence each other. Does that make sense from your point of view?"

Fifi nodded.

"Absolutely. Thoughts and emotions are indeed inseparable! Every time you have a thought, in addition to making *neurotransmitters* that move from one cell to the other along the *neural pathways*, your brain also makes another chemical—a small protein called *neuropeptide* that sends a message to your body to create a certain *neurochemistry* in your brain that triggers the emotion that matches the thought you were thinking. Today the most talked-about molecules that have elevating effects on our mood are dopamine (the molecule of motivation), oxytocin (the molecule of trust), serotonin (the molecule of happiness), and endorphin (the molecule of perseverance). These are known as D.O.S.E. But there are up to a hundred other neurotransmitters and neuropeptides that are known to create the neurochemistry in our brain and body that determines how we feel and influences what we think in any given moment."

I felt elevated by the clarity of this conversation, and Fifi continued.

"When the brain notices that the body is having a feeling, the brain generates another thought matching the emotions you are feeling. So, thinking creates feeling and then feeling creates thinking. This is a loop that goes on for years, until this cycle becomes so established that it creates a habitual state of being. And we literally become physiologically addicted to a certain neurochemistry in our brain and a certain way of thinking. We basically *live* in this emotional and mental state, creating the experience that we call our life."

Again Fifi paused for me to ask another question.

"Barbara had noticed that most people seem to spend the majority of their time in a rather negative state of being. Is that possible?"

"Absolutely. Most people live in a state of mild suffering most of the time. From an evolutionary point of view, this makes sense. We are creatures of survival whose main mission is to detect problems as early as possible to defend ourselves, which explains why our mind is not great at making us happy. We see an apple in the twenty-first century and our mind complains, 'Oh, it is not organic.' When we are disconnected from our heart and our body, we are often in a state of mild suffering. Our mind is really good for strategy, but on its own, it usually fails at contentment."

Act 2: Running on autopilot

I finished my notetaking.

"That explains a lot. But then I need to ask you the one-million-dollar question: Why is it often so difficult for people to change, even when they really want to?"

Fifi replied, "Good question, Leonardo. Maybe as a simplification it is helpful to imagine that we have two minds."

Now Fifi showed me the following drawing and then continued.

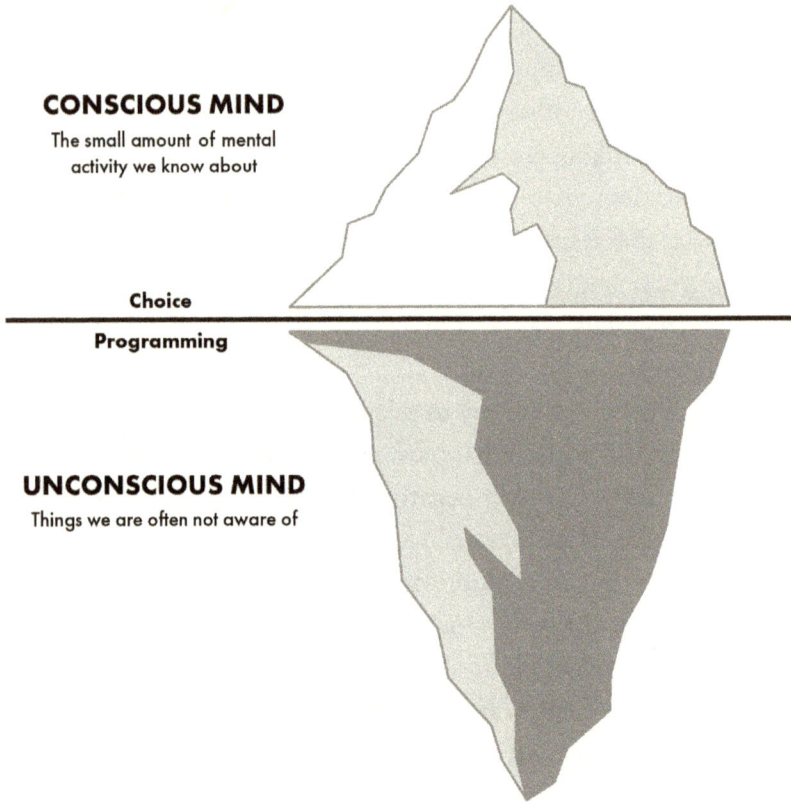

CONSCIOUS MIND
The small amount of mental
activity we know about

Choice

Programming

UNCONSCIOUS MIND
Things we are often not aware of

"The tip of the iceberg that extends above the waterline represents the conscious mind. The *conscious mind* consists of our mental processing that we can think and talk about in a rational way. However, beneath the water is the much larger bulk of the iceberg, which represents the unconscious mind, which directs the vast majority of our thoughts, emotions, and behavior. And what is going on there is redundant. Up to 90% of the thoughts we think each day are similar to the thoughts that we had yesterday, that we will think tomorrow, and every day after that in the future."

I reflected on this statement for a brief moment.

"So we are better off if some of these thoughts are positive ones."

"You bet! Because when we are thinking the same thoughts every day, we cannot be surprised that we are making the same choices, which lead to the same behaviors, creating the same experiences and creating similar emotions and feelings. It is a constant loop. And research shows that even 60 percent of our actions each day are the result of habit loops and not conscious decision making."

"Isn't that a mistake in how we are designed?"

"Not really! Even the most intelligent people can only process a very limited amount of information in their conscious mind in parallel, which is why the brain constantly converts any sequence of repetitive behavior, thoughts, and emotions to the most ancient, unconscious parts of the brain—the basal ganglia—to reserve the frontal cortex—the executive center of our brain—for higher functions. Being on autopilot most of the day is what allows us to go beyond primal functioning."

"What do you mean?"

"Think of when you learned to drive a car. Remember how you gripped the steering wheel and carefully executed every action? Later, you hopped into the driver's seat without giving it a second thought. This is because your brain laid down a multitude of neural pathways for the completion of this task, which operated in the background."

"I understand. But does this mean that we are doomed to live with the same neural pathways for the rest of our life?"

"Yes and no. The good news is, we are not doomed. These days we know that the brain continues to change throughout our life. This is called *neuroplasticity*. That means that the brain possesses the ability to constantly adapt and rewire itself. When certain thoughts, emotions, or behaviors are repeated often enough, new neural pathways are being created, and they are given more real estate in your brain. What fires together, wires together. And those neural pathways that you use less frequently will gradually wither away in the background, though they never fully disappear. It is a dynamic process."

"Very interesting, indeed. But how can people use this knowledge in practice?"

Act 3: Breaking free

Fifi drank a sip of water and put the glass back on the table.

"Another good question. Once you have decided what belief, emotion, or behavior you want to change, my recommendation would be to take advantage of the mechanism of the habit loop itself."

I looked at Fifi in anticipation. "How does this work?"

"Let me see how I can best explain this. A habit loop usually consists of the following elements: a trigger, a routine, and a reward. This, in essence, is the basic autonomy of all of our habits."

Fifi scribbled down a simple illustration that I copied in my notebook too.

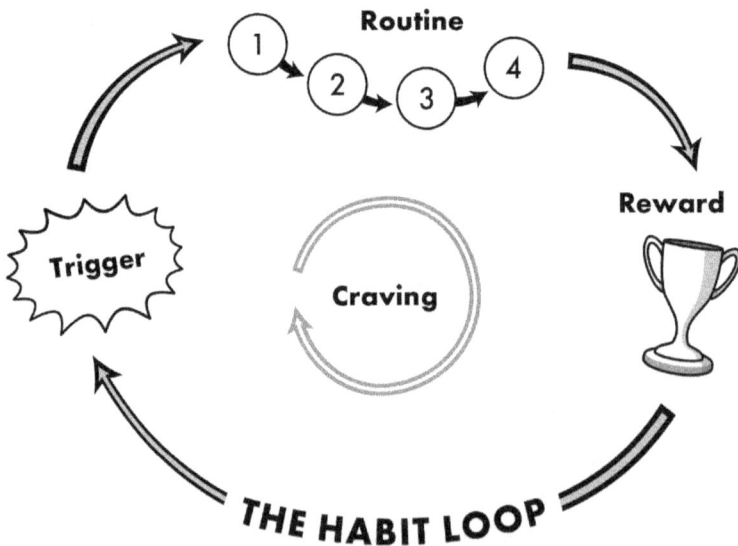

"Most habitual behaviors start off with a TRIGGER that transfers the brain into unconscious processing mode that automatically determines which habit to use. The TRIGGER for a habit can be anything that starts off the habit. Most often, it is simply how we feel in a certain moment that triggers a certain response, but it can also be a location, a time, or people we have met. Anything really."

Fifi paused for a moment.

"If you want to establish a new habit, my advice would be to intentionally prepare a cue that becomes a TRIGGER in advance. For example, putting your running clothes and shoes next to your bed could be an attempt to establish a trigger for you to exercise first thing in the morning."

"Okay, I see. What about the ROUTINE?"

"The ROUTINE is the change you want to establish. Let's say you want to eat a healthier lunch. Whether this new behavior actually occurs depends on a number of factors, such as the following:

- Motivation: What is your bigger goal behind eating a healthier lunch? What is really driving you?

- Clarity: What exactly will this healthier lunch look like? What are the options?

- Ease & Simplicity: When you want to eat a healthier lunch, it must be available around the time you plan to eat. If it is too difficult to get the right food in the moment you want to eat, it is less likely that the new behavior will occur. So, preparation is often the key for establishing a new habit. Things must be easy and simple for the change to work. That is of the utmost importance.

"Okay, got it. And what about the REWARD?"

"The REWARD is the reason the brain decides the previous steps are worth remembering for the future. The reward can be anything from something tangible—like the healthier lunch option being really tasty or enjoying a shower after the workout—to something intangible—like a feeling of self-worth—when sticking to the new behavior that moves us closer to our goals."

I nodded, and Fifi continued.

"Look, I am not saying that change is effortless now that you know about the habit loop. It still requires dedication and perseverance to establish a new way of being, particularly at the beginning, but the software to do so is between our ears. And once the necessary set of synapses are established to run this new behavior, it gets easier every day. That is the belief we need to hold onto!"

And this was the end of our conversation, and I hope you and our readers will find it useful too.

Making deposits

For Barbara and Sendhil, these insights came relatively late in their professional life, but they were a total game changer. When they learned about the power of the unconscious mind, they finally understood why so many of their patients had struggled to implement better lifestyle choices despite having the necessary knowledge, the means, and the intention to do so. Those people had literally been hijacked by their fast, unconscious minds.

One day, when Barbara and I had just completed our usual circuit training in the gym, she came up with an idea that proved to be tremendously helpful. "What about a fitness training for the mind?"

She put her towel down, and we both sat down on a bench.

"Look, when we assume responsibility for our physical health, one way of doing so is to visit the gym, eat the right things, plan in time to restore our energy, and more. This is how we make deposits in this area at the Bank of Life, and we see the positive impact in a matter of a weeks."

She paused again.

"However, many people never get there, despite their best intentions, as their unconscious mind—with its deeply ingrained patterns—always gets in the way. But now that we know about neuroplasticity and how the brain works, we might use this knowledge more intentionally. Instead of simply asking people to *exercise*, we might have to first show them how to *'innercise'* and explain to them how and why it works. If they understand the mechanism of the habit loop, they might be able to build up the belief and the necessary strengths to create the breakthroughs they're looking for. What do you think, Leonardo?"

I nodded in agreement. And we both knew intuitively that the answer was not to fight the power of the unconscious mind but to educate people in how to use its superpower to their advantage by forming new, constructive habits.

We therefore came up with a workout for the mind, which we also used ourselves whenever we wanted to establish a new habit. A mental coach offered a monthly workshop at the Peak Health Center where the habit loop was introduced, and people had the opportunity to do the mental and practical preparation for the lifestyle choices they envisioned. The success rates went up dramatically.

But this was only the beginning. In the spirit of the Bank of Life, we realized how important it was for people to find ways to nourish their psychology in a systematic way too. The power of the placebo effect shows that by thought alone, the physical reality of a person can change, not just the perception of it. That is how powerful our psychology is. And we all have access to this inbuilt magic ourselves. But in many cases, we let our inner voice do the opposite and activate the nocebo in us instead of purposefully using the energy of its brighter brother.

Maybe future generations will be luckier, with parents and teachers more equipped to show children how to nourish their psychology early in their life, helping them to build up neural pathways that work for them and not against them. From studying biology to geometry, everything would fall into place much more easily if children learned how to create mental and emotional wellbeing for themselves first and foremost. Much of the content they consume in school is forgotten soon after the test is passed. However, what will stay with these children forever is the psychological programming that they acquire during those early years.

And while we know that an inner landscape of self-doubt and fear can be rebuilt, we also know that it takes time, effort, and self-discipline, and we can still fall back into old patterns. So why not focus on what really matters, when our children's brains are still so malleable in the first place? Knowing how to make smart deposits into this account at the Bank of Life, like teaching children mindfulness or relaxation techniques or strengthening their feeling of self-worth and compassion, will provide them with high returns for decades to come.

For Barbara and me, engaging in our daily meditation and mindfulness practice was the most important deposit of all. "No training, no six-pack!" was the slogan that we used to motivate ourselves to stick to our daily mindfulness routine. But let's be clear, we would not have needed the neuroscientific explanation around the habit loop, neuroplasticity, and everything else to do so. We realized we had been given the key to our inner radio station long ago. However, learning about how our brain operated strengthened our and other people's belief that it could be done if we just kept at a new habit another day, and then another day. And knowing about the neural pathways and how to train them through repetition provided us with the necessary resilience to stick to new routines, even in the face of the initial setbacks.

And the Golden Habit that we dedicated our life to, when coming out of the shadow years, was the one we had been acquainted with in the forest in Florida. We started the day with some yoga and a ten-minute meditation to establish ourselves more firmly in the present moment and train the ability to watch our mind. Not to alter it, not to change it, not to control it. Just to be able to watch it and pull the inner voice out of our unconscious into our conscious awareness. And then, throughout the day, whenever we felt any kind of inner disturbance coming up— emotionally, mentally, and physically—we tried to consciously relax into it by slowing down our breath. Breathing in deeply into our tummy and breathing out very slowly. This was it.

And after a while, it had a game-like quality to it. And we were both almost looking forward to all these small annoyances coming our way, as they provided us with opportunities to enjoy becoming better at applying this new skill. Michael had taught us to look for the low-hanging fruit and not to wait for extreme emotional turmoil or something very bad to happen but to practice this Golden Habit with small things throughout the day, every day. This was the time where the most progress was being made.

Investments compound over time and so do habits—good and bad. And if I could recommend one and only one habit to adopt in life, it would be this one: the Golden Habit of Dr. Relaxation. It pays off big time.

Wrapping up

Sophia, I am drawing a line here now, as otherwise I could go on and on. After all, one could spend a lifetime studying psychology, in theory and practice, and now, with the field of neuropsychology and other interesting faculties coming into the picture, maybe even multiple lifetimes. The world is full of great insights on how to nourish your mind and make deposits into this account at the Bank of Life.

But the truth is that most people invest little or no time into this account, which is something of a tragedy. Every second of our waking life is influenced by the software that runs between our ears. If our phones update their software every couple of weeks, should we not work on better programming for ourselves too? Just practicing the Golden Habit regularly can create a different life experience. And that is not complicated at all. Nonetheless, knowing is not enough. Every person must do the inner work themselves to fully embody the wisdom entailed in this observation.

So, before you further engage with the endeavor of writing this part of our book, I would suggest that you also reflect about how you invest some of your time to purposefully nourish your psychology.

Are you making some regular deposits to strengthen your psychology that outweigh your withdrawals? Do you have a simple habit in this area of your life that compounds over time?

I know you are an expert in the field yourself, much more than I am, but with my old age I would dare to claim that this is a question worth asking, no matter what one's age, profession, or circumstances.

What do you think, Sophia?

I am finishing this letter now. Reflecting about Barbara and my life has once again been a deeply satisfying activity. Of course, my memory might have twisted and tweaked our story here and there. Sometimes, it seems to have a life of its own. Fifi said jokingly the other day, there is life and there is what our brain makes of it, and if we are lucky, these two different accounts overlap. But whatever the ratio between reality and distorted memory in my case is, I hope there is some longer-lasting truth in my writing that will be of use to you and others.

Yours sincerely,
J. Leonardo

CHAPTER 14

Sophia: Breaking Down Walls

Chronology: five months and twenty-three days after Leonardo and Sophia's brief encounter in San Francisco Airport.

Sophia looked over the vineyard terraces up to the beautiful yellow château on top of the hill. The view reminded her of Versailles, the famous palace near Paris. Sanssouci, in Potsdam in the outskirts of Berlin, was a smaller, more playful version of its French counterpart—reflecting everyone's wish of living without worry, *sans souci*, as the French saying goes. It had been raining softly earlier that morning, the sky was still a bleak gray, and Sophia was almost on her own sitting on one of the slightly wet steps of the staircase that was leading up to the château. She was holding Leonardo's most recent letter in her hands. In front of her was the Great Fountain, which the Prussian King Frederick, widely known as the Philosopher of Sans Souci, had never seen in operation, as the engineers three hundred years ago had not known enough about the hydraulics involved. Sophia's attention wandered back to Leonardo's letter. So many pages. So much life. So much inspiration.

It was true that much of the content about psychology, and even the part on neuroscience, was not new to her at all. However, Leonardo had a way of delivering his messages that really spoke to her. And watching her thoughts more carefully over the past couple of weeks, she had noticed what a slave driver the voice inside her head really was. Though she knew better, she was often on a quest to overtake herself: replying to emails, making phone calls, designing workshops, jumping from one video conference to the next. She was in a hurry but not always for good reasons, other than the voice in her head telling her to go faster and do more. And even reading these days, whether on a screen or on paper, was more often a race to finish the text than to absorb its meaning. A few years ago, she had taken a course on speed-reading to get more information downloaded in less time, which, looking back, felt ridiculous. An American film director had captured it brilliantly when he said, "I took a speed-reading course and read *War and Peace* in twenty minutes. It involves Russia." Did that not hit the nail on the head?

It was mid-July. But a few tiny raindrops fell on her face. And Sophia decided that it was time to get back on her bike and move on. There was another location that she planned to visit that day: Little Glienicke, a small village that had entertained her imagination ever since she first learned about what had happened there. Nicknamed the appendix of the GDR, the village had become a secluded island of East Germany within West Berlin during the division. Almost entirely encircled by the wall, the only way out of the village had been a very narrow road, just fifteen meters from side to side. The wall had zigged and zagged so much in this place that it had literally come up one side of the entrance road of Little Glienicke, snaked around the village through the backyards of several houses, splitting former neighbors from each other, and then down the other side of the entrance road. Outside was the forbidden territory of West Germany; inside was East Germany.

When Sophia arrived at her destination some thirty minutes later, she got off the bike and leaned it on a wooden fence, still pondering the history of this peculiar place. Strolling around the streets of the village now, it was not difficult for her to imagine just how oppressive being surrounded by the huge concrete wall must have been for its residents. They would have been constantly watched over by the border guards, who had the right to arrive at any time, day or night, to check cellars and make sure ladders were locked up securely. The villagers had reportedly felt like prisoners. And many of them had been diagnosed with "wall sickness," a psychological condition attributed to the depressing situation after they had been walled in. No wonder.

However, what had struck Sophia even more was to learn that after the wall had come down, many people were still suffering from the same condition. While the wall outside had been removed, the walls inside people's heads still remained. The wall sickness proved to be even more robust than the wall itself.

Sophia stopped walking, now staring along that narrow road, once the only one leading out of Little Glienicke, when a question suddenly emerged in her head: *Do we not all have walls inside of our mind that were built there in the past and now restrict us for no good reason?*

There were ample opportunities to improve one's life. Not distributed equally, far from it. But still, people had the power to play the given set of cards to the best of their ability and see how far they could get. But then they often didn't. Stuck in a negative state of being, those otherwise-free citizens of the world were literally held hostage by the constant negative chatter of their inner voice that was undermining their potential.

Of course, emotions were there for a reason, even the difficult ones. Grief, sadness, anxiety, anger, shame, doubt, fear—they were all designed to teach humans something about themselves. However, when a dark state became one's inner home, it was time to consider breaking down the walls and finding a better one. But how could one escape with a hostage taker as powerful as the nagging voice inside one's head?

The other day, when searching for an inspiring location to reflect on Leonardo's letter on psychology again, Sophia had read about the courageous people who had attempted to break out of Little Glienicke. Like the family with small children, who had been crawling through a long self-dug tunnel from the cellar of their house into the grounds of another building that stood in West German territory. Many people had been killed in similar attempts before and after them. Breaking out of a habitual inner state could also be difficult, but at least no risk to one's life was usually attached to it. People could fail, but they could try again and again. And there was often nothing to lose but much to gain.

Still, many people didn't deal with it that way. They sat there in Sophia's coaching sessions and told her that this or that needed to happen for them to feel good again. There were endless conditions people came up with in their mind so that they could feel fulfilled. But that was like being a hamster on the wheel. Now the wise person would get up one day and say, "I have a problem and the problem is not the outside world; the problem is that my mind will not leave me alone."

Sophia suddenly giggled about how ridiculous this situation really was. Michael Singer, whom she had actually looked up and to her delight found on the internet, had said in a podcast episode with the title "Breaking Patterns and Finding Inner Peace":

If someone's left arm constantly started going up and down, they would go and see a doctor immediately. But when their mind was doing the same, they were usually either so busy that they did not even notice it, or they otherwise accepted it. And all the while the mind, acting like a monkey out of control, never shut up for a second. It was constantly thinking and talking and worrying and plotting and planning and telling people everything that could go wrong, that already had gone wrong, or would go wrong in the future. Of course, if this inner dialogue got to be too much, then people would usually go and see a therapist eventually. But most of the time, people just accepted that their mind was restlessly going from one place to the other. And who could blame them?

Sophia hesitated for a moment and then turned to the right and continued walking along the street that once marked the outer boarder of Klein-Glienicke, further reflecting on the subject at hand. She too knew from painful experience that changing the mind with the mind in moments of emotional turmoil could feel like trying to catch fog with one's hands, as the smart neuroscientist Andrew Huberman had put it, which was why he recommended using one's physiology more intentionally to break out of a negative state in such intense situations. Like moving one's body. Motion created emotion. And moving forward changed people's neurochemistry every time by releasing dopamine. Or when the mind was particularly stubborn and stuck in redundant loops of anger or sadness, hot or cold water was also a trick that often worked to change the neurochemistry of the brain to calm the inner voice down. Taking a shower, switching intentionally from hot to cold water several times, could put people into a more positive state of being. Music was another wonderful state changer, as was being with other people. And there were more. Sophia usually suggested to her clients to be creative and observant to find out what state changers would work best for them when they were in trouble.

However, after reading Leonardo's letter, she had realized that it was time to extend her own took kit in a more profound way. Not just in theory but in practice. And fortunately, the Golden Habit neither required her to sit still, which was difficult at the moment, nor simply engage in positive affirmations. She did not believe in positive thinking per se. There was a time and place for it. But the mind was constantly working. All kinds of thoughts, also negative and even toxic ones, would inevitably arise, and suppressing those thoughts often made matters worse. But the idea that Sophia had become intrigued with was to become a witness of her thoughts and emotions and then work with the little irritating things coming her way every day.

Thus, whenever she now detected any emotional disturbance building up inside herself, instead of giving all her attention to her mind and the redundant thoughts that it produced in that state— as she had unconsciously done in the past—she would now try to *feel* the underlying emotions and bodily sensations. At the same time, she would consciously breathe into the deeper part of her belly and breathe out slowly, thereby releasing the upcoming tension. And then she would do this over and over again. If she felt a lot of emotional turmoil—like anxiety, anger, sadness, frustration about anything really—she would do this many times a day. Or if it was a big, lingering thing that bothered her and those disturbing emotions reappeared, she would continue to do this over a few consecutive days. But that wasn't a problem. *Consciously feeling* those emotions and *breathing into* them was not a full time job; she could do this while engaging with her daily life. Sophia smiled. And the great thing was that it really worked. Once those disturbing emotions got the *embodied* attention they needed, the hostage taker lost its power, and the redundant, agitated thoughts passed through her system much more swiftly than they usually would. And being freed from the sometimes deafening sound of the inner nagging voice for a while meant it was also easier to extract the learning out of any given situation and to actually process the pain, the upset, or whatever disturbed her instead of just mulling it over again and again in her head. And she could feel that this approach was equally powerful when it came to digesting her heartbreak. It took time to heal, but time was not enough; what made the difference was this form of very dedicated attention.

It wasn't easy though. In the beginning, it had been difficult to even know what she was thinking and feeling and how this affected her. But over the past couple of weeks, she had begun to notice the redundant mental activities when resistance or tension arose inside herself. Like when she got irritated or nervous over an email, or something made her feel defensive or lonely, or something did not go her way. Little things, really! And once she had acquired this awareness of what was happening inside of herself in those moments, she had been able to get a bit of distance behind it. It was almost hard to catch because it was happening so often throughout the day. But it was this new awareness about how ridiculous her reactions often were that brought humor to the situation, and she often had to acknowledge in amusement that everything wasn't life or death, even if the mind made it seem thus. Admittedly, it took some attention to establish this mindfulness muscle. Real neuroplasticity only started kicking in after about two or three months, and even then, the new patterns emerging were still fragile in those early days.

Sophia looked up. Big clouds were making moves in the sky. Having walked all around the small village, she now stood in front of the little bridge that had once been the only heavily guarded border checkpoint out of this place. Today people in kayaks were effortlessly passing underneath it, having a good time despite the misty weather. A smile flickered across Sophia's face. She was a coach first and foremost, and she had always been convinced that psychological wellbeing was at least partially a skill that people could become better at. Sometimes there were walls inside people's souls that had been built up for complicated, dark reasons, and she was careful not to touch those in her coaching work, as this, she firmly believed, required the attention of experts in those fields. However, for most of her clients, including herself, it was safe enough to do the inner work required to liberate oneself from becoming walled in unnecessarily.

Of course, practicing the Golden Habit would not prevent her from ever becoming hooked again or experiencing deeper emotional valleys. She knew that. But still, not many people would opt to live in a walled-in village, if they had any say in it, so why allow the mind to be one's prison guard day in and day out?!

Enlightened by this insight, Sophia walked straight over to her bike, which she had just spotted in front of her still leaning against a wooden fence, and unlocked the cable lock. In that moment, standing there behind this little bridge that had seen so much suffering over the decades, Sophia felt tremendously grateful that she had decided *to believe* in Leonardo's positive intentions. There was fear and there was belief. From a neuroscientific point of view, both of these feelings were *made up*, mere neurochemical reactions of the brain. But they could still serve as powerful weapons, creating very different outcomes along the way.

A few weeks ago, reading her favorite newspaper while having breakfast, Sophia had come across an interview with Reinhold Messner, a legend in the international rock climbing scene who had been the first human being to complete all fourteen eight-thousander peaks of the world without using supplemental oxygen. This man's life was certainly full of unlikely events. And one of them happened to his surprise on the ground and not high up on the mountain. One day, he was contacted by an old, retired lawyer with the unusual request to write a book about another rock climber, Wilhelm Welzenbach, who had been mistreated in the Nazi era and who then tragically died while climbing. This lawyer had been asked many years before to write this book himself by a very old lady, who had been his landlord in Munich. But as the lawyer was now getting too old himself to keep his promise, he sent all the documents that this old lady had trusted him with to Reinhold Messner, with the plea to take good care of it all. A true story.

And Reinhold Messner had indeed gone ahead to write and publish the book about 'Willo' Welzenbach titled *The Ice Pope*. Compared to this set of circumstances, Leonardo approaching her to edit and publish his letters about his and his wife's lifelong quest had suddenly almost seemed straightforward. And from then onward, Sophia had started to trust Leonardo even more whole-heartedly and she had stopped searching him on the internet. If Leonardo wanted his privacy in the last months of his life and the two of them did not meet again, so be it! He had mentioned in one of his first letters that he would offer assistance on how she could get "the message out into the world" once the writing of the book would be completed, and she still did not know what to make of that. But time would tell.

Sophia got back on her bike. Pedaling energetically through the forest, the humid air on her skin, she enjoyed the smell of this summer day and the wet forest soil underneath her. She was back in the driver's seat of her life again. "Whether you think you can or you can't, you are probably right"—she recalled it was Henry Ford who said this, and there was so much truth in it. Leonardo and herself both liked wise quotes. One of many things they had in common.

When she arrived at the shore of yet another lake, she briefly stopped cycling to enjoy the view. The sun was now peeking through the clouds, creating a wonderful atmosphere all around her. And she could see the pastel colors of a rainbow in the distance. Overlooking the large, shallow lake, Sophia imagined the castle of Sanssouci somewhere behind the colorful arche.

"What about the 'Philosopher of Sans Souci'?" she suddenly asked herself aloud. "Had Frederick, the king who had built this beautiful castle three hundred years ago, found peace of mind looking at the Great Fountain that he had never seen working in his lifetime?"

Sophia sighed and shook her head in amusement.

"If Frederick had had a mind like everybody else before and after him on this planet, this tiny detail had most likely distracted him from everything else that was luxurious and working just fine, more than he'd intended."

CHAPTER 15

Leonardo: Our Work

Life isn't simply about finding yourself. Life is about creating yourself.

—Adapted from George Bernard Shaw

Dear Sophia,

Would I still live and breathe were it not for wanting to write and finish these letters to you so badly? As you know, I am at peace with the idea of being reunited with Barbara sometime soon. Somewhere where the concepts of time and space might collapse, where eternity starts and spatial restrictions end. However, before that happens, I have something to do that is important and feels meaningful. Something that does not only circle only around myself: my pain, my losses, my disabilities. And while I am already in "extra time" and expect to hear the final whistle soon, I keep going strong. There is work that needs to be done. And I want to do my best until I can finally say: mission accomplished.

But before I get lost in the heroic thoughts of a foolish old man, let me introduce you to the next account at the Bank of Life, which focuses on our work, our career, our profession—choose the label that suits you best. Many people spend up to 80% of their waking life working, which often leaves little time to invest across the remaining accounts of the Big Five at the Bank of Life. Thus, from the perspective of a time investor, this is certainly an account of an expansive nature. And this means that the quality of this investment really matters! Therefore, allow me to ask you this question right at the beginning: Are you investing your time at work in a meaningful way that creates immaterial assets in your life beyond the money you earn?

Personally, I am feeling particularly excited about the prospect of writing this letter to you, as it will provide me with the opportunity to indulge in the memories of Barbara and myself traveling to an island literally at the other end of the world. A stunning place, where we stumbled across a thousand-year-old idea that helped us to solve the challenges we faced back then and that stayed with us for the rest of our life.

Running on empty

After a particularly busy period at work, Barbara started noticing that she was not feeling her best. Initially, she tried to hide it, even from herself. Working at the Peak Health Center, she felt embarrassed that she was now the one struggling with energy issues. She underwent a series of tests to find out what was wrong with her. When none of her ideas were backed up by evidence, I could finally convince her to share her problem with her colleague Sendhil who soon had a hypothesis of what was going on: Barbara's whole nervous system was in overdrive.

"Sometimes we are so smart that we are actually stupid,"

Sendhil said one evening when we were all sitting outside around our wooden table on the terrace. "And this is usually easier to notice in others than in oneself."

Sendhil looked at Barbara, smiling empathetically. I knew instantly that he had hit the nail on the head, and I was curious how Barbara would react.

After a prolonged moment of silence, it was me who eventually spoke up. "Maybe you have too much of what I don't have enough of."

Now Barbara looked at me with curiosity. "What is that?" she asked impatiently.

"Passion. Passion that somehow turned into an obsession."

I could see that Barbara knew that we were on the right track. Ironically, while consulting her patients on how to avoid stress, she had been creating it for herself for too long. Ever since her parents had died, she'd had a tendency to work hard, study hard, and exhaust herself in the process. And this way of approaching almost everything had become a pattern so ingrained in her brain that now a set of synapses seemed to occur every day to keep this pattern going, even when it was not helpful. She was applying a coping mechanism to a situation that no longer existed, which now produced unwanted side effects.

What did she usually say to her patients? It is not easy to solve a problem when one is part of the problem that needs solving. So true indeed.

However, this was not the only source of unease we were dealing with at the time. As it happened, Barbara's challenges coincided with me feeling unusually dissatisfied too. It was the first point in my career that I seriously questioned my existence at the bank. Of course, I had an in-depth understanding of banking and had been promoted various times over the years as a result of all the experience and skills accumulated. Nevertheless, something was missing—not just on the surface but deep inside myself.

And there was something else too. Maybe I was approaching an age where I wanted to reclaim my masculinity—I know this sounds silly, but I remember that it was important for me at the time. Barbara had been the driving force for most of the big decisions in our life so far, and this time I wanted to be the one moving things forward. Pondering over various options, I wondered if working abroad for a while could make a difference. Barbara could have some downtime and I could see my job through a new cultural lens and try to find a way to create more happiness for myself in my career along the way too.

After discussing this with my wife at length, I confided in my boss, talked about my lack of motivation and my desire to explore something new. And a few months later I was indeed approached by our global HR department with an interesting opportunity. Our bank had opened a series of branches all over Asia and were having problems with the leadership of some of them.

There were two positions on offer—a big role in Tokyo, which included extensive travel across Asia, and a smaller one in Okinawa, an island off Japan. When I put myself forward for the post in Okinawa, the bank was at first disappointed but then agreed to my transferring there. In return, I was prepared to take the lead on the overall project, and Timothy, a junior colleague of mine, would accept the position in Tokyo under my leadership.

This was a good deal for all of us. I was content and loved the nature of the challenge assigned to me. And luckily, Barbara was fully onboard with this big endeavor too.

Moving to Okinawa

Okinawans proudly call themselves "sea people" (沖縄人), and I remember weeks of endless rain, depressing at times, when we first arrived. Consisting of almost one hundred small islands, it felt like being in the middle of nowhere, detached from everything we had known before. However, the summer that soon followed the monsoon season in Okinawa was great, and we loved our small house covered with red tiles made of clay taken from soil of the island that we had moved into a few weeks after our arrival. With its black stone walls, it stood out against the blue sky. And from the rooftop, two Shisa dogs, symbols of good fortune in Japan, greeted us whenever we arrived home.

We often joked about our tendency to live in houses that were one size too small for us, but we soon settled into a new routine in this new environment and started enjoying our stay. When I was working in the bank, Barbara took time to relax and explore the island. And in the evening, we would discuss my work instead of hers. And while I had never minded the situation before, this was a nice shift in our relationship and created a new dynamic that I enjoyed.

At the dinner table we now focused on how I could best approach the tasks ahead of me. I had been welcomed into my new role with the utmost respect, and now I had to explore what was working well and what could be improved. In the following weeks, I initiated many one-to-one conversations to get to know all the people in the branch and find out what was going on. However, this was not as enlightening as I had hoped for. And when I was traveling to Tokyo to meet with Timothy, the situation he described was similar. People were doing their job but not more than that. They kept their head down and tried to stay out of trouble. And we did not know what to do about it. Somehow, we got stuck.

After exchanging further ideas with both Barbara and Timothy, we decided to dive deeper into the cultural aspect of the issue, to find the root cause of the problem. Barbara and I had already done things like whale watching and dragon boat excursions around the island. We had enjoyed going snorkeling at beautiful sandy beaches, diving into deep blue water, and swimming with wild sea turtles that had moved in the water as if they were flying in the sky. Nevertheless, after many weekends of pleasure, we now wanted to study the culture of the island more carefully. What immediately stood out were the many castles of the Ryukyu kings, dating from the Middle Ages when Okinawa had been an independent kingdom with its own culture and language. And we wondered if this theme of independence was still part of the identity of the Okinawan population. The other cultural aspect that we reflected upon was the American military presence on the island. My boss had told us that our employees didn't have a negative view of American citizens, despite the Okinawan love-hate relationship with the military bases. But was that really true?

And then it happened. One day, when traveling around the island, we noticed three Westerners standing in the middle of a small village, bending their heads over what looked like a map. Their car had broken down and we spontaneously offered them a lift to their hotel. Dan Buettner, an American journalist, shared with us that they were studying the Blue Zones—regions across the world where people had above above-average life expectancy. Residents of these places produced a high rate of centenarians and enjoyed more years of good health. In an inspiring car ride, we learned that Okinawa was home to the highest concentration of centenarians on the globe and was one of the world's few designated hotspots for longevity. The others were Sardinia, a beautiful island in Italy; Nicoya, a peninsula in Costa Rica; Icaria, another island in Greece; and Loma Linda in California.

Linda
California

Sardinia
Italy

Icaria
Greece

Okinawa
Japan

Nicoya
Costa Rica

BLUE ZONES

Longevity Hotspots

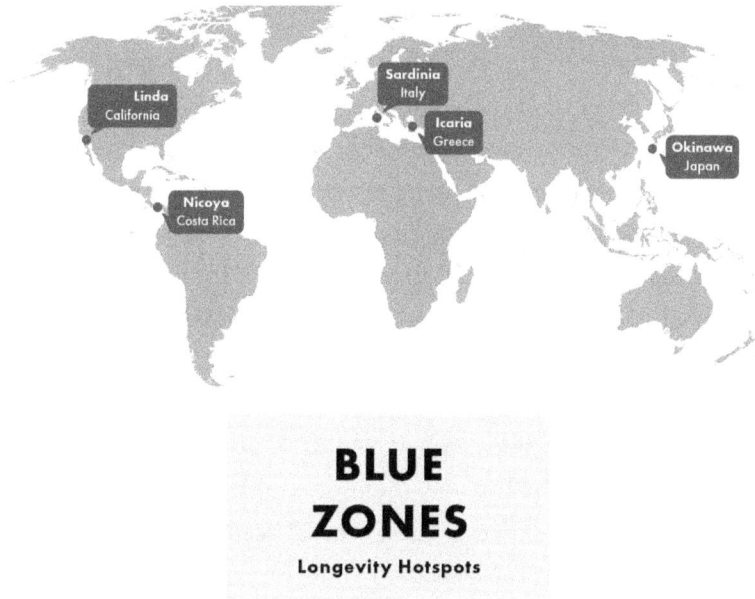

We were dumbstruck. Before meeting Dan, we hadn't heard about the Blue Zones, let alone known that we had unintentionally chosen to live in one. You can imagine how fired up Barbara was, so much so that I feared she would undo the recuperative work she'd put in since we'd arrived. Dan had said that they were fully staffed, but he had also mentioned that if Barbara wanted to accompany them when taking their interviews, he would be interested in getting her views. But my concerns were unfounded. In the following days, Barbara continued sticking to her new routines, using the time on the island to recharge her batteries, as promised. In the morning, she would still go out for long walks, engage with her meditation practice, and only afterward would she do some reading on the Blue Zones, before experimenting with some new Okinawan recipes in our kitchen later in the day.

Listening to the immortals

And nothing more happened until a couple of weeks later the telephone rang. It was Dan. Dr. Kinjo, a general practitioner who had lived on Okinawa for most of his life, was planning to check in on Yua, a 108-year-old woman living in the north of Okinawa. The culture of longevity was beginning to disappear, Dr. Kinjo had told Dan in an earlier conversation, and it was high time for him to complete his interviews. As Dan's assistant was coming down with a cold, he invited Barbara to join him on this visit, which she happily agreed to.

After driving up north for about an hour on a highway that was sometimes more dirt than asphalt, Dr. Kinjo parked his car in front of a small house, which stood there dreamlike with its tiny walls and windows, surrounded by a low coral wall, somewhat sunken into the ground, with a steep red roof. On top of the roof, two familiar Shisa greeted the group of three and encouraged them to come in. "Look at this," Dr. Kinjo whispered to Barbara in a low voice, pointing to the many herbs planted in the garden behind the house. "If you are looking for the secret recipe of health and longevity, its ingredients are growing right here!"

When entering the tiny house, they all took off their shoes, and Barbara—due to her height, which was average in the US but tall for Okinawa—instantly felt like the proverbial bull in a china shop. Inside, there was the traditional three-room structure made of warm wooden beams, separated by sliding doors and paper walls. In the middle of the living room, four elderly people were sitting on straw mats around a small table. Yua herself was dressed in a traditional kimono, and her white hair was put into a knot on the back of her head. Next to her were her children, who Barbara soon learned were all in their eighties. During the following hour, without speaking much, the unlikely group of seven enjoyed some jasmine tea. The calming effect of this quiet gathering soothed Barbara's mind and soul.

And eventually, when Dr. Kinjo had finished his medical

examination, Dan was allowed to ask a few questions to Yua, which Dr. Kinjo translated back and forth. The first one was about Yua's daily routines, and the old lady appeared vibrant when she dutifully shared how she usually approached her day:

"Every morning, I wake up at the same time. Around six, I make myself a pot of jasmine tea and eat my breakfast. Usually miso soup with vegetables. When I am finished with my breakfast, I put on my holy robes and my shoes and go to the sacred grove to pray for the health of the village. I thank the gods for supporting our village, for helping the village people to be safe, and for letting their hearts and souls be filled with peace. Around noon, I go into my garden to fetch vegetables and herbs for lunch. I do not eat much. Usually just vegetables and maybe some tofu or some fish. And before each meal, I take a moment to say, 'Hara hachi bun me.'"

Yua's eighty-year-old children giggled. Dan looked at Dr. Kinjo who smiled knowingly. "*Hara hachi bun me* (腹八分目) is a Confucian teaching that instructs people to eat only until they are eighty percent full," he explained. "Ancient wisdom strongly advises against overeating, which is why we present our meals on many small plates. Having five plates makes it seem like we eat a lot, when we don't."

"Hara hachi bun me!" Barbara and Dan said almost in unison.

And Barbara added, "Maybe this is a concept we should popularize at home too?"

"They do have a tendency to overeat, these Westerners, don't they?" one of Yua's daughters asked cheekily. Everybody chuckled in recognition. And Barbara reflected on how true this was. Whenever a Western fast-food chain decided to settle into a new environment, a few years down the line, things started to deteriorate. Just as was happening to the younger generations on Okinawa too.

After discussing this topic with Dr. Kinjo for a moment, Dan asked another question, this time addressing Yua again. "Yua, what is your secret of living for so long? Is there something that you can share with us?"

Dr. Kinjo translated the questions, and it took a while before Yua answered. "Maybe I have just forgotten to die!"

Yua started giggling again and then continued on a more serious note. "My father died when he was still very young. That taught me a lesson. He had quit his job when he was eighty years old and died at age eighty-eight. My mother, on the other hand, was a noro, working in service of others until she was 106. I figured that she was stronger because of her daily habits and living up to her ikigai. So a few decades ago, I decided that I would not repeat my father's mistake. And I am happy that my children follow my example too."

Dan nodded respectfully.

"Anything else?"

Yua looked at her hands.

"I guess, not thinking too much about oneself. Be kind to others. Often, you best take care of yourself by helping others. Grow and eat your vegetables. Smile and be optimistic. Pursue your ikigai with pride and dedication—the most important lesson of all."

And then Yua stopped talking. Not wanting to stretch the hospitality of their host too much, the group of three decided to call it a day. Touched to her core, Barbara dared to hug Yua when saying goodbye to her, which the old lady warmly returned. Beneath the silk fabric of her kimono, Barbara could sense her delicate body. She could hear and feel Yua breathing next to her. And in that moment Barbara realized that she was embracing more than one hundred years of life, a thought that left traces on her soul.

When I arrived from the office later than usual that day, Barbara did not mention what an extraordinary day she had had. I was suspicious though. My wife looked somehow more radiant and asked me to come home around lunchtime the next day. After quickly checking my calendar and kissing her on the forehead, I told her that I would be right there.

Barbara's tea ceremony

The next day I came home at noon as promised.

"Why don't we start with going for a walk?"

"Okay . . ." I said slowly. There had been a frustrating incident at the bank that morning that I had not been able to get my head around. But walking along the beach, the wind on my face, a taste of salt in my mouth, the smell of the ocean creeping up my nose, and the song of the seagulls in my ears helped me wind down. And when we returned home, I was curious what would happen next. Our living room was surprisingly empty, save for a few straw mats lying on the ground, and I was wondering where our furniture had gone but did not dare to ask. My wife sometimes had the tendency to overreact when I would spoil moments like these with irrelevant questions.

So, without further ado, we sat down on one of the straw mats. And in the subsequent hours we drank green matcha tea that Barbara carefully prepared, and she told me everything about the afternoon spent with Dan, Dr. Kinjo, Yua, and her children. And eventually she mentioned the philosophy of the ikigai that she now wanted to pass on to me, pointing at her notebook, which showed four Japanese characters on it.

生き甲斐

"Ikigai means a reason for being. The general gist of it is the thing that you live for, or what French philosophers might call one's raison d'être."

Barbara looked at her notebook again.

"Combining 生き, which means 'life,' with 甲斐, which means 'to be worthwhile.' 甲斐 can be broken down into the characters 甲, which means 'number one,' and 斐, which means 'beautiful' or 'elegant.'"

"When on earth did you learn all this?"

Barbara smiled and continued. "The Japanese believe that everyone is carrying their ikigai inside." She pointed at her chest. "It might be hidden, and searching for it might require patience, but it is there and it can grow, particularly when applied in service of others."

Interrupted by the boiling of the water, I got up to pour another matcha tea into the two delicate Japanese porcelain cups that Barbara had placed on the small table in front of us.

"The word describes a state in which the individual feels at ease. And living up to one's ikigai is all about devoting oneself to pursuits that one enjoys, in a way that it creates value for others too. Applying one's ikigai gives your life meaning. It is about having a sense of purpose in life, as well as being motivated. Does that make sense?"

I nodded.

"And Yua? Her ikigai is being a noro?"

After Barbara's vivid description of Yua and her children, I felt almost as if I had met them too.

"Yes. And imagine. At her age! Every single morning she puts on her white robe that symbolizes the spiritual purity of a priestess and then she walks to the sacred grove. And there she prays for the village and its wellbeing. I really believe she does not die because she feels she can't leave the village alone."

We both sat there in silence for a while. This was the first time I had heard about the ikigai, and like Barbara, I was intrigued by this ancient philosophy and the role it had played for people in Japan in everyday life for centuries.

"Do you think I could take this back to our bank? Somehow apply it there?"

Barbara's eyes brightened up.

"We need to figure out the details, but that sounds like a plan!"

Application at the bank

A few days after this conversation, I initiated a meeting with our Vice President, Haruto, and Yuki, my personal assistant, with whom I often discussed leadership matters despite his young age. Haruto was conservative and very experienced. Yuki, on the other hand, had only left university a couple of years prior, but he was a source of inspiration—future-oriented and incredibly capable of thinking holistically, which was somehow also reflected in the brightness of his brown eyes.

Yuki was my biggest hope for the unfinished idea I had in mind. Instead of forcing even more of our American working culture onto the Asian branches and their employees, my idea was to adapt to the Asian culture in a way that would allow us to have the best of both worlds: still living up to the headquarters' expectations, providing a similar customer experience around the world while having the flexibility to adapt to the cultural environment the branches were operating in. Like Barbara, I was convinced that we could learn from the mistakes in modern medicine. Arrogantly believing in the exclusivity of our superiority would not bring us to the next level. We were all on the same team in a game that we wanted to be best at, and the question was, how could the bank's American culture and the Japanese one marry on a deeper level?

Yuki was impressed, and he most likely wondered why on earth he'd been given the honor of participating in this meeting. Haruto seemed to think the same. However, I ignored any questions about hierarchy and went on to share what I had learned so far about the ikigai. Maybe we could build a higher level of employee engagement by building on this one-thousand-year-old idea?

Now Yuki looked as if Christmas, Easter, and his birthday had fallen onto the same day—not that any of these Christian feasts existed in the Okinawan culture, of course. Haruto's face showed an expression that I had not seen before. He was not smiling—he did not show his emotions so bluntly—but I still sensed that he felt touched by my words. I did not expect any immediate answers from the two of them, and I asked them to meet again in a couple of days to hear their initial thoughts. When Haruto had left the room, Yuki hesitated and looked at me, as if he wanted to share something but did not dare to.

"Yuki, if we always do what we have always done, we will always get what we always got. Albert Einstein. Spill the beans!"

Yuki seemed surprised but started to relax a bit.

"My great-grandmother celebrates her birthday next week. She lives in Ōgimi. I don't know if you have heard of it. It is known as the Village of Longevity. People there have the highest life expectancy in the world. Maybe you can come with me; I am sure she would feel honored. And once there, we could speak to some of her friends about their ikigai, as this is a philosophy most present among the older generations."

Yuki turned away. "But I am sure you have better things to do."

"Yuki, this is a brilliant idea. Do you think I could bring my wife along?"

"Of course you can!"

Yuki's face brightened up, and he high-fived me back somewhat awkwardly.

A birthday party in Ōgimi

It was a typical Okinawan summer morning when we got ready for the weekend trip to Ōgimi. The sun was already baking the countryside, but the air around our little house was still fresh. In our khaki shorts and short-sleeved shirts, Barbara and myself probably looked like tourists, except for the stethoscope hanging around my wife's neck and the medical kit under her arm. Yuki's grandmother had mentioned on the phone that a friend of hers had fallen the other day, and of course Barbara was more than happy to be of help.

During the car ride, Yuki and Barbara hit it off instantly, and time literally flew by during the two-hour drive up north. And soon a stone marker welcomed us to Ōgimi, displaying an ancient proverb:

> *At seventy you are a child.*
> *At eighty you are merely a youth.*
> *And at ninety, if the ancestors invite you into heaven,*
> *ask them to wait until you are a hundred.*
> *And then you might consider it.*

And these were not just words. Ōgimi was a place where energetic great-grandparents lived in their own homes, tended their own gardens, and on weekends were visited by grandchildren who, in the West, would qualify for senior citizenship. The birthday party itself took place in a community garden, which was carefully prepared for the gathering. Beautiful, handcrafted lanterns were hanging from the trees, and other Okinawan artwork made this place a treat for the soul. Yuki's great-grandmother greeted us warmly and introduced us to the rest of the group. As only a few of the younger people spoke English, we mostly communicated nonverbally: smiling, exchanging views with the birthday guests, gesticulating with our hands.

There was a welcoming atmosphere, and the elderly party guests were much more active than one would imagine. They laughed and talked with each other; sometimes they got up and started singing songs that were popular in the village, as Yuki explained to us. They even chanted "Happy Birthday" in English with a heavy Okinawan accent that, to our surprise, they all mastered. Barbara and I happily joined in. And in the evening, before we left to spend the night at the house of Yuki's cousin, we even ended up dancing in the garden as though this was the birthday of a twenty-something.

The next day, we then had the pleasure of talking to the village people about the philosophy of the ikigai and the role it played in their daily life. Sitting at the large table in the community center, drinking jasmine tea, we heard similar stories. People in their seventies, their eighties, nineties, and centenarians shared with us how their ikigai had kept them going throughout good and bad times in their life. And we learned that there was not even a word for retirement in the Japanese language. Having a purpose that comes to fruition through meaningful work has always been so important in the Japanese culture that the Western idea of retirement simply did not exist here. Yuki took minutes of this conversation, and I still have these notes in the drawer of my desk to this day, as I found them so inspiring.

"Working is my ikigai. If you don't work, your mind and body break down," a ninety-five-year-old said, who at his age still worked as a consultant in a company that published educational materials. He still walked three-quarters of a mile to the office every morning, and afterward he did some desk work before he then hit the streets again, making rounds of the bookstores in town. "Working and being of use for others is what keeps me going," he said proudly.

"When I wake up, I go to the altar and light a candle. You must keep your ancestors in mind. It's the first thing I do every morning. That is my ikigai," said another woman, well into her nineties. A message that sounded very much like Yua's ikigai of being a noro.

And there were more statements like these.

"Planting my own vegetables is my ikigai. I share some of my vegetables with my neighbors every day. That makes me happy. It is a lot of work, but it is my reason for being."

"Supporting my friends is my ikigai. We all get together, and I lighten up their mood and make them think of something that gives them joy. That is what I enjoy most in life," another centenarian added to the discussion.

"I make things with wicker. That's my ikigai. The first thing I do when I wake up is pray. Then I do my exercises and eat breakfast.

A soup with vegetables and tofu. At seven, I calmly start working on my wicker. When I get tired at five, I go visit my friends," an eighty-seven-year-old man said with a smile on his face.

"My ikigai is to learn and help others to learn. Every day I learn something new and pass it on to others is a day worth living." This lady was just over a hundred, and we wondered what new things there were to learn every day in her age. This was a statement that I thought about a lot, and it really helped me to understand what had been the missing part in my life until then.

At the end of the morning, another old lady summed it all up: "Once you discover your ikigai, applying it will bring meaning to your life. But it is about the doing, not the searching. Everything is fleeting in life. Time never stops. However, if you have a clear sense of your ikigai, each moment will hold so many possibilities that it will seem like an eternity."

The Year of the Ikigai

Back in the bank on Monday morning, Haruto, Yuki, and myself decided to set up a small project team to take this further, and within days, we came up with a three-step plan. First, we wanted to do a town hall meeting, where we would announce the "Year of the Ikigai" and ask everybody to gather stories about their family's ikigai and what role it had played in the Japanese culture over centuries. Second, we decided to design a series of workshops where we would invite our employees to reconnect with their personal ikigai and explore opportunities to apply it inside the bank. And third, the decision was made that, at the management level, we would use the idea of the ikigai to think again about reshaping the purpose of the bank. And we soon set about executing this plan.

The beginning of the process was a little bumpy. After the first town hall meeting, nobody said a word and people just went back to their desks when the event was finished. However, within days, Yuki heard more and more about how people were gathering stories about the ikigai of their relatives. They were talking to their parents, their grandparents, and their great-grandparents and started sharing these stories with each other. And soon the communication around the ikigai sparked a level of excitement within the branch that we had hoped for but could not have anticipated.

The workshops that we conducted were similarly successful. The teams that had been responsible for designing those workshops, which we also rolled out across other branches throughout Japan, had come up with a practical tool illustrating the idea of the ikigai and its different aspects.

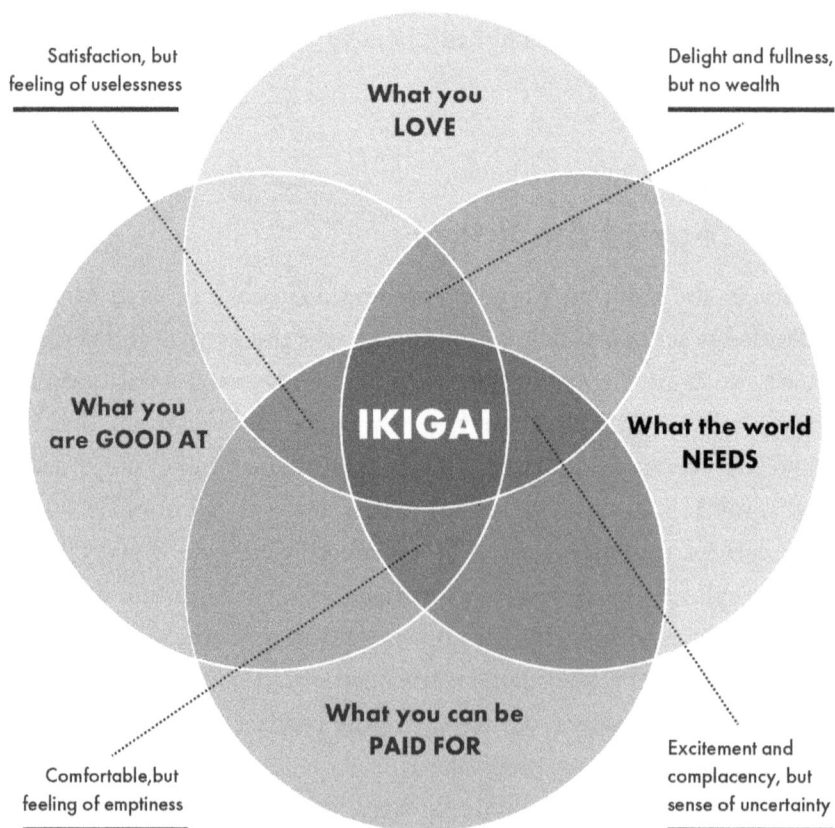

Satisfaction, but feeling of uselessness

Delight and fullness, but no wealth

What you LOVE

What you are GOOD AT

IKIGAI

What the world NEEDS

What you can be PAID FOR

Comfortable, but feeling of emptiness

Excitement and complacency, but sense of uncertainty

The ikigai flower, as we soon referred to it, was fairly self-explanatory, and maybe, Sophia, you would find it worthwhile to explore each segment for yourself too. The ideal is to create a working life for oneself consisting of activities that you are good at, that you feel passionate about, that the world needs, and that you can get paid for. This might not be possible all of the time. But with patience and hard work, most people can create at least some ikigai moments in their professional life and then nurture and cultivate those with care and determination.

And this is why the Okinawan people loved the metaphor of the flower, as it illustrates the belief that the seeds for our ikigai are within all of us, but once discovered, they still need to be watered, nurtured, and cultivated for them to blossom. Just discovering those seeds is not enough. It is about the doing and not the searching. These words often echoed in my mind.

The third step of our overall plan was tricky at first. Timothy, and other senior leaders from across Japan, joined us for meetings in which we tried to develop the cornerstones of the bank's ikigai strategy that wouldn't contradict our headquarters' philosophy. And as we explored the matter further, we discovered that the four basic questions sparked by the ikigai flower were similarly relevant for organizations as they were for the individual.

The first dimension of the ikigai flower focuses on motivation. There are organizations in which one can feel the shared passion for the business, an excitement of being part of it all. And on the other end of the spectrum, there are organizations that seem to drag the energy out of their employees. Most of the subsidiaries of our bank in Japan belonged neither to the first nor to the latter category. We reckoned that we were somewhere in between, but there was a lot of room for improvement—that was for sure. The second aspect of the ikigai flower refers to skills and competencies. The strengthening of this dimension in an organization, we agreed, was strongly linked to the generic human resources development task. And the Year of the Ikigai was aiming to provide our employees with possibilities to harness their skill sets while fulfilling their purpose. The third dimension of our business ikigai fell into the classical management category. The basic task was to create value for our customers, producing a good margin for ourselves. However, reducing a business to mere profit generation was not enough from the perspective of the ikigai.

And it was indeed the fourth dimension of the ikigai flower that had an additional, hugely positive impact on the bank in Okinawa and on all the other subsidiaries across Japan. We dared to ask what the environment that the bank operated in needed. It wasn't easy to convince the New York headquarters that we aimed to put up a fund for local sustainability practices so that the employee committees could invest into local projects. But this new twist in doing business got traction. Okinawan people were socially responsible citizens, believing in an ethic of conservation in all they did. And when the bank decided to support community-friendly efforts, the reputation of the bank increased, and our employees beamed with pride.

Looking at the world today, I cannot believe how advanced we were in our thinking. Words like "sustainability" or "corporate citizenship" were not even part of our vocabulary back then. So, by using a one-thousand-year-old idea, we designed a management approach which was much ahead of the time. Of course, the ikigai project was not a quick fix for every problem the bank encountered in Japan and Asia, but it did make a difference, and looking back, those memories still make me feel proud and content.

Insights from Okinawa

Our time on Okinawa went by like the proverbial twinkling of an eye. Every day we saw, heard, felt, smelled, and sensed something new. And before we knew it, our stay on this beautiful island was coming to an end. To say goodbye to Okinawa in a proper way, we decided to visit a lighthouse the day before we boarded the plane to Tokyo and then to Los Angeles. Barbara and I both loved lighthouses in all shapes and forms. For us, they stood for so much that reflects so deeply on the human condition: a call for light and a desire for darkness, a need for belonging and a thirst for adventure, a craving for truth and the comfort of the illusion. It was all there. So much ambiguity and so much unity.

And the lighthouse we visited that day did not disappoint us. It was a white, well-maintained building, surrounded by a rocky terrain that looked like the moon, even though the rocks were probably coral or limestone. The water that day was of a deep blue, and the greenery around the building was so verdant that every cow in California would have been speechless. A handful of people were still strolling around when we arrived. But once the museum on the first floor of the lighthouse closed, we had this beautiful place all to ourselves, and we soon started unpacking our picnic.

It was a windy day, and the waves were spraying our late lunch. We began reflecting about what we had learned living on the island over the past few months. We both agreed unanimously that the Okinawan people had discovered something quite unique, something that had been the quest of so many cultures past and present. Centenarians like Yua, Yuki's great-grandmother, and many others had shown us that it was possible to live healthily well into old age. In the West, most people hit their peak between their twenties and thirties and then start declining year by year. If there was a pill that could achieve the same results as the Okinawan lifestyle, it would represent the biggest pharmaceutical advance of all time and sell in the millions.

But what did this Okinawan lifestyle look like?

One of the common characteristics seemed to be that their days all started with a morning routine. For some it was praying, for others it was meditation, while for some it was preparing their first cup of tea in silence and contemplation. This mindful start into the day seemed to strengthen and center them.

Furthermore, there were those healthy eating habits. Food was considered medicine and great attention was given to maintaining a balanced diet which mainly consisted of vegetables, some fish, and some tofu. Not overeating also seemed important, and we later added "Hara hachi bun me!" as a slogan to our refrigerator. Most of these centenarians had endured long periods of hardship in their life, with periods of little nutrition. And we wondered if, in that way, that they made use of what science regards as the most effective longevity biohack known today—autophagy. This is a mechanism activated when the body is in fasting mode that helps the cells to clean themselves and get rid of dysfunctional materials that could otherwise turn into cancer and other problems. Getting daily moderate exercise was also part of the Okinawan lifestyle, with many of the elderly people still growing their own vegetables to ensure their flavor and freshness.

Another element that stood out was the exceptionally strong sense of community across Okinawa. The ties and relationships between family and community seemed hugely important. There was singing and dancing and other communal events taking place wherever we went. And it was obvious that the traditional Okinawans nurtured all their relationships very carefully—with the living as well as with the dead, the relationship with themselves, their spirituality, as well as with nature and the wider cosmos. This really seemed to be the foundation of Okinawan life.

And last but not least, what all these longevity studies suggested was that applying one's ikigai was just as important as the famously healthy Japanese diet. And for Barbara and myself, reflecting more deeply about our purpose was an eye-opening exercise too. My ikigai, I discovered on Okinawa, was to learn and inspire others to learn. The bank had given me ample opportunities to engage with the first part of my ikigai in the past, which I was grateful for. However, what I had missed in my career as a banker was the second part of my ikigai. Learning made me feel alive, but inspiring others to learn too provided me with a kind of meaning that I had not experienced enough in my professional life so far.

Barbara, on the other hand, realized that she had been living up to her ikigai all along. Helping others to live a healthier and longer life had provided meaning for her over the past decades. So, her biggest insight was not to discover her ikigai, but to realize that if she overdid it, she would sabotage her ability to apply it in service of others. A healthy passion was a source of energy; an unhealthy one that leaned too much toward compulsion could easily have the opposite effect.

Our lighthouse moment

Deeply immersed in our reflections, we had not noticed that the sun had been coming down over the ocean. The atmosphere was changing, and we stowed the rest of our picnic into our backpack. It was time to climb up the lighthouse which, to our amusement, proved to be a challenge. The narrow, winding staircase seemed endless, and we were out of breath when we reached the top. But what greeted us was worth the effort. Despite having seen so many views of the ocean in Okinawa, this spot was still different with the colors and force of the waves. The vastness of the ocean soothed us, and after a while, induced by the pure contemplation of nature, Barbara started speaking calmly.

"One day, we should bring all of this together. All the pieces of wisdom that we find. And maybe write a book about it all. A book about the essence of life. A book of wisdom, if you will. Not our wisdom but the wisdom that we have been fortunate enough to experience with our eyes, our minds, our hearts wide open. And maybe our only task will be to connect the dots, or at least some of them. Everything seems so interconnected from this perspective, so much more than we usually realize. And if we are lucky, we sometimes get a glimpse into this wholeness. Finding wisdom is not something that can be prescribed. There is no one recipe, but there are ideas that can give orientation, provide clarity, but also offer enough flexibility to adapt the essence of it to everyone's liking. Maybe writing such a book would make a small contribution, bringing more orientation into some people's lives, like this lighthouse has been a beacon for hope over centuries."

She looked at me for a moment and then turned her eyes slowly back to the ocean.

"Perhaps we are able to offer such an organizing idea."

She paused again.

"Not to restrict people but to inspire and motivate them or offer a set of guiding principles in times when they might need them most. Something simple and applicable, and still flexible, to reflect people's uniqueness. Certain topics in life seem so essential and so universal that they endure the passage of time. And if we look after them more carefully, everything in life might be more likely to fall into place too. I am talking about those topics that are so important that, without them, you could not imagine human existence to be the same. You know?"

Her gaze was still wandering over the vastness of the ocean while I was looking up into the darkening sky, noticing some evolving stars. I turned to her.

"You mean, like the Big Five?"

Barbara now looked at me with curiosity in her eyes, and I continued.

"You couldn't imagine Africa without those elephants, could you? The elephant, the giraffe, the lion—they belong to Africa like the water belongs to the ocean."

Barbara's eyes lit up in the twilight surrounding us.

"Wow," she said with a tender voice, and after a brief moment she said it again, and then again once more, which made me smile. "We need to think carefully about what those essential elements in our life are. No hurried judgments. There is still so much to do. I just hope we will have a long and healthy life to be able to accomplish it all!"

Making deposits

And that is what we did. We took a long time. Most of our time. And it was worth the investment. Throughout our life, we often examined those pieces of wisdom, thousands of them, if not more. Sometimes we evaluated them against our better intentions, then postponed judgment to consciously look at them from different angles. Many of these pieces of wisdom were collected close to our home, through conversations with patients and customers, through introspection, reading, and accessing research. Others stemmed from journeys that we undertook. It was a long and worthwhile pursuit and provided us with meaning beyond our withdrawal from our respective professions.

And this is what the philosophy of the ikigai is all about, Sophia—pursuing happiness as the main goal in life, as many people in the West do, is a delicate game to play. Do we feel like a failure when happiness is not there? Our time in Okinawa taught us to favor a deeper human experience. Humans want to be happy, and that is understandable. But happiness is fluid and ever-changing. Meaning, however, can move into our life like a loyal friend who is there to stay during good times and bad, acting like a guiding star even when our perception of the world is momentarily clouded.

So to make deposits into this account at the Bank of Life, I would strongly encourage people to discover those activities in life which energize them and build a skill set around them. The next step is to find ways to perform these activities in services of others and eventually get paid for it. This is what the ikigai flower shows us. If we are able to create a working life for ourselves consisting of activities that we are good at, that we feel passionate about, that the world needs, and that we can get paid for, we will always know that our time is well invested. This might not be possible in each moment, but with patience and hard work, most people can create more and more ikigai moments into their professional lives and then nurture and cultivate those with care and determination.

In finance, the purpose of investing is to generate a return from the invested asset. And that is true at the Bank of Life as well—only that we invest our time and not our money. However, in the world of finance, the chances for higher returns on one's investments usually come along with higher risks attached. And that is where we luckily part ways with the world of finance. Investing one's time wisely, like discovering and applying one's ikigai in service of others in different moments of our life, offers the chance of deeply satisfying returns over decades often without risking much at all.

But again, our ikigai is not a meaning-producing machine on its own. And this is how the concepts of purpose and passion are often misunderstood. It does not stop with discovering one's ikigai, one's purpose, or one's passion. Working hard is part of the game. Flow comes from doing things, including challenging things, again and again, not from seeking alone. Floating from one thing to the next to find pleasure carries the risk of never arriving, which seems to be happening a lot to materially satiated people these days. Deprived of deprivation, they seek joy and happiness and yet end up feeling empty and disoriented.

Wrapping up

Most of us know from experience that this area of our life attracts time like a magnet. Unlike the other accounts at the Bank of Life that often get neglected for too long, this one usually gets more than its fair share of attention, which is why the quality of time invested in this area of our life matters so much.

So, what about you, Sophia? Have you discovered your ikigai? Are you investing your time at work in a meaningful way that creates returns beyond the money you earn?

Studying you on the internet, watching your videos, reading your books, and listening to you in San Francisco giving your speech on the neuropsychology of leadership, I am quite certain that this is an account that you feel passionate about and that you already master in your life. But still, you may wish to reflect on these questions again. In essence our ikigai often stays the same over decades, but how we express it can change over the years, and it might make sense to evaluate this from time to time.

For now, this was what I wanted share with you. One more letter to go . . . and we might be dunking the ball just in time. Sometimes I wonder if my writing gives the impression that Barbara and I were always living and traveling abroad, going on some kind of great adventure. That is actually not true, Sophia. But maybe the time we spent on the road has triggered so much learning that these memories jump the queue and squeeze themselves into the forefront of my attention. When new impulses are coming our way, long-term memories often form by the minute, while our memories of everyday life frequently seem to vanish into thin air. And yet ordinary life is what occupies most of our time, which is why having an ikigai that one pursues on a daily basis can make such a huge difference overall.

By the way, I can imagine that you are preoccupied about how to put all these different strands of our story into one book.

I sometimes compare writing with exploring new territory. We might have an idea of the direction we are taking, but we do not see much of the road ahead.

It takes faith to still move on, as creating something new always does.

Yours sincerely,
J. Leonardo

CHAPTER 16

Sophia: Creating Purpose

Chronology: six months and twenty-two days after
Leonardo and Sophia's brief encounter at
San Francisco Airport.

Sophia's new strategy, to randomly pick a location in Berlin some-how inspired by the theme of Leonardo's letters, was still working out well for her. Climbing up the enchanted spiral staircase of the Japanese-style café situated in Berlin-Mitte, the charming space of the House of Small Wonders had immediately appealed to her. The interior, dotted with vintage curiosities, looked as if it had been put together over a long time like a Japanese patchwork quilt, with its many plants and floor-to-ceiling glass windows evoking an urban greenhouse. Sophia studied the fine milky leaf covering the grass-green matcha latte that had just been placed in front of her. She was in a reflective mood.

Leonardo and Barbara's life perhaps wasn't perfect either, but to her it seemed as if their relationship had almost a fairy-tale quality to it. All those journeys together, their shared sense of purpose, their willingness to make things work for both of them. She had never heard of Okinawa before, but she now vividly pictured the exotic island in her mind's eye. And what had captivated her attention most was learning about the Blue Zones, getting to know people like Yua, the old centenarian, and of course, hearing about the idea of the ikigai, which very much reminded her of the work she did with her clients. And she could easily imagine why longevity researchers believed that people's overall wellbeing was so tightly entwined with living up to one's ikigai, and she assumed that this was possibly truer today than ever before—given all the fundamental change people were constantly facing these days.

Of course, change itself was not a new phenomenon. Societies had always been changing since the dawn of time. However, the depth, the breadth, and the speed of change that could be witnessed today was unprecedented in the history of humankind. Life, as one knew it, was being turned upside down.

And what happened on a macro-level all around the globe was also reflected in the microcosms of the organizations Sophia was working for. In the past, when she assisted an organization embarking on a transformation process, there had been a starting point (A) and a new desired status quo (B). In between, there was the change process, and when this had been completed, a phase of relative stability had followed, in which people had the chance to settle into a new normal. Sometimes this new normal had not been as attractive as the old one, but still it had existed. But this phase of relative stability, which often lasted for years, sometimes even decades, was now missing. Before the dust could settle down, the organizations were changing direction again, now targeting a new status quo: C, D, or E. And while everybody was waiting for a new phase of relative stability to arrive, it didn't come, which was disorientating to say the least and often manifested itself in a collective state of unproductive stress. This wasn't surprising, since *when emotions go up, intelligence goes down.*

Sophia often explained this relationship to her executive clients showing the picture below:

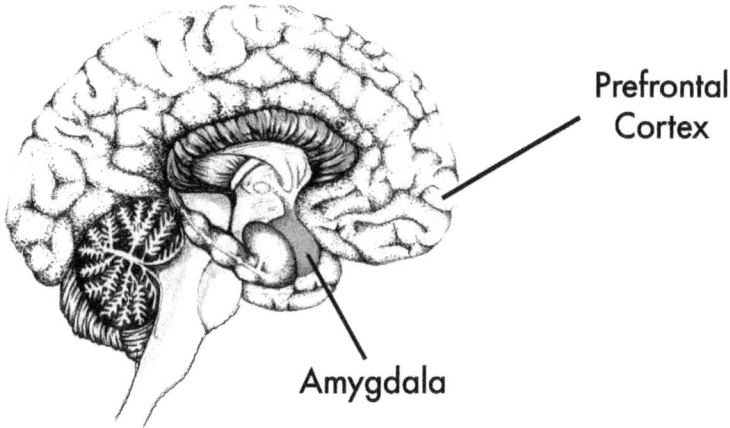

Whenever people feel nervous, anxious, angry, fearful, or resentful, the amygdala—a tiny structure in the oldest part of the brain—plays a crucial role. Demanding all the attention for itself, it gets flooded with an extra supply of blood and oxygen, thereby leaving the prefrontal cortex—the brain's executive function, where rational thought and judgment reside—literally hanging out there to dry. And when this occurs in a group of people, not just within one individual, these intelligence-lowering effects often spread like wildfire on a hot summer's day, suppressing people's capacity to think holistically, synthesize, or empathize with people outside their circle. In such moments, all those brains care about is their own survival and how they are right and others are wrong.

But what to do about it? Providing a compelling purpose was believed to help people reorientate in those turbulent times.

However, there was a crack in the system somewhere. While many organizations spoke about the importance of purpose these days, often with long and flowery words, global surveys showed that more people than ever were walking through life feeling stressed out, disengaged, dissatisfied, and disconnected, showing lower levels of productivity and performance in their work.

Sophia had her own theories on what had gone wrong here. And one of the problems that she identified was that people were often implicitly told to only start looking outside for a sense of purpose, while what they were really looking for were activities that made them feel alive and gave them possibilities to grow and express their potential. And this is what excited Sophia about the idea of the ikigai, as it seemed to bridge this gap between the *big* purpose outside and the *small* purpose inside the individual that makes every moment count.

For example, when someone disliked doing administrative work and yet their job revolved around the behavior that came with this activity, then the wider purpose of their company, no matter how noble and attractive, usually did not lead to this person's fulfillment. However, if people could apply their strengths, which made them feel alive, thereby helping a company pursuing a noble purpose, then this gap could be closed, and true meaning could emerge. When this happened on a broader scale, people had the chance to reenergize and believe in themselves, and that was noticeable in the whole organization, even contributing back into the bottom line as research overwhelmingly demonstrated.

Sophia picked up Leonardo's letter again to study the different facets of the ikigai flower. This philosophy very much resonated with a modern coaching tool that she had come across a year ago that helped people to identify their "Sparketype"—which described a specific set of activities that brought more fulfillment to our lives. Jonathan Fields, a best-selling author who she had once met during a leadership conference in New York, had spent thousands of hours researching motivation at work and found that most people fell within ten different Sparketypes that he identified in his book *Sparked* and which Sophia now scribbled down into her journal to reflect about them again:

The Maven

The Maven loves acquiring new knowledge and is energized by the very act of learning.

The Maker

The Maker is motivated by creation and seeks to transform ideas into reality.

The Scientist

The Scientist thrives off of the challenge of solving difficult problems, putting in as much time and effort needed to reach a solution.

The Essentialist

The Essentialist strives to distill order from even the most chaotic of circumstances and is satisfied by the task of organization.

The Performer

The Performer enlivens all interactions and moments, creating an energy in all their conversations with others.

The Warrior

The Warrior is a leader of people, driven to organize and direct groups to reach common goals.

continued

The Sage

The Sage teaches and shares wisdom with others, transmitting their learnings with the goal of inspiring others.

The Advisor

The Advocate is a champion for others, supporting the people and ideas they believe in and bringing attention to others' contributions.

The Nurturer

The Nurturer dedicates themselves to taking care of others through an extremely acute sense of empathy.

Sophia loved this free online assessment tool for its simplicity and its explanatory power.

In her case it had validated what she had known before. Her primary Sparketype was the Sage, the person who was driven to learn in order to teach and share wisdom. After a meaningful conversation with a coaching client, she often asked herself who should send the invoice to whom, as she felt so energized as the result of having assisted a person in their self-discovery process. This was her ikigai, and she now realized that she had this in common with Leonardo. Learning and inspiring others to learn was what excited the Sage.

Her secondary Sparketype was the Performer, a quality that she had not been able to make much use of recently, though she remembered how much she had enjoyed giving the speech in San Francisco after a long period of working from home.

And in addition, this tool also offered an indication of one's Anti-Sparketype, highlighting those activities that made a person feel least alive. In Sophia's case this was the Essentialist—she too appreciated smooth processes and order, but she often found it energy-draining to create or maintain them.

But of course, there was probably no one perfect strategy to connect with one's ikigai or the *purpose within*, as she referred to it. Identifying one's Sparketypes could be one great starting point. Another was to simply use one's intuition more intentionally and reflect on those activities that one had already felt naturally drawn to during one's childhood or adolescence, as those patterns of thought, emotions, and behavior that provide people with feelings of pleasure and meaning usually emerge early in life. A third mechanism that Sophia often recommended to her clients was to focus on those activities that felt energizing—emotionally, mentally, maybe even physically, in the here and now. But in essence, it was all the same philosophy.

And the beauty was that the advice was not necessarily to quit one's job but to first search for opportunities to apply those behaviors within one's current profession or even within one's leisure time. Applying one's ikigai in service of others meant making deposits continuously. And even when doing this in the wrong job, this could hold true. The skill set built around one's ikigai could always be put to better use in a better environment later.

Sophia looked around the House of Small Wonders. Her eyes wandered over the fine Japanese artwork on the wall appreciatively. Could working on this book also become part of her living up to her ikigai? Writing did not always come easy to her—it was often hard work, but she did certainly experience moments of flow once she got into it, particularly when she was editing her work and she imagined how it would help her clients to initiate real change in their lives. She noticed a tingling warmth in her chest.

But how could she find an innovative way of contributing to Leonardo's writing that would do his and Barbara's ideas justice? And then she remembered what she herself had said to a dear client of hers the other day who had felt stuck in the pursuit of a business idea.

"Imagine you have an identical twin endowed with the same brains and talents that you have. You're both given a week to accomplish a special task. During that week, you come up with your ideas alone in your office. In contrast, your twin talks to three people from different walks of life, visits three innovative start-ups to observe what they do, experiments with a number of different ideas, and shows one of those ideas to three different people and asks for their opinions and critical questions. Who do you bet will come up with the more innovative and doable idea?"

She had gone on to explain that research at Harvard Business School by Dyer clearly showed that leaders who were more innovative than others spend 50% more time on activities that ask them to apply what researchers call the innovator's DNA—namely networking, observing, experimenting, questioning, and associating.

And now, remembering this conversation, Sophia suddenly thought about all those urban workspaces that had popped up everywhere around the globe. Opening her laptop, she searched for coworking spaces in Berlin and found many. Would that not give her all the opportunities in the world to apply the five discovery skills that could make her more innovative in her approach to editing Leonardo's work?

She had decided a few weeks ago that she would first wait for all of his letters on the Big Five to arrive before she would start planning the book itself. So there was still time . . . but there was nothing stopping her creating a better network for herself in this city.

Sophia got up and paid for her breakfast. Climbing down the enchanted spiral staircases of the House of Small Wonders, she noticed that she again had a list of things to do and luckily enough time to explore and pursue them further. For the beginning of September, it was an unusually warm day. Rolling up the sleeves of her blue summer dress, she stepped outside and started walking along the street, which since reunification had become one of the most exciting and well-known centers of contemporary art in Berlin. For Sophia, Berlin-Mitte was more than just the central neighborhood of the city. It was the place where her grandmother had lived most of her life and, interestingly, also the cradle where Berlin itself was born. Growing from a small settlement founded along the River Spree in the thirteenth century, it was now one of the boroughs that most embodied the spirit of an open, world-beating city.

Sophia stopped walking, her gaze falling on an unusual arrangement of bamboo decorating the spacious sidewalk. Wasn't living up one's ikigai somehow like stepping into green energy that was always renewing itself? Or was she experiencing a dopamine peak that would soon be balanced out? Probably both, and that was as good as it could get. She knew too that many people were under the illusion these days that living up to one's purpose was all about pleasure, passion, flow, excitement, having fun, while in truth, living a meaningful life was a combination of working hard in alignment with one's values, enjoying moments of fulfillment, and then doing it all over again and again. That had been Leonardo's message too. And Sophia was prepared to do precisely that.

She was in the wonderful pursuit of something that she really cared about and was ready to take on the highs and lows of this project that she had been miraculously trusted with.

CHAPTER 17

Leonardo: Our Relationships

Love is why we're here.

— Adapted from Brené Brown

Dear Sophia,

Today I woke up to the sun peeking through the blinds, shining light on my face, bringing with it new hopes and aspirations. A small team of nurses is sharing shifts to look after me these days. And I do not mind that at all. I need their assistance and receiving it makes me feel grateful. I usually spend the mornings in bed now, before Sandra or Eric or Monica move me out onto the terrace in my wheelchair. While my mental radius has been expanded much in the past months when writing to you, the radius of my physical performance now stretches from the bedroom to the kitchen and, when I am lucky enough, out onto our terrace, which is where I am sitting now, slouching over the wooden table, my head barely higher than the stack of pancakes beside me, starting to write this letter to you.

My aim is to finish this last mission of mine in style. At least on paper. Visually, I probably bear a resemblance to a disappearing ghost, but that is luckily of no particular importance here. There is, by the way, another letter in the pipeline. Over the months, I have put together some final notes, sharing with you the best time investment principles that I have collected over the years for all novice and seasoned investors at the Bank of Life alike. It is unlikely that I will have the time to turn these notes into a more coherent story. But you can use them as you see fit, Sophia.

Everything else is already organized, and Fifi will know what to do when I am no longer here. Next to my desk waits another envelope, ready to be shipped to Berlin after my departure. It will contain those notes and everything else too.

And now, without further ado, onto the final element of the Big Five at the Bank of Life: our relationships and our relational wellbeing. Without health, the Bank of Life closes down. Our psychology determines how we perceive every second of it. Work is what allows us to make a meaningful contribution toward others, applying a skill set that makes us feel alive and helps us pursue our purpose. Finance provides the basis for our worldly existence. But love and relationships are what glues it all together. Why bother doing it all if we cannot share our life with others? What is a world without love, friendship, and the feeling of deeper connection? It is a beautiful topic to write about indeed. And yet for me it is not easy to tackle this one topic in particular, which is why I might have unconsciously saved it for last. But it is time to share.

The other side of the story

You might have thought that my storytelling reminded you of some kind of fairy tale. Me and Barbara having the perfect relationship. Health. Love. Happiness. Meaningful careers. Exotic travels.

Finances in check. A house at the beach in Santa Barbara, even if a very small one. What more could one ask for? And that is true, and we were grateful for all of that, yet there is more to it. And this is what storytelling is all about. I could have told our story without mentioning the skeletons in our closet, and it would not have been a crime. We are all selective storytellers all along, all of us. We leave certain things in and others out. We constantly edit and distort reality a bit here and there. We want our audience to hear our side of the story in a way that will make us seem right, capable, and lovable. However, the biggest pitfall is not that our storytelling is selective, flawed, and never complete. The biggest pitfall is that we pretend not to notice. But one usually pays a price for such "under-the-counter" editing, often ending up with a version of our story that prevents us from learning and moving on.

So, what are the threads of our story that I have left out so far, that are still lingering? Part of the truth is, not everything was fantastic all the time. There were years of suffering and despair, a passage of time which involved disappointment, secrets, and even betrayal. It sheds light on the one relationship we longed to have but unfortunately lost sight of due to all the other exciting things that happened in our life—all the journeys across the world, all the work projects, and everything else that felt so important at the time.

To make a long story short, we never had children. All those years when we might have been able to start a family easily, we were always too busy with our projects, our dreams, our work. I wasn't concerned and quite honestly, it didn't even occur to me that we might be missing the perfect moment. But as it turned out, we did. Barbara went into menopause prematurely, which shook us to the core. And for many years we tried everything that modern and holistic medicine had to offer, which eventually put a strain not only on Barbara's health, but our relationship too. But all our efforts were not rewarded, and when we were almost too old for all of it, we explored one last avenue—adoption. I will not go into detail about this, but the painful summary is that we didn't find our happy ending here either. The baby that we had wanted to adopt died a few weeks after being delivered prematurely.

So what did we do then? At first, nothing. A long period of grief and sorrow hovered over us like a dark cloud. For Barbara it was even worse. My feelings floated rather quietly over my emotional universe, like the disconnected thoughts of a sad daydreamer. Barbara, however, struggled more tangibly and had to stop working for a while. For weeks, she started and ended the day in her pajamas, not capable of imagining the light at the end of the tunnel. And when the worst was over, she did what she had always done, reverting back to her default setting—working more than she had ever done before. And while this was most likely the best she could do in the circumstances, I began questioning the idea of fighting our loss with the same medicine that had gotten us into trouble in the first place: work and more work. Had we not simply taken our work so seriously that we had missed making deposits into the other accounts at the Bank of Life? Whatever the reason, we now had to deal with reality as it was, and if possible, learn from it.

Nonetheless, this was easier said than done. We often did not speak for days or quarreled over stupid things. It might have already started in the years of continuous trying, but it worsened after the adoption fell through. So, if you had thought that things were too good to be true, you now know that we had our dark moments too, and many of them. But I remember one moment in the middle of one of these stupid fights, literally waking up from it all. I watched the two of us from above with grim expressions on our faces, exchanging uninspiring words. And I recall asking myself, What the heck had become of us? For how long had this been going on? For how many years? Things had to change. The question was how.

It was a difficult and delicate problem to solve, as I was caught up in this misery too. But then, a few days after this incident, when watching TV, an informercial caught my attention. I had seen it many times before but never paid attention to it. While it struck me as odd, I dialed the number provided in the ad and spontaneously signed up for one of the upcoming self-development events advertised. I did not include Barbara in my plans, as I could easily imagine how she would react. "You would be successful with your glued hair, when I buy your tapes," I once heard her saying in a cynical voice when that same commercial was on TV. This might have amused me once. Tony Robbins, the orchestrator of the event that I had signed up for, did indeed have funny hair back then. But there was a bitterness to Barbara's comment, resulting from the years of sublimated depression, which took the playfulness out of it.

However, I was determined to attend the event and be as unjudgmental as possible—*just rolling with it*, as the travel agent organizing our trip to Africa had once said. And that is exactly what I did. Talking to unknown neighbors, jumping around like a rubber ball, seeking liberation, redemption, and relief—whatever Tony invited us to do, I did it. For three days, I was fully into whatever was happening around me, acting as much out of character as one might imagine. And there were moments in which I admittedly felt grateful that neither Barbara nor my colleagues could witness my cathartic attempts to free myself from the emotional prison I had lived in for too long. But what can I say?! I was rewarded big time. Three days into the workshop, I felt alive in a way that I hadn't for a long time. Maybe this was a temporary new state of mind—I didn't care. I wanted to simply enjoy it and find a way to share some of the insights gained during the seminars with Barbara in the weeks to come.

Love is not enough

"Meaningful connection is formed when we bravely share our truth."

—Michelle Maros

Following up on this intention, I booked a lodge in the San Rafael mountains for a weekend retreat, like I had done many times before entering those shadow years, as I always referred to those dark times of our relationship. During the day, Barbara and I went outside to explore the countryside. In the evening I built a fire and eventually shared the concept that had stood out to me the most when attending the seminar two weeks prior—the human need psychology. Barbara was skeptical, to say the least, and she wondered if the scientific foundation for this concept was solid enough. But I tried to gently challenge her on this. Impact, after all, had always mattered more to her than generic evidence.

And with that I showed her an illustration of the concept that I had received at the seminar.

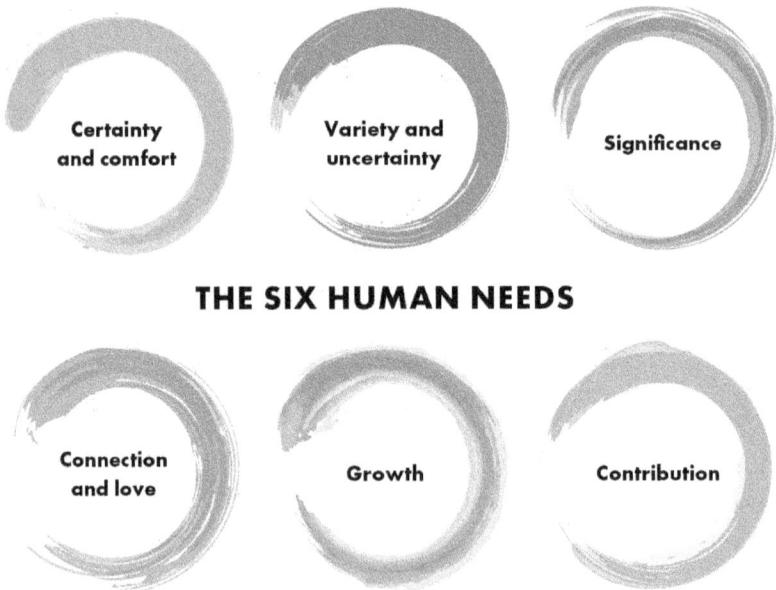

Certainty and comfort

Variety and uncertainty

Significance

THE SIX HUMAN NEEDS

Connection and love

Growth

Contribution

"These are the six human needs. The assumption is that when we meet all those needs for ourselves at a high-enough level in a constructive, positive way, we feel content and fulfilled. That is the theory, at least."

Barbara remained silent, but I saw that the expression on her face was slightly changing. So, I went on.

"And the same applies in relationships. If you're in an intimate relationship and you both meet four or five needs of your partner at a high-enough level, as said before, in a healthy way, the chances are that you're going to have a great relationship."

I looked at her and added spontaneously, remembering Tony's joke, "Six out of six, and you have a love slave who is not going anywhere."

But Barbara barely raised an eyebrow.

"I see. So that is the reason why we are both still here?" Barbara responded, quick-witted as always. She had meant it as a joke, but there was again this bitterness underneath the surface. She was not open to this conversation yet, I could tell. But any beginning was better than none.

"Let me see. The first human need that we are all striving for is to satisfy the need for certainty. We all want to feel safe and have a level of predictability, control, and consistency in our life," I explained. "So what do you think? Do we make each other feel safe? Do I make you feel safe, Barbara?"

I could see that Barbara started thinking about my question, even if only reluctantly. And after some discussion that still felt awkward, we agreed that we at least did nothing to provoke the opposite. There was no concern that one of us would run off with somebody else or similar. And we still had a lot of stability in our life through our jobs, our finances, our home.

So, in many ways, we did feel safe. But the question that popped up in my mind at that moment was if Barbara actually believed that she would ever feel complete or happy again. This was a certainty that she had lost along the way. I didn't say anything, and Barbara interrupted my thoughts with another observation. In the past, we'd had all these routines that had somehow provided a structure around our day and possibly also around our relationship. Our

morning routine, with yoga or meditation and then enjoying a cup
of tea together, and in the evening preparing dinner for each other
and often going for a walk afterward, enjoying a glass of red wine
on the terrace. But this structure no longer existed, and we certainly
felt the effect of it.

Barbara looked at me. "So, what now? Are we making a list of
things we should start doing again?"

I thought about it for a moment. "Maybe we just talk and see
where it leads us to before we turn it into a plan. What do you think?"

Barbara nodded. "What is the second human need in this
framework?"

I contained a smile. The conversation no longer felt like me giving a one-sided presentation.

"Paradoxical as it may sound, this is the need for uncertainty and
the excitement of the unknown. When everything in our life—our
relationships, our job, etcetera—becomes predictable, we stop feeling alive. And we start craving variety and some sort of adventure.
So are we doing enough to make each other feel alive?"

Barbara responded with an interesting facial expression. "Can
we skip this?" We both chuckled.

Satisfying this need for each other had been effortless in the
past. We had done small things to make our daily life interesting
and different, like cooking a new recipe, inviting each other out for
dinner, writing little notes that the other would find throughout
the day, sometimes going to the movies or a festival spontaneously.
And we had also done big things to satisfy this need for variety and
adventure. All our travels around the world had kept us on our toes.
But none of this happened now. And maybe that was understandable. When the need for safety and certainty was not fulfilled, the
need for variety did not get much attention either.

"Are two sets of data enough to identify a downward trend?"
Barbara asked me with her old sense of humor back in place. Again,

we both giggled. The six human needs analysis was a good way of having this conversation—not going too deep right away, but not staying on the surface either.

"Alright, number three then, bring it on, Leonardo!"

I studied the drawing and then continued.

"This is the need for love and connection. I guess this is the most obvious one when talking about the quality of a relationship. Are we fulfilling this need for each other on a high-enough level?"

The answer was not debatable. We no longer did. And, what was worse, we both admitted that it had not bothered us too much. Most of the time, we hadn't even noticed it. And it had gone further than that. We had not only lost a sense of connection toward each other, but also to our inner selves, as this was the place where our deepest pain resided. We knew that we still loved each other, but love was not enough when we could not find a way to connect and heal at a deeper level.

"Maybe we leave this need alone for now," I suggested after a prolonged period of silence, aware of the sensitivity of the topic.

Barbara nodded again, putting on a brave smile. And I continued.

"The next one is about our need for significance. People want to feel recognized, needed, wanted, unique, and important, you name it." And then I added, "Tony claimed that this is even more important for men than for women. Obviously not true."

Barbara ignored my attempt to lighten the mood, instead asking me on a more serious note, "Did I make you feel any of those things in the past few years?"

It was a rhetorical question, and it went both ways. We had not only not made each other feel significant, we had almost stopped caring about each other's approval, which somehow made things worse.

"It doesn't get better, does it? How many bottles of wine have you brought along?" Barbara said mockingly.

The level of honesty that characterized this conversation amazed us both. It was possibly the most refreshing exchange we'd had in years. While it was painful to openly acknowledge where we were at in our relationship, it triggered a weird kind of enthusiasm too, at least on my side. And when we looked at the next two human needs, which Tony had described as needs of the spirit that could bring a deeper sense of fulfillment into people's lives when met at a high-enough level, we both agreed that they had been our star qualities in the past.

There was the need for growth, progress, and self-actualization on the one hand, and the need to contribute, to do something that matters, to live a life of purpose, and to provide value to others on the other hand. And that is what we truly had been all about. We loved learning and we loved pursuing our ikigai in service of others. But we had to admit that while we still somehow fulfilled these needs in our respective professions, we had stopped doing this with, and for, each other.

When we finished our conversation, I moved closer to Barbara. For the rest of the evening, we just sat by the fire, our thoughts drawn into the flames, drinking more wine than we usually did. And when we went to bed that night, we felt a sense of togetherness that we had almost forgotten about.

Of course, not everything changed after this weekend. Getting out of this valley of our life was more like a zigzag than a straight line. And sometimes I would get tired of it all. But then one Sunday morning, I found Barbara out on the terrace in her nightgown, already preparing breakfast for the two of us. When our eyes met, I could sense that something out of the ordinary was coming my way.

"You were right," Barbara said. "There is still so much to be grateful for!"

Tears were rolling down her cheeks. And when I hugged her, she started crying harder. But these were cathartic tears. And she soon told me about her new point of view. Every book, she said, consisted of different chapters. And for us it was now time to turn to a new one, a new chapter in our life. The red thread of our book was love. The kind of love that could flourish between people when they felt seen, heard, and valued . . . and when they dared to love and accept their deeper inner selves, despite not being perfect either. She looked at me intensely. And I knew her well enough to realize that she was talking as much to herself as she was talking to me, using a concept of time that had served her well on similar occasions in the past. Nodding as empathetically as I could, I tried to give her all the encouragement that she was looking for.

If we both pretended that a new chapter in our life would start at this very moment, this could serve as a springboard to a more joyful future for the two of us. I wanted that too.

Health, love, and meaning

In the weeks to come, sitting around our wooden table on the terrace, sharing a glass of red wine, or going for long walks on the beach, we often discussed what a vision of this new chapter of our life could look like. The deepest insight coming out of the shadow years had been that we had lost a deeper sense of connection. Not just between the two of us, but also to our inner selves and others around us. And we wanted to do what was necessary to change that.

For Barbara this was the beginning of a deep spiritual journey, which from the outside expressed itself in numerous long meditation and yoga sessions, ceremonies, and many rituals that she engaged in. But the shift inside was even more profound. It might sound odd, but she somehow changed into a more fluid, wiser version of herself.

During those years we also met Michael again, the spiritual teacher who had taught us so much many years earlier. And being reminded of the Golden Habit again, we started practicing it almost every single day until the moment Barbara died. And it was this habit that opened the door for a new level of self-love and the possibility to relate to each other from a very different place. It was like another awakening from the constant chatter of the mind that had been closing us off from our love for each other and from our love for life in general for too long. I know I said it before, but if there was one habit that I wish people would start practicing early in life to make daily deposits at the Bank of Life overall, a deposit that leads to dividends across all the other accounts too, this would probably be the one.

For me another important step to feel more connected again was buying a surfboard. In my earlier years, I had pursued various forms of martial arts, even if only at a very amateur level. And now in this new situation that I found myself in, I decided to do something that might sound insignificant, but for me it wasn't. I loved being out on the board. Being well into middle age, I sometimes thought it was ridiculous, but most of the time it made me feel deliciously alive. In those moments out there in the ocean, I felt a connection to myself, to nature, and to life itself that showed me what true presence was all about.

And it did not stop there. Barbara and I consciously opened our hearts to bring more joy to our circle of friends and the community of Santa Barbara. At the beginning Barbara exaggerated this new behavior, as she would usually do. She planned barbecues, parties, and all sorts of other meetings with friends or soon-to-be friends, which exhausted both of us. Later, we took a more balanced approach toward the relational side of our life and started doing so by raising an interesting question: If our life was indeed the story of our encounters, as the saying goes, who were the people we would like to spend more time with?

And the first answer that came to mind was the two of us. While we wanted to open ourselves to the world around us, we also noticed that we needed a lot of our precious time just for our respective selves, and our intimate relationship. I guess when you share a friendship within a marriage of such depth and breadth, as we had the pleasure of experiencing, being somewhat isolated as a couple sometimes might be a natural side effect. However, we now made sure that we invested some of our love and energy into nourishing the relationships outside our marriage too, and we established a few rituals like a monthly barbecue date at the beach during summertime or an annual trip to Yosemite in the fall with our friends.

In those days, I often thought about what a centenarian had said to us on Okinawa: "These doctors thought it is all about the food. But the real secret of living a long and rich life is being part of a circle of family and friends. That is what being rich is all about." I don't know if there was a mistake in the translation, but as a banker, I found this extremely interesting. And one day, inspired by the memory of this brief encounter, I did some research on the topic too. Did investing one's time into relationships make people feel more fortunate than investing in bonds and shares? And believe it or not, I found empirical evidence that I instantly shared with my wife.

"Barbara, did you know that friends can be worth $134,000 of bliss and happiness?" I asked her one evening. "I'm not making this up. A behavioral economist at the University of London calculated that an expansion in relationships and social involvement adds as much to our happiness as receiving a $134,000 increase in salary, which most people would never experience anyway. It is empirical proof that the Okinawans were right. Relationships do matter!"

Barbara looked at me in a way that I knew that I would not receive the recognition that I deserved.

"There is really no hope with bankers!" she responded, rolling her eyes and letting out a theatrical sigh of exasperation. "You didn't really need these numbers to figure this out, Leonardo. Did you?"

We were obviously back to playing pitch and catch with each other. Our shared sense of humor had always been one of the elements that I had enjoyed most about our relationship. It showed me that we were on the right path again. And Barbara and Sendhil did a fair amount of research on the impact that relationships had on health and happiness over the years too. They soon found out that maintaining positive relationships, cultivating love and friendship indeed had a measurable encompassing effect, not only on the mind but also on the body, just as the Okinawans and ancient philosophers had already known all along. A feeling of connectedness provides humans with purpose and meaning at the deepest possible level. Without it there is suffering and despair, and that affects people's health on a mental, emotional, spiritual, and even physical level. Deeper connections not only give people pleasure, but also influence their short-term and long-term health in ways every bit as powerful as adequate sleep, a good diet, and exercising do. Humans are hardwired to love and connect.

Strong and healthy relationships, modern research proved, could help to protect us from disease and even lengthen our lives.

The Japanese teahouse

Another visible sign that we had left those unhappy years behind was the Japanese teahouse that we built in our garden. Just as we had envisioned on the top of the Okinawan lighthouse more than a decade earlier, it consisted of two rooms. There was one room with a small desk and shelves for books, materials, and journals containing our notes from our journeys around the world: starting with our honeymoon in Africa, to our trips to Israel, India, and Japan, and later our holidays to Italy, Greece, the South of France, and Costa Rica, covering all the Blue Zone areas that Dan and other researchers had identified. The other room was almost empty, only furnished with tatami mats on the floor and an altar with a golden Buddhist statue on top. This was a space for meditation, spirituality, contemplation, and, as it turned out, lovemaking on very rare occasions.

"In Chinese medicine, sexual energy is a form of healing. It is life's qi, which resembles the importance of breath and food in its role in maintaining health. Isn't that fascinating?" I would lecture Barbara lying on the tatami mats next to me, and for once she would receive this wisdom with a smile.

Designing and building the tiny house had taken almost two years and lots of highly qualified helping hands. But it was worth the effort. And when it finally stood there in all its glory, we simply loved it. I still remember the day when Barbara and I were standing in front of the finished masterpiece, and my wife uttered in wonder that this could well be her deathbed. It makes me shiver remembering this scene now, and I often asked myself in the past years if her saying this was a form of anticipation or just an odd way of expressing her feeling of awe. Back then, I shook my head in calm disbelief and subtle amusement. For Barbara, you must know Sophia, this was an uplifting thought, and I knew then and there that she had made it to the other side of the deepest valley of our shared life in one piece. Before the shadow years, she had always had a fascination with death and endings. Wherever we traveled, she had to visit every graveyard she could find. Wandering around those serene spaces, silently reading the gravestone inscriptions, she would say things like, "This was wonderful, Leonardo, so peaceful; now I feel more like myself again."

My approach to life was different. I had never felt the desire to focus on death to feel alive or concentrate on the dark to appreciate the bright side. I often joked that if I was a melody, I would be like Mozart, floating along innocently, like a small stream through a green landscape gently embedded in its environment, whereas

Barbara reminded me more of Beethoven and *Symphony No. 9*, covering a much wider range of emotions. Needless to say that Barbara challenged me on these facile comparisons.

Glimpses into wisdom

"As our island of knowledge grows, so does the shore of our ignorance."

—John Archibald Wheeler

In the later stage of our life, when Barbara and I had both stopped working full-time, the teahouse became the place where Barbara spent much of her time. Most of our days started with the two of us having breakfast together on the terrace of our beach house, and when I would ask Barbara what she was up to that day, more often than not she would answer, "Finding glimpses into wisdom, if I am lucky enough today," and then she would retreat to the teahouse to engage with her ceremonies, her rituals, and her writing, which, from my perspective, all seemed perfectly intertwined.

Barbara had never wanted to become an academic, which is why she had never gone out of her way to write scientific papers about any of the subjects she had researched over the years. The only piece of writing she ever felt drawn to was the book about the essentials of life. And the overarching theme that attracted most of her attention in those later years was the interconnectedness of all things in the universe. For her, strengthening the relational side of our life had many emotional, spiritual, and practical implications, but it also extended into an intellectual activity that influenced her view of her profession. And she often pondered over the question of whether all those "either/or" approaches in the world of medicine and psychology actually made sense. Conventional medicine versus holistic medicine; the science of disease versus a science of health; a person-centered approach versus a systemic approach. The list of dichotomies went on and on. And increasingly Barbara asked herself if these seemingly combatant views could not be held in one's mind simultaneously for the benefit of the patients.

Could it really be true that all the arguments presented were incompatible?

And together we wondered what would possibly happen to a scientific field or even a society as a whole when the gap between all those opposing approaches would be filled with a genuine sense of curiosity, when people were humble enough to at least be interested to see what the other side had to offer.

Over the years, Barbara and Sendhil had seen with their own eyes that conventional medicine and other healing systems could indeed inspire each other, even when human intelligence could detect mutually exclusive ideas on the other side. In conventional medicine, principles like rationality, analysis, cause-and-effect thinking were seen as superior, and the idea of separation a necessary requirement in the process of analysis. As a result, the body and the mind were treated as separate entities, and the connection between them was largely ignored by the leading medical research institutions of the Western world for more than a century. And it had gone much further than that: Not only the body and the mind, but even the different parts of the body were looked at separately, as if they were not part of the same system. One doctor per organ! And not many doctors or patients had questioned that.

Advocates of a more holistic approach to medicine strongly rejected the underlying assumption of separation, and Barbara even considered it to be the cause for much suffering in the world. But unlike many of their colleagues, Barbara and Sendhil recognized the achievements of modern medicine without mitigation. After all, the emergence of this field had led to some of the most amazing advancements in human history. The diagnostic instruments invented allowed them to scrutinize the human body in unprecedented ways. The pharmaceuticals discovered and the surgical method developed—the two most important weapons of treatment of conventional medicine until today—helped save millions of people every year, which is why Barbara and Sendhil both agreed that it would be irresponsible to not make adequate use of them.

However, acknowledging the credits of modern medicine did not mean that one had to ignore its shortcomings. Starting with a century-long lack of interest in creating a science of health as such, modern medicine often seemed to fail to understand the root cause of why people became ill in the first place. Despite trillions of dollars spent on healthcare, people in our societies are getting sicker, heavier, and more depressed every year. This is a scientific fact, not an opinion. And nine out of ten of these chronic diseases are directly attributable to poor nutrition, heightened blood sugar levels, and poor lifestyle choices, like physical inactivity. Of course, the design of societal life and the food industry is not helpful in this regard either. But while the World Health Organization points out that the vast majority of factors related to individual health today are associated with lifestyle choices people make, most medical schools do not expect students to take at least one course in nutrition during their education or attend a seminar on how to create health in more general terms. And that still holds true today.

Sendhil, Barbara, and I often discussed these observations while enjoying a good dinner on our terrace. It was difficult to understand why progress in science occurred at such a fast pace on the one hand but at the same time was so incredibly slow on the other. Sendhil, as so often happened, nailed it with his dry sense of humor, claiming that things would change "one funeral at a time!"

There was a lot of truth in this. Looking into the field of modern medicine, it was not difficult to notice how dismissive many professors, researchers, and medical doctors were toward holistic medicine. They claimed publicly that this was because there was no scientific proof that lifestyle medicine worked. But this was simply untrue, as demonstrated in applying the same scientific principles and diagnostic measures they so believed in. So, maybe the main obstacle in the way of taking on a more integrated view was a struggle of the ego rather than the incompatibility of different ways of thinking . . . well-educated people wanting to be right and be recognized for their uniqueness and their expertise, instead of more openly relating to other researchers and their patients in more meaningful ways.

Luckily, Sophia, today the majority of the leading institutions in the medical community admit that there is no real division between mind and body, and an increasing number of leading medical schools have at least small departments devoted to lifestyle medicine, and there is also research being undertaken reflecting on how one's position within society affects one's health.

And there is more. Much more. There is a revolution on the way, brought about by those inside but also outside modern medicine, creating a new science of personalized health literally at the speed of light. Enabling patients to measure parameters of their health themselves wearing tiny devices, soon producing results a thousand times per second. And well-educated, well-off patients will no longer exclusively be at the receiving end of top-down services from experts in the field but will be able to take their fate into their own hands, ideally working hand in hand with open-minded doctors and healers around the world.

Nevertheless, these positive developments should not distract from the fact that those insights are not yet integrated into the approach of millions and millions of doctors still operating within the old paradigm. And Barbara, when still alive, often said that while change might happen one funeral at the time, people should make sure that it is not their funeral first!

Making deposits

Over the decades, I have seen the world change, Sophia. Not just the events, but our community, our society, and our environment. I have seen the subtler changes and how people were at different times. And the older I became, the more I was convinced that it truly is the quality of our relationships, our love to ourselves, to others, and to the wider cosmos that glue everything together. People who are deeply connected with themselves and their loved ones seem to be happier, more fulfilled, healthier, and live a better life in general. The good life. It's not money or fame or good looks, it's love, connection, and relationships. And if you ask people about what they value most in their life, they often say their families, their children, and their close friends.

And as that is what they say, we'd therefore assume that we see that reflected in how they invest their time at the Bank of Life too. But that is where common sense and the practical realities of our lives part ways. Unlike the account of work that attracts time like a magnet, this account often doesn't get the attention it deserves. At the Bank of Life, where all human time spent is being registered, the investment into this account is often not in accordance with what people say they value. This is particularly true in the most industrialized parts of the world. And to be crystal clear, I am not simply referring to quantity of time invested. In this account, the *quality* of time is what makes all the difference. Paying undivided attention to someone, having moments of shared pleasure, truly being there, supporting each other.

We have all heard it. At the end of their life, people do not regret having spent too little time in the office or at their desk. And I can subscribe to that notion too. However, millions of people have regrets about not having spent more dedicated time with the people they love and hold dear. Which is why, in the spirit of the Bank of Life, I want to invite you to carefully think about how you will make your deposits into this account throughout your life.

And, if you like, pause for a moment to ask yourself—What could possibly stop you from following up on your positive intentions? What could be holding you back?

During one of our walks along the beach at the time, when Barbara and I were still trying to find our way out of the shadow years, we drew a diagram in the sand to reflect about how we wanted to nourish the relational side of our life more carefully again.

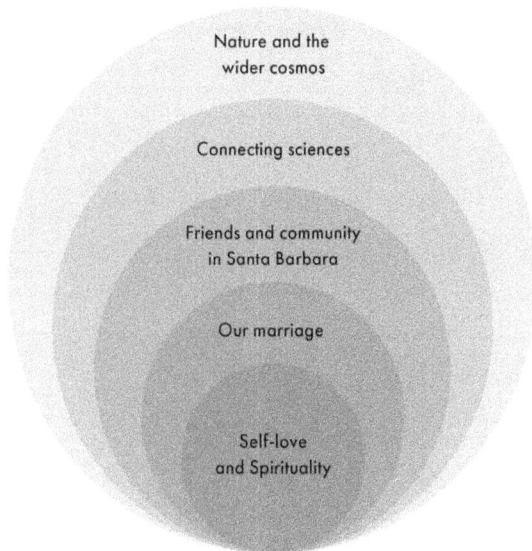

Nature and the
wider cosmos

Connecting sciences

Friends and community
in Santa Barbara

Our marriage

Self-love
and Spirituality

These circles might look different for different people. For Barbara, the circle around connecting different ways of thinking across sciences was more important than it was for me. But we both felt that integrating a deeper form of spirituality, nature, and the wider cosmos into these circles was important so as not to lose perspective. Just acknowledging that the sun comes up, day after day, to shine light on us. To marvel at the fact that water rains from the sky and allows trees to grow. To be aware that our bodies are made up of trillions of cells that all work together simultaneously to keep us alive. Cultivating this sense of awe for the little and big things around us in nature and the wider universe made us feel more connected to ourselves in a deeper way.

So, while you engage with the endeavor of writing this part of our book, I would suggest that you also reflect about how you invest some of your time to purposefully nourish the relationships that matter most to you in your life. And you might draw these circles in a different way. You decide. But the questions that remain will be the following:

Are you making some regular deposits into this account at the Bank of Life?

How are you nourishing the relationship with your deeper spiritual self?

What are other relationships that you would like to invest your time and love in going forward?

How can you use the human needs psychology to strengthen the relationship with yourself and others?

Wrapping up

My storytelling is as complete as our perception of life always is. Completion is a myth. And still there are things that I need to share with you to feel that I am done. And to start tidying up those loose ends that I have carefully avoided touching upon so far, I want to tell you what actually happened to Barbara's book project. Because as you will see, I am the one who is responsible for all of that. I must admit that I sometimes wondered if I had to tell you. Would I be sent to court if people knew what I did? I will never find out. But deep in my heart, I hope that truth leads to trust and then to more truth and even more trust.

It all happened the night after Barbara's funeral. These were the darkest days of my life, the most painful ones. This is not an excuse for what I have to say next. But I want you to know that this was the context in which I operated. And I hope by sharing what I must share, I will be able to forgive myself and find some peace too.

The evening after the funeral, I was wandering around the teahouse restlessly for hours on end. I listened to Beethoven's *Symphony No. 9*, especially the "Ode to Joy," which we had both loved so much. And after what felt like an eternity, I lay down on the tatami mats on the ground of our teahouse, where Barbara had lain down so many times before, and I listened to the "Ode to Joy" again and again and again. And then, when the night was almost over, I suddenly got up. As if guided by a higher force, I walked straight into the garage to fetch a small petrol can with such certainty, as if I had planned for this to happen, which was not the case at all. And without much hesitation, I spread the petrol across the floor of the teahouse, lit a match, and burned it all down. The rice paper walls flickered in the fire, and when I saw Barbara's deathbed being eaten by the flames, the "Ode to Joy" still playing in my mind, I felt it all made so much sense. Barbara had died of toxification of the lungs due to a smoldering fire in the entrance of the teahouse ten days prior when I had been away traveling to LA to meet with a former colleague of mine. A toxic fog had taken her life away when she had peacefully rested on those tatami mats next to the golden Buddha she had adored so much. And now the teahouse and the golden Buddha received the ending that they deserved.

Of course, I must have been out of my mind. An old, wounded

lunatic gone crazy. But during that moment, I stood there almost triumphant. And I waited calmly until it was too late to save anything of substance before I went inside our beach house to call the fire department. It was very early in the morning, and when the firefighters left, believe it or not, I slept deeply and soundly. It was only when I woke up again many hours later that I gradually realized what I had done and what a stupid old fool I had been. I had burned it all down. Not just the teahouse but everything else too. All of Barbara's work. All the words she had written. All the sentences she had worked on so meticulously over such a long time, edited again and again, polished like exquisite silverware. In horror, I contemplated my sin.

The following days, two police officers, who I was coincidently acquainted with, came to find out what had started the fire, and they concluded that it had been the same cable that had caused the first tragic event too. I did not lie to them. I was simply too shocked to speak at all. And they did not expect me to. No further investigation was undertaken. I was lucky in that sense, but I could not have cared less. To the grief of having lost Barbara came an overwhelming sense of guilt, which left me emotionally frozen, not capable of doing much for a year.

Today, I am sure that Barbara would say that it all happened for a reason. She had often emphasized how, in retrospect, every ending in our life had miraculously led to new beginnings. And even the destruction of our research for Barbara's book project, as unjust and foolish as my actions had been, has led to something new. And while I could not see it that way for a long time, I now hope that by handing over the baton to you, Sophia, this circle of destruction is transforming itself into a circle of growth and inspiration. Even if you still wonder why I chose to approach you out of all people on this planet. Rightly so! And I am not sure if I can provide you with a satisfying set of answers to this hypothetical, but legitimate, question.

When I think of you, Sophia, I am often thrown back in space and time, being reminded about my first overseas travels to Prague. I don't know if you remember it, but I mentioned this journey to you in one of my earlier letters. Back then, I was visiting the last living relative of my mother. And it was there and then that I met the girl from Berlin that ultimately led me to finding you all those decades later. As it happened, she was on a study trip at the same time I was visiting my aunt, residing in the house next door, which is how we met. We instantly liked each other and spent some time together exploring the city of Prague. On the last day of my visit, we went to the old famous town bridge in the center, possibly the most beautiful Gothic gateway in the world, when she predicted how my life would turn out. We had sat down in a little café behind the bridge in a tiny old building, when she unexpectedly offered a tarot card reading, which I agreed to. And while I considered it a joke at first, I was also impressed. She seemed so skillful at what she did. And she predicted a great future for me, a long life and a happy marriage. And she even foresaw that I would be on a lifelong sacred quest of some sort.

And with this magnificent claim and a grand theatrical gesture, she gave me an old pocket watch. Inside the old shabby watch that no longer functioned was an inscription in English—*Lost time is never found again.* She had found the watch in an old, deserted building in Berlin, and she had sensed that it would have a special meaning to someone someday. I didn't know what to make of this. But then she looked me in the eyes so intensely and insisted that, at the end of my very long life, it would come to my rescue.

It wasn't like I believed her. But I was intrigued. And for many months after my return to New York, I often looked at the watch. Mostly amused but baffled too. And then, without really intending to, I kept the watch over the years. Admittedly, there were a few instances in my life when decluttering my belongings that I almost got rid of it. But at the end, I kept it as a memory of my journey to Prague. I did show it to Barbara too. She loved the story behind it and suggested I take good care of it as a symbol of good fortune.

And then, exactly one year after Barbara's death, when cleaning up the house, I stumbled across the small watch again, and I looked at it in wonderment. The simple fact that I had kept it over a lifetime suddenly felt like a miracle. And when I saw your picture on the internet a couple of days later, I decided this was it. I think you have the same surname, if I am not mistaken, and you are living in Berlin. Seeing your picture on the internet, Sophia, was pure coincidence, but recognizing you was not. And even if you are not who I think you might be, this still holds true. I told you that my explanation, why I contacted you, would possibly not fully satisfy you.

First it was the timing, and the mindset I was in, when I saw the picture of you. It was the watch, the superstitious idea that you could well be the granddaughter of this woman I met in Prague all those decades ago, and that this watch would come at my rescue at the end of my long life, just as she had predicted. You really look like her, with your dark hair and those unusual, bright green eyes. And in addition, it was your background as a psychologist, a coach, and an author, and your videos on the internet that brought me to believe that destiny had meant for the two of us to meet in this particular way. I know it all sounds unlikely. And it most probably is. But isn't all of life more than unlikely, and still it happens. We are on a planet that is spinning around in the middle of nowhere. In fact, the universe is 99.99999999999999999999% empty space. According to scientists, it exploded into existence 13.8 billion years ago, an incomprehensible amount of time. The fact that we are here and can do and experience *anything* is nothing short of miraculous. So why not extend the imagination that little much further, that it was meant for the two of us to cross paths at this moment in time!

There is a longing for truth in all of us, and there is the comfort of the illusion. And to have the energy to do what I had set out to do, I was thriving on the latter. But I can honestly say that I have no doubt in my mind that you will do something with my letters that is going to be of value to you and others. So, forgive me for creating this one-way street of communication, and thank you so much for respecting my privacy all along. With the little energy I have left, all I managed to do was to stay withdrawn from the world and pursue what I had set out to do in silent contemplation.

And now I am sitting here in Santa Barbara in my final days, working on these pages that will eventually travel from California right into the heart of Germany, in the middle of Berlin. Maybe to an address not so far away from where the girl who gave me this watch once lived. And when you will have published our book, Sophia, who knows—some of these words that I am putting to paper right now will later travel back to California where a reader might pick up a copy of our book in a store here in Santa Barbara, reading it on a flight to Berlin. Unlikely but possible.

Life is fascinating. We are going in circles. Thousands and millions of times, again and again. And not just geographically but also mentally, emotionally, spiritually. In Western societies, circles are often looked down upon. As the outcast of geometry, they are used in our language to describe things that are not working. When people are stuck on a task, the recommendation is to stop going in circles. We are told to sit up straight, to think straight, talk straight, and to be a straight-A student. Straight lines and right angles receive the utmost appreciation, while circles are often treated with less courtesy.

For a long time, you must know, Sophia, I also suffered from such an anti-circle bias. Only when traveling through Asia did it dawn on me that I had been ignorant in some ways. Circles seemed to be everywhere. The mandala, the prayer wheel, the ensō in Japan. Circles in those Eastern cultures symbolize the eternity of life and the possibility to create wisdom. And circumambulation, the act of walking in a circle, is considered to bring the soul closer to enlightenment. Like many Westerners, however, Barbara and I for a long time even viewed time as such in a linear fashion too—literally picturing a linear timeline that resembled the one drawn in our history lessons in school, starting at point X on the left and ending at point Y on the right. But then I got support from a former investment banker-turned-Buddhist, Eric Weiner, who had settled down in Santa Barbara after spending a decade in India. One evening, I admitted to him that I found it troubling when going in circles in any area of my life, as success, productivity, and advancement were usually on my mind.

He looked at me and said, "Ultimately, Leonardo, there is nowhere to go, no progress to be made." Letting the words float into the sunset, I was waiting for him to shed some more light on the matter. When he added, "The circle unveils the lie that is seen in progress and success. From a spiritual perspective, it is nothing but an illusion of the mind!" I wasn't sure if I understood, but I decided to let the message sink in.

And now reminding myself of stepping into the circle that joins the two of us, Sophia, decades ago, before you were even born, I feel a sense of peace. Real or imaginary, it is a circle that I like and appreciate. And mind me, one that feels like progress too.

Some people say there is a book in everyone. Is that true? Barbara liked to say that the most important stories are the ones we tell ourselves. And we should be careful editors when rewriting our narrative from our point of view. Instead of being the authors of our own unhappiness, we might have the chance to be the hero and not the victim, as we ourselves get to choose what goes on the pages that lives in our minds and shapes our realities.

Looking back, I think that this is what we did most of the time. And I hope you do too. However, what I didn't see until I started writing it all down were the connections between the different stories of our shared life. And looking at all those letters from where I am today, I realize how much these different periods of our life are in conversation with one another.

Now it might look clear, but I really struggled with the structure of my writing. And I cannot imagine that what I am asking of you is easy. So just write a little every day, without despair. When you have a great and difficult task, something that almost feels impossible, if you work at it a little at a time, suddenly the work will finish itself.

And as I write these final lines, I feel my hands unclench, my mind expand, pieces of poetry falling through my imagination. So be it, heart: bid farewell without end.

J. Leonardo

CHAPTER 18

Sophia: Making Connections

Chronology: seven months and twenty days after Leonardo and Sophia's brief encounter at San Francisco Airport.

It was an overcast morning when Sophia started walking the last sequence of the Berlin Wall Trail, following the Iron Curtain that once cut off West from East Berlin and the rest of Germany. This was the street where the wall had claimed its first victims and some of the most famous tunnels were dug. How heart-wrenching it was to think about it. Sophia looked at a display portraying some of those unlucky people who had been killed in their attempt to cross the wall in the first months of its existence. In this place, one could agree with Barbara that the idea of separation could be the root cause of much suffering.

But was integration always the higher aim and separation evil, speaking from a broader, philosophical perspective? Sophia had recently read the amazing book *The Master and his Emissary*, written by one of the few true polymaths of current times, Iain McGilchrist, in which it was argued that in the world at large, not just within society, but within nature, there was always a combination of division and union coexisting with one another. Take the brain as an example: an organ which was all about making connections but was still divided in two hemispheres separated by the corpus callosum, inhibiting connections and stopping the left and the right hemispheres from interfering with each other while at the same time transferring information. Just to be wholly unified did not seem to be the answer, but to be wholly divided and atomistic was not very helpful either.

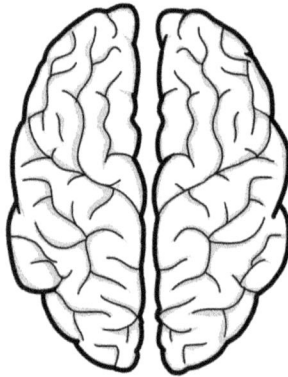

Sophia checked the photographs on the display again and then continued her expedition along the remnants of the wall, passing tourists from all over the world huddling around further points of historical interest. The street was covered in leaves from the trees. Fall was an intriguing time of the year, and today it resonated with Sophia's mood. Things were coming to an end with Leonardo. He had achieved what he had set out to accomplish, and while this made her happy, it saddened her just as much. The idea that she would lose Leonardo without meeting him ever again was unsettling. Early this morning, tossing and turning in her bed, she had even considered engaging a private detective to track Leonardo down before it was too late. But of course, this was ridiculous—how could she disturb an old man during his final days after everything he had done for her?!

Nonetheless, Sophia assumed that Leonardo perceived the situation differently. He probably felt he owed her for taking care of the book and solving the puzzle of getting it out into the world. But for Sophia, it was the reverse. She was tremendously grateful for everything he had given her. And there was a pressing urge to tell him at least that. To give something back while he was still alive.

His last letter had arrived almost two weeks prior, and she had read it several times. Sophia had not been surprised in the least that Barbara and Leonardo had identified relationships to be among the Big Five accounts at the Bank of Life. One did not necessarily have to dig deep into the research about the positive effects that love, friendship, and the feeling of connectedness had on people's happiness to assume that this was the case. But it was interesting to learn about the huge impact positive relationships had on health and longevity, too. And it also seemed to work the other way around. The isolation that came with the challenges of modern life took a huge toll on people's health. What a strange thought anyway that the richest countries in the world had the highest rates of mental health issues, the highest rates of chronic illness, and the poorest diet of all time. And all the economic growth did not seem to make a difference within the Western, educated, industrial, rich, democratic nations, known by some as the W.E.I.R.D. countries. And it was weird indeed that the leading countries of the world seemed to have lost *connection* to what a good life on and for this planet could look like.

Sophia stopped patrolling along the former wall to glance at the statue of reconciliation showing a man and a woman embracing each other.

And what about herself?

Months ago, walking the streets of Berlin not far from where she was now, she had asked herself whether she could transform herself at least once, when this city could reinvent itself so relentlessly over centuries. And today, Sophia knew that she could. And of course, she had known this before. As a coach, it was her job to help people do exactly that: go through various transitions in life, challenge their limiting beliefs, and achieve their goals. But progress was not necessarily linear when it came to personal development—just like Leonardo's Buddhist friend had suggested, people were going in circles many times and even being a psychologist or a well-respected coach, for that matter, did not save her from going through life with all its up and downs too. Sophia herself had been caught in a downward spiral for quite some time, but over the past months she had managed to turn things around. There was still work to be done, construction sites to attend to, across the Big Five accounts at the Bank of Life and beyond, and this would probably never change. A life without challenges was not to be expected. However, Leonardo trusting her without reservation had motivated her to gather her strength and move on to something new. She knew that she would have gotten to this point without receiving Leonardo's letters, but they had served as a catalyst. She did indeed look at the world through a different lens now. And her relationship toward time and how she invested it had changed substantially.

She was no longer sitting on the fence making one-dimensional decisions at the Bank of Life. In England, she had been part of a circle of expatriates, which she had loved. Intellectually stimulating people open to new experiences, knowledge, and insights. And she was now meeting similar people in the coworking space that she had signed up to. However, she was careful not to overtake herself like Barbara had done when coming out of the shadow years. To nourish the relational side of her life was as much a short-term as a long-term decision. But when making deposits into this account of her life became a habit, the positive results would accumulate over time. And that belief centered her. Of course, it still sometimes saddened her that her relationship with Ruben had not worked out, but it neither triggered the panic nor the pain she used to feel months ago. She knew that she was genuinely better off without him.

Walking alongside a double row of cobblestones marking the former course of the wall, Sophia thought about Leonardo's recommendation to work with the human needs psychology when investing in a relationship.

One observation was that at the beginning of most relationships, everybody was eager to satisfy the needs of the person one was falling in love with. But once the relationship was cut and dry in one way or the other and the need for certainty was met, the focus gradually shifted from wanting to satisfy the needs of the other person to observing what this other person did or did not do for oneself. And that did not work particularly well.

Spotting an empty wooden bench in front of her, Sophia spontaneously sat down, got her notebook out to write down six questions people could ask to develop their relationships further, just as Leonardo and Barbara had done. She amended them several times. Maybe she could share those questions with her clients too.

1. How would you like me to create safety and certainty for you in our relationship?

2. How can I make you feel alive and surprise you?

3. How do you wish to be recognized?

4. How would you like me to show my love for you?

5. How are we learning and growing together?

6. How can we contribute to something beyond ourselves?

What works for me?

What works for you?

If people were courageous enough to ask each other such questions and were interested enough to listen to the answers, this could possibly make a real difference.

However, there was one potential pitfall in all of this. Due to different personality types, preferences, and value systems, people differed very much in how they wanted and needed those needs to be fulfilled. And so for this to lead anywhere, both sides had to be interested in finding out what worked for the other person. Admittedly, Sophia never had a conversation like this with Ruben. And looking under the surface of their former relationship now, she realized that Ruben was not the only one to blame. It usually took two to tango. She had probably stifled him with an oversupply of certainty while not being able to satisfy his need for excitement and connection when it came to his outdoor sports dreams and ambitions that made him feel so alive and that he wanted to share with his partner. And by the way, he hadn't satisfied her need for variety either, at least not on a deeper intellectual or even spiritual level! There had been no alignment around a vision of a shared life together, and despite his analytical intelligence, their way of communicating had not stimulated her desire for learning and growth. Yes, he had made her laugh, but it wasn't like they had connected on a deeper level.

Sophia sat up, leafing through the pages of her notebook. A couple of weeks prior she had also used the human needs psychology to quickly diagnose her relationship to other parts of her life, like her profession, using a scale from 1 to 10.

My professional life:

1. . . . provides me with enough security, structure, and certainty? _____

2. . . . makes me feel alive, offers enough variety, surprise, and unknown possibilities? _____

3. . . . makes me feel significant and gives me the level of recognition that I am looking for? _____

4. . . . offers opportunities to connect with other people? _____

5. . . . provides possibilities to grow, learn, and progress? _____

6. . . . gives me the chance to contribute to something beyond myself? _____

On a scale from 1 to 10, her job scored 7, 8, 9, or 10 on all fronts, which was probably the reason why this area of her life provided her with so much satisfaction overall. And of course, she had done a lot to shape it this way. After all, this was the account at the Bank of Life that she had invested most of her time and attention in. And she would usually also challenge her clients to think about how they could influence things both inside and outside themselves at work to create higher scores on those fronts too, following the motto to never simply be the passive spectator of any situation but an active player on the field.

Sophia wrote down another note on the page in front of her and then closed her notebook, striking her fingers softly across the gentle leather cover as she had done so many times in the past months. The human needs psychology was indeed a great tool, both when wanting to invest more consciously in a relationship or when thinking about one's personal satisfaction in different areas of life. And it could also shed light on all kinds of relationships, not just an intimate one, which would be of use in her consultancy business too.

Great leaders, for example, make people feel safe in their environment, they offer a variety of experiences, they give recognition generously for contributions made, and they build genuine connections. And of course, when those leaders would aim to generate true followership and not just execute formal power, they would offer people opportunities to grow and learn while pursuing a goal with a noble cause.

Sophia was feeling content and got up. The sun was now peeking through the clouds, and she felt its warming effect on her skin. After sauntering along the footpath for half an hour, marveling at the changing colors of the trees lining the former death strip where the wall once stood, she reached yet another memorial. And that meant that she had now officially completed the trail, covering the distance of 160 kilometers, divided into several individual sections each between seven and twenty kilometers long.

Over the course of three months, she had biked all the longer sections and walked some of the shorter ones. Remains of the old wall had alternated with stretches of natural beauty, like in the north of the city where the trail, to Sophia's great surprise, had led her deep through the woods marked with sandy embankments, grazing horses, and picnic areas. But even biking along those sparkling shorelines, the tales of the Berlin Wall had never been far away, with memorials and information prompting a dissonance to the beauty of the present moment that her heart had absorbed like a sponge. For Sophia, embarking on this trail had been about reinforcing a more active lifestyle, and even if it wouldn't count as an athletic achievement for others, she had enjoyed the process of completing it, since it had opened her heart toward this city she now lived in. And maybe even more importantly, it had also helped her to find and love herself again, the very thing that would allow her to go out and love again. This time more wholeheartedly, with courage and compassion.

Would this qualify as closing another circle? Sophia smiled. Conducting imaginary dialogues with Leonardo had become a normal activity for her to engage in.

She examined the photo exhibition in front of her, depicting scenes from the night when the wall fell. In contrast to the people she had seen on the first information post earlier that day, the faces in these pictures were jubilant, triumphant. Those were the lucky ones, the ones who had lived to see the wall fall, who danced on it, smashed at it with hammers, who crossed it, optimistically anticipating the future. Celebrating the end of separation, freedom, and reunion. Sophia raised her eyebrows, creating wrinkles in her forehead. Of course, the idea of separation was not right or wrong. It was the implementation of this idea that could cause problems. When it became the headline of one's life, a scientific field, or a whole country for that matter, it could indeed blind people from seeing the bigger picture.

In stark contrast, the wisest leaders she'd had the privilege to work with in recent years had the capacity to hold completely opposing ideas in their heads. Without panicking or simply settling for one alternative or the other, they were able to produce a synthesis that was more enlightening than any of those seemingly opposing thoughts. Distinctions were necessary. However, without those impermeable walls and divisions, there was more potential for true insight and development. But in business, as well as in academia and the public discourse, things were too often presented in silos, as if they were unrelated, while a more sensible goal would be to strive for a multifaceted understanding of the matter in question.

Sophia took a deep breath of the autumn air. The former death strip had indeed been turned into a beautiful place that now underscored the country's good fortune of reunification. But even that was a matter of perspective. She shook her head empathetically, thinking about the rabbit colonies she had read about on another information post earlier that day. During the years of the German separation they had led a wonderful and peaceful life here. Hovering around the watchtowers, floodlights, and trip-wire machine guns, these rabbits had grown their communities in unimaginable ways. But with the reunification of the country, those rabbits had been separated, and the few who had survived had fled to different parts of the city. Sophia shrugged her shoulders almost invisibly. All wisdom ends in paradox—no arguing with that.

*   *   *

When arriving at her new apartment situated on the top floor of a renovated historical building in the middle of Berlin later that afternoon, Sophia noticed a flat package with Leonardo's handwriting sitting on her doormat waiting for her. She stopped walking. She had not expected to hear from him so soon. With a fluttery feeling in her belly, she picked up the package, opened the door, and stepped inside the spacious flat. Fiddling through the kitchen drawer, she took out a sharp knife to rip the package wide open. Her eyes narrowing, she stared at the contents inside.

It had happened. Really happened. The last envelope had reached its destination. Sophia looked up the ceiling, letting out a deep sigh. Everything in life was temporary—that was so true. Touching the reinforced envelope like a sacred treasure, she opened it and carefully placed the five things that she found inside on the kitchen table in front of her. Following an impulse, she adjusted her phone to take a photograph of this ensemble before opening the letter containing Leonardo's final notes.

CHAPTER 19

Leonardo: Final Notes

We have two lives. The second starts when
one realizes that we have only one.

—Confucius

There is a dream that keeps coming back to me, Sophia. And in this dream, I am an old professor who one day speaks to a group of leaders from different walks of life. Standing in front of these people who seem to be willing to write down every word I say, I slowly meet the eyes of each person in the room before I tell them that I am about to conduct an experiment.

From under the table that stands between the audience and myself, I pull out a bag of rocks, each the size of a tennis ball, and a big glass jar, both of which I put on the table in front of me. Slowly, I start placing the rocks in the jar, one after the other. I do so until there is no room to add another rock into the jar.

Lifting my gaze to my sophisticated audience, I ask, "What do you think? Is the jar full?"

There is a beat or two of silence. And then I see some people nodding.

"Yes," I hear a few of them saying.

I am content. This is exactly the answer I was hoping for. I pause another moment to heighten the anticipation and then reply, "Is that really true?"

The audience remains still. And with the gravitas of a wise old professor, I reach under the table another time and pull out a bag full of pebbles. I pour the pebbles into the jar and shake it a bit until all the pebbles settle in all the spaces between the big rocks. I lift my gaze and ask, "What do you think? Is the jar full now?" At this point, my audience begins to understand my intentions.

"Obviously not," I hear a woman in the front row saying.

And I continue the experiment by pulling out a bucket of sand from under the table. Cautiously, I pour the sand into the big jar until every little empty space is occupied. And again, I ask, "What do you think? Is the jar full now?"

Without hesitation, people shake their heads.

"Right," I respond, and as is by now expected of the smart students of the Academy of the Bank of Life, I reach for the big bottle of sugary lemonade that is on the table and pour it into the jar until it is absolutely full.

"What can we take away from this experiment?" I ask.

Silence for a moment.

"As busy as we are, it is always possible to add more items to our calendars, at least fluid ones," a handsome man in an expensive-looking suit then says jokingly.

The audience laughs.

"That, my friend, would be a great tragedy." I smile, looking warmly across the room. "There is a greater lesson that we can take away from this experiment."

I briefly pause again, and then I continue, lowering my voice to emphasize the importance of the message I want to convey. "Whatever our idea of a good life is, we must include the large rocks first. Because if we don't, we are likely to miss out on them altogether. If we give priority to the things that don't matter, our lives will be filled up with pebbles, sand, and cheap lemonade— things of minor importance. Leaving little and sometimes no time for the topics in our lives that are most important to us. Therefore, ask yourself, 'What are the large rocks in your life?' And once you identify them, be sure to put them into the jar first."

I hear a murmur of recognition. And with a wave of my hand, I bid farewell to my audience and slowly walk out of the room. And this is how my recurring dream usually ends, and if it reminds you of a story that has been widely circulated in management circles in the last few decades, you are spot on.

Some think that a dream is a microscope through which we look at the ambitions of our soul. And it is true: From the perspective of a banker, who has been almost a century on this planet, I still, in these final days of my life, would argue that the single most important investment you will ever make in your life has little to do with money.

The most important currency, I believe, is your time, your presence, your heart. And while you might say, "Yes, but making a great monetary investment will buy me precisely that—time," I would argue that it starts with how you invest your focus first.

When somebody would throw away money, we would find that ridiculous. However, when somebody throws away time, a much more valuable resource that cannot be replicated, we regard this as a regular occurrence. The Roman philosopher Seneca said it well in a letter to Paulinus: *When time is squandered in carelessness, we perceive it has passed away before we were aware that it was passing. It is not that we have so little time, but we waste so much of it!*

And therefore, as my final act as the secret director of the Bank of Life, I am going to share those five principles with you, which I have borrowed from the world of finance, that in its modified version seems to work quite well in relation to time investment too.

1. Identify the "big rocks" in your life first

This one you are already familiar with. The first principle, when aiming to become a good time investor, is to identify the big rocks in your life first. And interestingly, these big rocks are often the same. Reading ancient philosophers, like Aristotle, who already discussed the idea of the good life thousands of years ago, as well as listening to what the experts have to say these days, the essence of their conversations are much alike. As human beings, we will always need to take care of our bodies, as this is the vehicle which carries us through life. We need to nourish our psychology—our mind, our soul, our spirit—as this influences all of our life experiences. We need to nurture our relationships, as this is what glues it all together. And to feel alive and useful, we have to engage in meaningful work, and to develop skills to make a positive contribution toward others, which gives us purpose, confidence, and a sense of self-worth. And of course, last but not least, the majority of us will have to make sure that we have the financial means to create the material side of our life too.

These are the Big Five accounts at the Bank of Life as we identified them, and we would advise you to put them into your calendar first so that they all get some of your precious attention.

But of course, as the wise statistician George E. P. Box once said, "All models are wrong, but some are useful!" So, if you find out that there is another topic or two that deserves more attention in your life, make your amendments as you see fit. Some might want to add the topic of spirituality as a rock of its own. Others might include

Our Physiology

Health
Energy & Fitness
Sleep & Relaxation
Nutrition
Exercise

Our Relationships

Love
Connection
Family & Friends
Community
Spirituality

BIG FIVE

Our Psychology

Belief
Power Within
Thoughts & Emotions
Mindfulness
Meditation

Our Finances

Abundance
Gratefulness
Financial IQ & EQ
Wealth
Focus

Our Work

Ikigai
Purpose
Contribution to Others
Perseverance
Passion

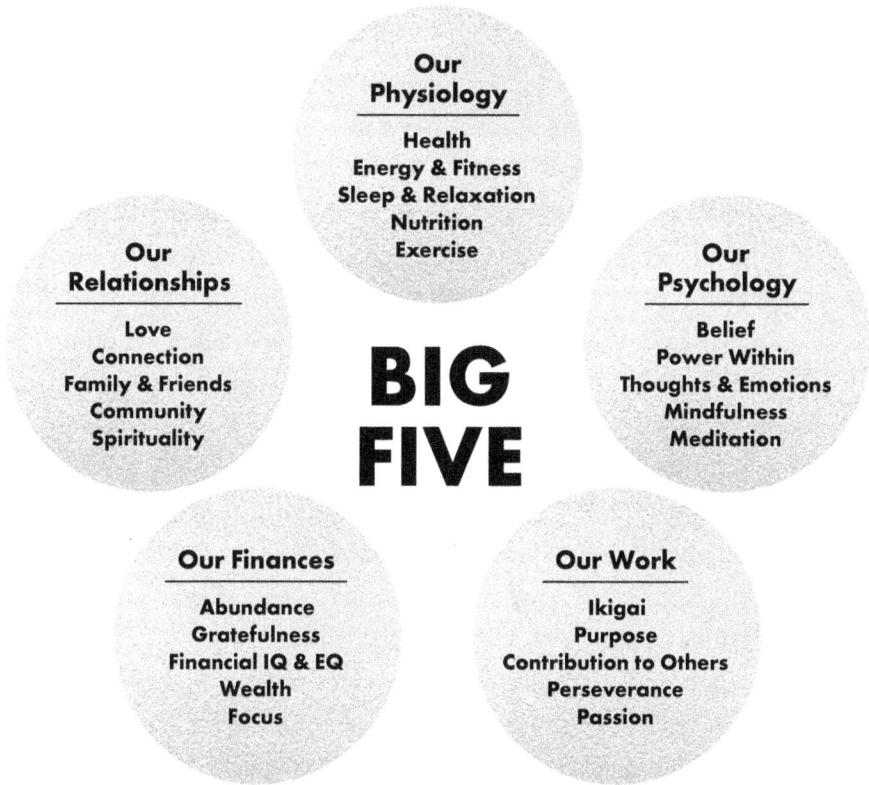

it in the pocket of relationships, as we have done, as our assumption was that it all starts with the relationship that we have with our deeper inner selves. You might have an area of interest so important that it deserves an extra account at the Bank of Your Life, and you might end up with the Big Six to Fix or the Seven Made in Heaven. You decide. After all, these big rocks do not represent all of life. But they serve as a simple reminder to give the essential topics in your life the attention they deserve. And of course, in reality these big rocks are not completely separate entities either. Not at all! They all blend into each other, as life always does. But working with these distinctions might help you to build a solid all-weather portfolio that supports you to navigate through good and bad times in your life ahead.

2. Rebalance your portfolio

Another important principle is to rebalance one's portfolio at the Bank of Life at regular intervals. In practice this means that we have to take a look at the different areas of our lives and make sure our time allocations are still in the right ratio. From time to time, a particular part of one of our buckets may grow significantly and disproportionally to the rest of our portfolio and throw us out of balance. We might have started out with a great portfolio in mind, but it washes away over the weeks, months, and years. If building your career, for example, ends up consuming too much of your time for too long, you might run the risk of diminishing your health or feeling disconnected. Most humans run into debt at the Bank of Life, not because they have not started off with a good plan; most will fail due to poor asset-rebalancing practices.

But the good news is that it is not all about the quantity of time spent that makes the biggest difference at the Bank of Life— often the quality of time is even more important. For example, if a great deal of one's available time is being invested into one account (and this account is often called work), one can still grow wealth in the other accounts by being exceptionally present, for example, during a mediation practice or when being with the people you love.

So think about it: What core accounts of your life deserve more of your precious time and attention? How can you rebalance your time, energy, and presence to counteract on the imbalance created?

3. Settle on smart ways of investing your time

Every banker knows there are smart and not-so-smart ways of investing. The same is true for the way we spend our time. Some of our daily behaviors lead to great returns, while others do not. I am simplifying things here, but to increase your self-awareness as a good time investor, I differentiate between four different ways of spending our time:

Disaster Strikes Activities: These are activities that are not particularly enjoyable in the here and now and then lead to negative outcomes in the future. You might wonder—Why on earth should I engage in such activities at all? And that is a good question to ask. But still many of us unconsciously choose short-term discomfort in order to experience even more long-term pain in the future. Even if this does not make sense at all. What are such activities for you? Think twice if your immediate answer is you do not have them in your life. For some it might be to hold on to a bad relationship for too long; for others it might be being stuck in the virtual world for no good reason or eating addictive food that you have a love-hate relationship with.

Ice Cream Activities: These are activities that are enjoyable in the here and now but may lead to negative outcomes in the future. Like drinking alcohol, indulging in delicious food that might not be particularly healthy, spending money for consumption's sake— there are many other such examples. In the right dosage, these kinds of activities can make life more enjoyable, but if you overdose those ice cream activities, which happens easily, they will lead to many negative returns in the future. What are these ice cream activities for you? And how can you make sure that you engage with them in the right dosage?

Willpower Activities: These are activities that require willpower to engage in but lead to positive outcomes in the future. Doing a hundred sit-ups in the morning, eating healthily, switching off from screens in the evening—all of these could be willpower activities for you. However, with time and the right attitude, we can often turn this kind of activities into which I refer to as "five-star activities." If your life is filled up with those, you are on the right track to diminish wasting time in your life and maximize your returns.

Five-Star Activities: These are activities that are enjoyable in the here and now and lead to positive outcomes in the future, for oneself and for others. So if you could turn eating healthily, exercising, relaxing, sleeping, innercising, pursuing your ikigai, nurturing your relationships, and so on and so forth into five-star activities, you will invest your time to your very best abilities. Writing a book that will help people make better decisions on how to spend their time and enjoying the process of doing so, might also land in this category. These kinds of activities receive a triple-A rating at the Bank of Life.

So, the question is: What classes of behavior do you engage in on a daily basis?

4. Automate your sunshine habits

If we had to reinvent the world every day, we would run out of time in no time. And if we had to relearn everything every day, we would not be able to develop ourselves beyond primal functioning. This is why much of what we think, feel, and do is automated. And at the Bank of Life, we take advantage of these deeply ingrained mechanics inside our brain. Just like in the world of finance, where we advise our clients to automate certain procedures to operate efficiently, we do the same at the Bank of Life. Whatever your portfolio looks like, we ask you to automate some of your behaviors that will consistently pay into these different accounts. Habits compound over time. Even small ones. And that is true for bad habits, which lead to capital depreciation, as it is true for good habits, which help us to build a good life for ourselves. So, when you settle on the Big Five accounts that we have put forward, we would give you the following five questions to reflect about:

1. Health: How do you want to invest your time to nourish your physical wellbeing? What habits do you want to establish and commit yourself to?

2. Psychology: How do you invest your time to cultivate and nurture a psychology that serves you? What habits do you want to establish and commit yourself to?

3. Relationships: How do you invest your time to create meaningful relationships in your life? What habits do you want to establish and commit yourself to?

4. Work: How do you invest your time to create a work life that provides meaning to you and others? What habits do you want to establish and commit yourself to?

5. Finances: How do you invest your time to create the financial means that you need to live a good life? What habits do you want to establish and commit yourself to?

5. Keep a longtime perspective and have faith

The last principle is also borrowed from the world of finance. Every good investor knows that the sun is not always shining. There are bull markets and there are bear markets. There will be sunny days when things will feel easy and fall into place, and there are going to be some cloudy days when things will be more challenging. However, a change in our orientation to time can dramatically affect how we think about life itself. The challenge is to learn from one's past, nurture a strong sense of well-being and deep gratefulness in the present, and find excitement in thinking about one's future. However, overthinking does not help at all. Just invest calmly and steadily in the right accounts, stay the course in the face of setbacks, and your assets will grow. And do not forget that in life, there is no such thing as perfection—and to search for it is often nothing but a vain activity of the ego and not worth your precious attention. Life usually brings a lot of hardship as well as joy. But if you choose to seek health, love, and meaning and to be of service to others first and foremost, most likely you will have a good chance of succeeding. And there will be many moments of happiness to enjoy too.

In the last months, working on these letters has been my source of meaning, Sophia.

And thinking about you completing this book now, in whatever shape or form it will take, makes me very happy indeed.

What an unexpected twist the universe had in mind for me.

Good luck to all!

CHAPTER 20

Sophia: Snow in London

Chronology: ten months after Leonardo and Sophia's
brief encounter at San Francisco Airport.

Sophia watched the London Eye slowly moving around in the distance. It was a cold day in the middle of December. The weather
had changed overnight, and a harsh wind had brought cold air and
unexpected snow with it, covering the city in a magical white blan-
ket. Although it was only a little after three o'clock in the afternoon,
the pallor of a winter evening seemed to have descended upon the
river Thames, cloaking everything in an almost mythical mist.

Sophia had taken the flight to London early in the morning,
using the tickets that Leonardo had sent to her a couple of months
prior. The address and the time she had been expected to be there
had been scribbled on the map that had been in Leonardo's final
envelope, together with the name of a person she was supposed to
meet: Edward. And now she stood in the old-fashioned conference

room of one of the most prestigious publishing houses of London, looking out of the window in awe.

Luckily it had only started snowing more heavily after her plane had already hit the ground. Sophia remembered how the British themselves had joked about how everything seemed to stop working as soon as a few unexpected snowflakes made their appearance when she was still living there. And as suspected, the airline company had informed her right after her arrival that her return flight to Berlin the same evening was canceled. But Sophia did not mind in the least. She would book a nice hotel nearby and enjoy strolling around the snowy streets of London, which were all decorated for Christmas. What a wonderful treat. Perhaps she would meet up with a friend of hers, but she would be just as content spending time on her own. It somehow fitted the occasion. She had missed this city! It truly felt like coming home.

Sophia looked at the River Thames and the boats passing by. Dreamily, she reflected on everything that had happened since meeting Leonardo all those months ago in San Francisco. Receiving Leonardo's letters had sent her on a journey that she could not have anticipated. It had taken her to many different places, inside herself and across Berlin. As invited, she had opened five accounts at the Bank of Life, too, to invest her time more consciously into her health, her psychology, her work, her finances, and her relationships. These were the big rocks in her life. And then she had added another one, which she had called *recreation*. The Big Five + 1. She consciously made sure that she spent more time engaging in activities outside work—exploring the city, visiting art galleries, museums, and cafés more regularly than she had done before. As much as she loved her work and living up to her ikigai, and she truly did, there was a risk attached that it would consume all of her time, and she wanted to be more careful about creating a solid all-weather portfolio and rebalance her time investments regularly just as Leonardo had suggested. Sophia's face brightened up. Leonardo's letters had indeed made a real difference in her life. And as he had predicted early on, they had influenced her thoughts, her emotions, and her behavior in many ways. And Sophia wondered if this would also happen to other readers of the book she was about to publish. Wasn't that the whole point of it all?

And still, despite all the good things that made her feel hopeful about the present and the future, there was a real sense of sadness too. Flying to London marked the end of her journey with Leonardo—at least that was how she perceived it.

A ringing noise stopped her introspection. Was that Big Ben chiming? Sophia checked her mobile phone and saw that Edward was due to arrive any minute, when another thought crossed her mind. She looked at the date and then quickly scrolled through her calendar. It took a moment for her to digest the information, and she felt stupid when she did so. Exactly ten months ago today she had met Leonardo at the airport in San Francisco. Sophia smiled again. These were the kinds of details that Leonardo would have cared for. And in that moment, she felt tremendously grateful but also mystified that she was part of this improbable endeavor.

"Hello, Sophia. So glad to finally meet you."

Sophia flinched. Turning around in a fluster, she looked at the man entering the room, dressed in a casual brown suit, wearing a cream-colored jersey.

"I'm sorry. I didn't want to scare you. I'm Edward," he said as he came closer to her, and Sophia noticed his dark brown eyes, long eye lashes, and prominent jawline.

"That's okay. No worries. Hello Edward. Nice meeting you," Sophia said in a friendly way, moving toward him as well.

"I have been really looking forward to meeting you, Sophia!" Edward added, and the two of them started chitchatting about the unusual weather and how wonderfully Christmassy snowy

London looked. Sitting down at the large conference table, they soon talked about Leonardo and the book project. Leonardo had passed away around the time the final package had arrived on Sophia's doorstep, just as she had suspected. Edward's grandfather had been a close friend of Leonardo's in New York when they were children, and Leonardo had written a letter to Edward, asking him for help, as he knew that Edward, like this father, was a publisher too. Sophia listened attentively, and she noticed that Edward seemed to be almost as intrigued about this project as she was. So far, she had been on the receiving end of Leonardo's letters, but this communication had been a one-way street, and now to speak to a real person about it felt somehow unreal and liberating at the same time.

Edward opened his laptop.

"Have a look. What do you think? It's a rough idea for the cover design."

Sophia stared at the screen. It looked so professional.

Edward smiled. "You like it?"

Sophia didn't move, her eyes still captivated by what she saw on the screen.

"Yes. It's . . . it's beautiful. Really. Very modern. And engaging too. With the golden circle, and the stars."

She paused and Edward waited for her to continue.

"But . . . I'm not sure about the title. Does *Living with Sophia* not sound pretentious? I mean, the book isn't about me."

In the past ten months, Sophia had already invested a substantial amount of time editing Leonardo's writing. In some cases, she had slightly rearranged some of it and amended a few parts here and there to increase the readability of his and Barbara's life story. But in essence, the content of Leonardo's letters had remained the same. In addition, she had collected a notebook full of her own thoughts and experiences that had come to mind in the past ten months. Her idea was to start the book from her point of view, tell-ing the reader about the brief and unlikely encounter that she had had with Leonardo on Valentine's Day ten months ago at the San Francisco Airport. Maybe she would share some of her personal introspections and reflections around her own journey to provide the reader with a sense of orientation, and maybe she would choose a pseudonym to hide her identity. However, she was not going to share *her* life story extensively too—that much was clear. This was Leonardo and Barbara's book, and nothing would change that. Edward interrupted her thoughts.

"I think the title is quite subtle," he added, alluding to the orig-inal Greek meaning of her name. "Sophia (Σοφία), as I am sure you know, means wisdom in ancient Greek."

But Sophia shook her head calmly. "I love how professional it all looks. I really do. But I'm still not sure," she said diplomatically.

Edward nodded and Sophia tried to digest all the information coming her way. And then she added with her eyes lightening up, "What about *The Bank of Life* as a title? I mean that is what it is all about. Isn't it? It is about how we invest our time in life wisely to create a good life for ourselves and others. And it is about Leonardo and Barbara's quest for health, love, and meaning. A quest that we can all feel inspired by."

Edward looked at her and nodded.

"Sophia, this is a special project that we are running on the side, and the usual publishing procedures will not apply in this case. We can discuss these questions later."

Sophia looked grateful and relieved. And then her green eyes sparkled again.

"If I ever get stuck with my writing or the editing of Leonardo's letters, can I contact you?"

Edward's face brightened to a smile. He seemed delighted. "Of course. Whatever contribution I can make, I will."

And then they were both looking at the rough cover visual on the screen again.

"I still like it. *Living with Sophia* sounds great to me," Edward said, pleased with his initial idea.

"Are you interested?" Sophia asked, sounding a bit too flirty. Being quick-witted was a quality of hers that she had cultivated. But she sometimes frightened herself with how words could come out of her mouth seemingly without passing through her brain first. She blushed and Edward started laughing.

"Don't worry, Sophia. I'm happy that Leonardo has picked you out of all people and then contacted us. And I will consider the offer!"

Now they both laughed, and Edward added, "There are two more things that I need to cover."

Sophia raised the index finger of her right hand. "And I have one too."

"Then you go first."

Sophia hesitated—she did not want to jump the queue—but then she opened her bag and took out the key that Leonardo had sent to her two months prior.

"What is this about?" Sophia asked.

Edward smiled knowingly. "This might be one of the two things I wanted to explore with you too."

He fiddled through his documents and handed her a piece of paper.

"Leonardo has arranged a meeting for you with a notary here in London at the beginning of the new year. Here is the address, the name of the notary, and your appointment. The key most likely belongs to his beach house in Santa Barbara. I think he intended to turn it into a writers' retreat, but I'm not sure how this involves you exactly."

Sophia was dumbstruck. Now she really felt like she was part of a movie. She'd had this sensation many times since meeting

Leonardo at the airport in San Francisco ten months ago, but it felt even more surreal now. She stared at the piece of paper in her hand.

"There seem to be more surprises out there for you, Sophia. Let me go to my office—I have one more, and it isn't even Christmas Eve yet."

Edward chuckled and Sophia went over to the window again, wondering what could possibly happen next. There were people on the street rushing around for work, for love, for Christmas shopping. London, a place both old and new, where the most historic buildings were right next door to its newest skyscrapers, had always spoken to her. For her it had been an inspiration, and it had hurt her badly leaving it behind just to escape an unhappy relationship. For quite a few years, she had thought that this was the city where she would want to settle for life. But Berlin was now entering into her heart too. And maybe she would return here someday. She shrugged her shoulders; at that moment, it wasn't important to know that for sure. Turning her head to the right, she glanced over to the London Eye. Though it was snowing, the giant wheel was still making its rounds.

A few minutes later, Sophia heard footsteps behind her, and she saw Edward approaching her with an envelope in his hands. Filling her lungs with air, she sat down at the table. This was possibly the last time she would receive one of Leonardo's messages. Carefully opening it, she identified the watch that Leonardo had sent a picture of, together with his final notes, the key, the flight tickets, and the map of London. With great care, Sophia took the old watch in her hands, identifying the inscription on the back of the watch case that she had expected:

**Lost time is
never found again.**

She put it down, intuitively pressing her thumbs down the watch back until it snapped open. There was a tiny photograph inside, which showed the face of a woman who indeed looked a little bit like her grandmother. Sophia opened her mouth and closed it again, her hands shaking slightly.

Everybody had always said that Sophia and her grandmother looked alike. However, as suspected, the woman in the picture was not her grandmother. But that didn't matter. It really didn't.

What mattered was that Leonardo had thought this could be the case and that this vague possibility had come to him at that moment in time when he had stumbled across the old watch again, which had made him seek her out of around eight billion people on the planet. And what also mattered was that Sophia had accepted to deliver a speech at this global leadership convention in San Francisco. If she hadn't, none of this would have ever happened. Her picture would not have been on the website of the pharmaceutical company that Leonardo had scrolled through, and he would have never contacted her either. Sophia made a mental note to send a thank-you note to Spencer, her long-term client who had talked her into this assignment despite her initial resistance. Life truly was a mystery. How often this idea had crossed her mind in the past ten months!

Immersed in her thoughts, Sophia walked over to the huge window again, ignoring Edward for the time being. The London Eye caught her attention once more. The Buddhists, with their love for circular thinking, must have gotten this right, she thought to herself. It was the end of the year, Christmas was around the corner, and Sophia was no longer afraid of her attachments to the past. She savored the present moment, and she was open to what the future would bring. There were so many questions out there to be explored, bigger ones and smaller ones. Maybe she should visit the Greenwich Observatory where east meets west at longitude 0° and time all over the world was measured from. It was only half an hour away if she took the tube. Had Leonardo been there as well?

Turning her back to the window, Sophia noticed how Edward had been observing her. And when their eyes met across the huge conference table, she sensed what a great comfort it was that the responsibility of finishing and publishing this book was now a shared one. Of course, she was willing to make the most meaning-ful contribution to it herself, but it was good to know that she could count on a partner in crime to make it happen. Edward smiled at her warmly.

All of a sudden, Sophia wondered if she had just gotten a glimpse into eternal wisdom too, when she had not even been looking for it. This was not the beginning of the end, she suddenly realized, but the beginning of many new beginnings.

There were many more circles to trace, to embark upon, and she was ready for the ride.

✴

Mission for
The Bank of Life

My idea for this book was first and foremost to write a *story* that would encourage readers around the world to

- increase *their feeling of agency about their health* and their life in general and

- generate an interest in the emerging science of health creation.

Struggling with some debilitating health issues myself for decades in the past, I found out the hard way that the health care system, as it is set up right now, is not necessarily designed to treat or even cure chronic conditions or to support us in accessing maximum health and wellbeing for ourselves.

Of course, one shall not ignore the achievements of modern medicine. After all, as already pointed out by Leonardo in this story, the emergence of this field has led to some of the most amazing advancements in human history. And it would be ignorant not to be in awe of those developments and, indeed, irresponsible to not make adequate use of them when in need.

However, many of the chronic health challenges we are facing these days as a society must be met with a more holistic approach to health creation, which follows a bio-psycho-social paradigm, to be successful. Fortunately, a new science of health and longevity is being created at an unprecedented speed these days, and there is a new generation of open-minded, holistically thinking doctors emerging who are willing to work alongside their patients to help *them* to help *themselves*. Because within this new paradigm, everybody is seen as an active player in the process and not just a passive spectator of one's health and wellbeing. This comes of course with a new sense of responsibility for one's fate in this area of life, but it leads to more empowerment, too.

In another life, I might become a medical doctor and healer myself to help other people create more health for themselves. In this life, in addition to being a coach for many, I hope to make a small contribution with this book toward inspiring people around the world to learn more about health creation and increase their feeling of agency in the process. The biggest opportunities to create health and wellbeing for ourselves across the different areas of our lives are more often than not either within us or within our reach!

If you feel that you want to support this mission, you can help by recommending *The Bank of Life* to others who would enjoy reading it or by leaving a review on Amazon; this would be much appreciated.

Kindest regards,
Katja

Acknowledgments

This book is the result of a lifetime of accumulating insights and being at the receiving end of love, friendship, education, and a career that offers many exciting opportunities for learning and development. The fundamental ideas that this book is built upon have been percolating for decades. Still, moving from concept to creation takes many people. And I would like to acknowledge those people who have been most instrumental in the process of writing this book directly or indirectly:

My parents, Irmtraud and Helmut Krückeberg, for their pure existence and often making it possible to work on this book at all. My daughter, Jolanda, whose input genuinely made this book better. Dominik Wakeford for being an outstanding, critical editor in chief. Christoph Martin Schmidt for being the number one motivating force and feedback provider behind the scenes. Carola Conze for being my best friend, first reader, encourager, and editor. Simone Owzarek for giving me enlightening feedback that shaped the final version of the book. Peter Krone and Felix Maria Arnet for providing critical insights during the design process. The wonderful Greenleaf Publishing team from Austin, Texas—Anna Jordan, Danielle Green, Daniel Sandoval, Jen Glynn, Jen Rios, Neil

Gonzales, Madelyn Myers, and Tess Newton—for being awesome, professional, and genuinely interested in the art of publishing. Felix Wegeler and the real Dancan Sandys for being a lighthouse of inspiration for the Africa episode in the Bank of Life and beyond.

And, last but not least, I want to say thank you to: Alicia Molina Parra, Daniela Dosch-Boden, Desi Kimmins, Dr. Gerald Wiegand, Dr. Hajo Schulz, Dr. Martin Schulz, Dr. Paul Aitken, Dr. Scott Lichtenstein, Dr. Walter Kromm, Dr. Walter Samsel, Inger Buus, Jerome Doherty-Bigara, Jolanda Anna Marie Krückeberg, Jon Morton, Jorgen Thorsell, Lothar Diete, Kerstin Krückeberg, Luca-Sophie Krückeberg, Marco Bode, Maria Costa, Nina Conze, Oliver Wagner, Prof. Dr. Ben Bryant, Prof. Dr. Carola Hillenbrand, Prof. Dr. Jane McKenzie, Prof. Ian Turner, Prof. Dr. Wolfgang Amann, Professor Dr. Erich Barthels, Rebecca Abigania, Sandra Raca, Saskia Osterhold, Sigrun Conze, Tim Osborne Jones, Dr. Sally Bonneywell, Dr. Dena Michelli, and Zoltan Kaszia for acting as my mentors, supporters, and sources of inspiration in the book writing process and at different stages of my life.

Bibliography

Amen, Daniel. "Change Your BRAIN, Change Your LIFE! These Hacks Will Improve Your BRAIN | Dr. Daniel Amen." Tom Bilyeu. August 26, 2021. Video. https://www.youtube.com/watch?v=1zrg2Vanfco.

Antonovsky, Aaron. *Unraveling The Mystery of Health: How People Manage Stress and Stay Well*. San Fransisco: Jossey-Bass, 1987.

Antonovsky, Aaron. *Health, Stress and Coping*. San Fransisco: Jossey-Bass Publishers, 1979.

Aristotle. Aristotle's Theory of the Good Life. In: Hall, Edith. *Aristotle's Way: How Ancient Wisdom can change your life*. Penguin Books, 2020.

Assaraf, John. *Innercise: The New Science to Unlock your Brain's Hidden Power*. San Diego: Waterside Productions, 2018.

Bach, David. *The Automatic Millionaire: A Powerful One-Step Plan to Live and Finish Rich*. New York: Crown, 2016.

Bilyeu, Lisa. "How to Take Full Ownership of Your Own Health | Lisa Bilyeu on Health Theory." Tom Bilyeu. September 5, 2019. Video. https://www.youtube.com/watch?v=YBxWS26CdfI.

Blixen, Karen. *Out of Africa*. Victoria: Reading Essentials, 2019.

Brown, Walter A. *The Placebo Effect in Clinical Practice*. Oxford: Oxford University Press, 2012.

Brueck, Frank. *Ikigai for Leaders and Organizations: The Way to Individual and Collective Purpose and Meaning.* Self-published, Lulu, 2020.

Buettner, Dan. "504: Dan Buettner on the Secrets for Living Long & Well." *The Rich Roll Podcast.* March 9, 2020. Podcast. https://www.richroll.com/podcast/dan-buettner-504/.

Buettner, Dan. *The Blue Zones: Lessons for Living Longer from the People Who've Lived the Longest.* Washington D.C.: National Geographic Partners, 2010.

Buettner, Dan. *The Blue Zones of Happiness: Lessons from the World's Happiest People.* Washington, D.C.: National Geographic Partners, 2017.

Bulsiewicz, Will. "Gut Health Expert on How Fiber Optimizes Your Microbiome | Dr. Will Bulsiewicz on Health Theory." Tom Bilyeu. April 8, 2021. Video. https://www.youtube.com/watch?v=sXe6cvROhVg.

Chatterjee, Rangan. "5 Minute Habits to Change Your Life | Rangan Chatterjee on Health Theory." Tom Bilyeu. October 8, 2020. Video. https://www.youtube.com/watch?v=QUPGDThiRM0.

Chatterjee, Rangan. *Feel Better in 5: Your Daily Plan to Feel Great for Life.* Dallas: BenBella Books, 2020.

Chatterjee, Rangan. *The 4 Pillar Plan: How to Relax, Eat, Move, Sleep Your Way to a Longer, Healthier Life.* London: Penguin Life, 2017.

Clear, James. *Atomic Habits: An Easy & Proven Way to Build Good Habits & Break Bad Ones.* New York: Avery, 2018.

Cooley, Mason. "Regret for wasted time is more wasted time." Goodreads. https://www.goodreads.com/quotes/160251-regret-for-wasted-time-is-more-wasted-time#:~:text=Quote%20by%20Mason%20Cooley%3A%20E2%80%9CRegret,time%20is%20more%20wasted%20time%20E2%80%9D.

Covey, Stephen R. *The 7 Habits of Highly Effective People: Powerful Lessons in Personal Change.* New York: Free Press, 2004.

Dispenza, Joe. *Breaking the Habit of Being Yourself: How to Lose Your Mind and Create a New One.* Carlsbad: Hay House, 2013.

Dispenza, Joe. *You Are the Placebo: Making Your Mind Matter.* Carlsbad: Hay House, 2014.

Doctorow, E.L. "Writing is like driving at night in the fog. You can only see as far as your headlights, but you can make the whole trip that way." Goodreads. https://www.goodreads.com/quotes/53414-writing-is-like-driving-at-night-in-the-fog-you.

Duhigg, Charles. *The Power of Habit: Why We Do What We Do and How to Change.* New York: Random House, 2013.

Dweck, Carol S. *Mindset: The New Psychology of Success.* Rev. ed. New York: Ballantine Books, 2007.

Dyer, Jeff, Hal Gregersen, and Clayton M. Christensen. *The Innovator's DNA: Mastering the Five Skills of Disruptive Innovators.* Boston: Harvard Business Review Press, 2019.

Epstein, Mark. "Believe In Yourself, Get Uncomfortable & Find PEACE | Dr. Mark Epstein." Tom Bilyeu. April 5, 2022. Video. https://www.youtube.com/watch?v=gxmNsA_F33o.

Fields, Jonathan. *Sparked: Discover Your Unique Imprint for Work that Makes You Come Alive.* Nashville: HarperCollins Leadership, 2021.

Ford, Henry, "Whether you think you can or you can't—you're right." Goodreads. https://www.goodreads.com/quotes/978-whether-you-think-you-can-or-you-think-you-can-t--you-re.

Frankl, Viktor E. *Man's Search for Meaning.* Boston: Beacon Press, 2006.

García, Héctor, and Frances Miralles. *Ikigai: The Japanese Secret to a Long and Happy Life.* New York: Penguin Life, 2017.

Goleman, Daniel. "Psychologist Daniel Goleman Reveals How to Strengthen Your Emotional IQ." Tom Bilyeu. January 7, 2021. Video. https://www.youtube.com/watch?v=kQnEvSU1Buc.

Goleman, Daniel and Richard J. Davidson. *The Science of Meditation: How to Change Your Brain, Mind and Body.* New York: Penguin Life, 2018.

Gottlieb, Lori. *Maybe you should talk to someone: A Therapist,* Her *Therapist, and Our Lives Revealed.* New York: Harper, 2019.

Graziosi, Dean. "The SECRET HABITS Millionaires Use Everyday That YOU CAN COPY! | Dean Graziosi." Tom Bilyeu. September 18, 2018. Video. https://www.youtube.com/watch?v=7Jye1ZwgxaM.

Hesse, Hermann. *The Glass Bead Game.* Edited by Richard Winston and Clara Winston. New York: Picador, 2002.

Honda, Ken. *Happy Money: The Japanese Art of Making Peace with Your Money.* New York: Gallery Books, 2019.

Huberman, Andrew. "Master Your Sleep & Be More Alert When Awake." *Huberman Lab.* January 11, 2021. Podcast. https://hubermanlab.com/master-your-sleep-and-be-more-alert-when-awake/.

Huberman, Andrew. "This Neuroscientist Shows You the Secrets to Obtaining A Growth Mindset | Andrew Huberman." Tom Bilyeu. May 21, 2020. Video. https://www.youtube.com/watch?v=OGa_jt3IncY.

Hyman, Mark. *Food: What the Heck Should I Eat?* New York: Little, Brown Spark, 2018.

Hyman, Mark. *The Pegan Diet: 21 Practical Principles for Reclaiming Your Health in a Nutritionally Confusing World.* New York: Little, Brown Spark, 2021.

Hyman, Mark, and Casey Means. "489: The Worst and Best Foods for Your Blood Sugar." The Doctor's Farmacy. Febuary 2, 2022. Podcast. https://drhyman.com/blog/2022/02/02/podcast-ep489/.

Jamieson, Joe. "5 Things You Need to Know About the Maasai." *Work the World* (blog), https://www.worktheworld.com/blog/5-things-you-need-know-about-maasai.

Kirsch, Iriving. *The Emperor's New Drugs: Exploding the Antidepressant Myth.* New York: Basic Books, 2010.

Kuhn, Thomas S. *The Structure of Scientific Revolution.* Chicago: University of Chicago Press, 1962.

Lempke, Anna. *Dopamine Nation: Finding Balance in the Age of Indulgence.* New York: Dutton, 2021.

Lugavere, Max. "Max Lugavere On What to Eat to Optimize Your Brain | Conversations with Tom." Tom Bilyeu. March 19, 2020. Video. https://www.youtube.com/watch?v=I7_Ay7snzQ0.

Malkiel, Burton G. *A Randowm Walk Down Wall Street: The Time-Tested Strategy for Successful Investing.* 12th ed. New York: W. W. Norton & Company, 2020.

Maslow, Abraham H. *Motivation and Personality.* 3rd ed. London: Longman, 1987.

McGilchrist, Iain. "Everything You Know About the BRAIN is WRONG! Here's How the Brain ACTUALLY Works | Iain McGilchrist." Tom Bilyeu. November 11, 2021. Video. https://www.youtube.com/watch?v=6Dtp1-BCZzc.

Mindell, Phyllis. "'War and Peace' in 20 Minutes? If You Care What It Says, Read." *The New York Times.* September 3, 1995. https://www.nytimes.com/1995/09/03/opinion/l-war-and-peace-in-20-minutes-if-you-care-what-it-says-read-449395.html.

Mittelmark, Maurice B., et al. *The Handbook of Salutogenesis.* New York: Springer, 2017.

Mylett, Ed, and Lewis Howes. "Struggling in Life? What You NEED to Know to Get AHEAD & MAX OUT Your life RIGHT NOW | Ed Mylett." Lewis Howes. May 15, 2020. Video. https://www.youtube.com/watch?v=tt1hCwalT58.

Perlmutter, David. "THIS CAUSES DISEASE – The Worst Foods You Need to AVOID At All Costs! | Dr. David Perlmutter." Tom Bilyeu. February 15, 2022. Video. https://www.youtube.com/watch?v=Qp2erf1IICs.

Perlmutter, David. "This Neurologist Shows You Weight Gain Traps and How to Avoid Them | David Perlmutter." Tom Bilyeu. March 25, 2021. Video. https://www.youtube.com/watch?v=iavLy8ss6lY.

Piatt, Julie. "465: Stop Trying To Fix Other People: Julie Piatt." The Rich
    Roll Podcast. September 4, 2019. Podcast. https://www.richroll.com/
    podcast/julie-piatt-465/.

Piatt, Julie. "637: Julie Piatt Wealth Is The Community You Keep." *The
    Rich Roll Podcast*. October 28, 2021. Podcast. https://www.richroll.com/
    podcast/julie-piatt-637/.

Piatt, Julie. "672: Julie Piatt Intuition vs Intellect." *The Rich Roll
    Podcast*. April 4, 2022. Podcast. https://www.richroll.com/podcast/
    julie-piatt-672/.

Powdthavee, Nattavudh. "Putting a price tag on friends, relatives,
    and neighbours: Using surveys of life satisfaction to value social
    relationships." *Journal of Socio-Economics* 37, no. 4 (2008): 1459–1480.
    https://doi.org/10.1016/j.socec.2007.04.004.

"Project Reports." Round Table School of Hope. Accessed November 23,
    2022. https://rtschoolofhope.wordpress.com/besonderes/berichte/.

Reynolds, Grant. "Berlin: A City Transformed." LinkedIn,
    November 28, 2018. https://www.linkedin.com/pulse/
    berlin-city-transformed-grant-reynolds/.

Richards, Rachel. *Passive Income, Aggressive Retirement: The Secret to
    Freedom, Flexibility, and Financial Independence (& How to Get Started!)*.
    Self-published, 2019.

Robbins, Tony. *Money Master the Game: 7 Simple Steps to Financial
    Freedom*. New York: Simon & Schuster, 2016.

Robbins, Tony. *Unshakeable: Your Financial Freedom Playbook*. New York:
    Simon & Schuster, 2017.

Robbins, Tony. "Why we do what we do." TED Talks. March 4, 2014.
    Video. https://www.ted.com/talks/tony_robbins_why_we_do_what_
    we_do?language=en.

Robbins, Tony, Peter Diamandis, and Robert Hariri. *Life Force: How New Breakthroughs in Precision Medicine Can Transform the Quality of Your Life & Those You Love*. New York: Simon & Schuster, 2022.

Seneca, Lucius Annaeus. "On the Shortness of Life." Translated by John W. Basore. London: William Heinemann, 1932.

Siegel, Cary. *Why Didn't They Teach Me This in School?: 99 Personal Money Management Principles to Live By*. Self-published, CreateSpace, 2013.

Sinclair, David A., and Matthew D. LaPlante. *Lifespan: Why We Age and Why We Don't Have To*. New York: Atria Books, 2019.

Sinclair, David A., and Matthew D. LaPlante. "What to Eat & When to Eat for Longevity | Lifespan with Dr. David Sinclair #2." David Sinclair. January 12, 2022. Video. https://www.youtube.com/watch?v=wD8reCw3Kls.

Singer, Michael A. *The Untethered Soul: The Journey Beyond Yourself*. Oakland: New Harbinger Publications, 2007.

Singer, Michael A., Tony Robbins, and Sage Robbins. "Tony Robbins and Michael A Singer | Breaking Patterns and Finding Inner Peace." Sounds True. November 15, 2019. Video. https://www.youtube.com/watch?v=Sl7UwUOlTLQ.

Sisson, Mark. "How To MELT YOUR FAT & Get In The BEST SHAPE Of Your Life." Tom Bilyeu. September 10, 2020. Video. https://www.youtube.com/watch?v=_PMedVdBFPQ.

"Sparketype Assessment." Sparketype. Accessed November 23, 2022. https://sparketype.com/sparketest/.

Sullivan, Paul. "Guardposts and gardens: walking the Berlin Wall Trail." *The Guardian*, November 5, 2014. https://www.theguardian.com/travel/2014/nov/05/walking-berlin-wall-trail-germany.

"The power of the placebo effect: Treating yourself with your mind is possible, but there is more to the placebo effect than positive thinking." *Harvard Health Publishing*, December 13, 2021. https://www.health.harvard.edu/mental-health/the-power-of-the-placebo-effect.

Trost, Steward G., Steven N. Blair, and Karim M. Khan. "Physical inactivity remains the greatest public health problem of the 21st century: evidence, improved methods and solutions using the '7 investments that work' as a framework." *British Journal of Sports Medicine* 48 (2014): 169–170.

Walker, Matthew, and Andrew Huberman. "Dr. Matthew Walker: The Science & Practice of Perfecting Your Sleep." *Huberman Lab*. August 2, 2021. Podcast. https://hubermanlab.com/dr-matthew-walker-the-science-and-practice-of-perfecting-your-sleep/.

Wang, Zheng, and John M. Tchernev. "The 'Myth' of Media Multitasking: Reciprocal Dynamics of Media Multitasking, Personal Needs, and Gratifications." Journal of Communication 62, no. 3 (2012): 493–513. https://doi.org/10.1111/j.1460-2466.2012.01641.x.

Weil, Andrew. "The Power of Words and How They Can Affect Your Health | Dr. Andrew Weil on Health Theory." Tom Bilyeu. August 27, 2020. Video. https://www.youtube.com/watch?v=MdDCecYr0-4.

Weiner, Eric. "How I learned to go in circles in Kathmandu." *BBC*, February 21, 2018. https://www.bbc.com/travel/article/20180220-how-i-learned-to-go-in-circles-in-kathmandu.

Willcox, Bradley J., Craig Willcox, and Makoto Suzuki. *The Okinawa Program: How the World's Longest-Lived People Achieve Everlasting Health—And How You Can Too*. New York: Three Rivers Press, 2002.

Wilson, Sarah. "Why You Should Quit Sugar, Appreciate Anxiety, and Experiment with Everything | Sarah Wilson. Tom Bilyeu. October 3, 2019. Video. https://www.youtube.com/watch?v=hx4Kr1HJ79E.

Winn, Marc. "005: Marc Winn on Merging Ikigai with the Venn Diagram of Purpose." *The Ikigai Podcast*. December 29, 2019. Podcast. https://ikigaitribe.com/ikigai/podcast05/.

Praise for
The Bank of Life

"*The Bank of Life* accomplishes something powerful: it is as entertaining as it is educating and makes you want to apply the insights gained. Its emphasis on time, self-renewal, and the understanding that life needs us to tap into our own physical, mental, emotional, and spiritual resources are exactly what we need now."

—Deborah Zwilling-Ikpoh, Client Director, Duke CE, London & New York

"Katja Kruckeberg provides a well-founded framework that helps people to orient and reenergize themselves in times of constant change and disturbances. A perfect blend of storytelling, scientific insights, wisdom, and life experience."

—Gero Götzenberger, Global Head of Strategy and Transformation, Mercedes-Benz Mobility AG

"*The Bank of Life* offers an empowering concept that supports people to renew and re-center themselves in this era of unprecedented change and transformation around the globe. This book is insightful, thought-provoking, and rich with scientific ideas and practical experience."

—Maria Cristina Bombelli, founder and CEO, Wise Growth; author; former professor, University of Milano-Bicocca, Italy

"In *The Bank of Life*, Katja Kruckeberg offers an opportunity, not a 'how to guide.' With all the responsibilities placed upon people in today's fast changing world, *The Bank of Life*'s timeless principles can help guide anyone to focus on the things that matter in life and to move towards a stronger, more centered version of themselves."

—Desi Kimmins, Partner, Ernst & Young, London, UK

"Insightful, charming, and full of life's big questions, *The Bank of Life* is an intelligent book you will enjoy reading from the beginning to the end. Inducive storytelling and a real page turner! This deserves to be classic!"

—Prof. Carola Hillenbrand, PhD, psychologist, author (*Harvard Business Manager*, etc.), Henley Business School, UK

"Every so often a book comes along that is somehow different and leaves an imprint on how books are being written. *The Bank of Life* encompasses timeless principles that can help guide anyone towards more health, happiness, and meaning. Compelling and incisive, this will become the new way of storytelling in the context of self-leadership."

—Marco Bode, author, business leader, TV producer, UEFA European Football Championship winner, FIFA World Cup finalist, Germany

"A wonderful book, a real story of the heart shared by a writer with soul. It captured my attention from the beginning to the end. This book truly provides the reader with a holistic guide to the practices and mindsets that create a healthy, fulfilling life. Inspiring and entertaining alike."

—Alicia Molina Parra, lawyer, DEI expert, NGO activist, Director of Global Leadership Development Programs, IE Business School, Madrid, Spain

"*The Bank of Life* is an invitation to explore those factors in life that have a positive influence on one's health and overall wellbeing with curiosity and an open mind. What generates health? That is the question that we need to ask before we start to manage people's diseases! Inspiring, provocative, and entertaining."

**—Prof. Dr. Walter Kromm, medical doctor, researcher,
author, & lecturer, Hannover Medical School and
Frankfurt School of Finance & Management, Germany**

"In this fictional account of one couple's pursuit of health and meaning, the author reveals the key to making the most of our lives. Examining the five accounts that comprise the Bank of Life—physiology, psychology, work, relationships, and finances—she weaves scientific principles into a compelling story to demonstrate how we can get the best returns out of our time."

**—Jérôme Doherty Bigara, coach, consultant, entrepreneur, founder, Circle of
Life (global initiative for transitioning executives), London & Mauritius**

"What is special about this book is not only the content, but also the way in which know-how and practical knowledge are conveyed. What made all the difference was getting to know and like the characters of the story. Katja not only leaves the reader with prose that is fun to read, but also provides tips on the practical implementation of what has been learned . . . clear and crisp."

**—Dr. Gerald Wiegand, MBA (INSEAD),
Country Director, Moderna, Inc., Germany**

"This is a must-read book. In a world that is only getting faster, Katja Kruckeberg gives us an opportunity to pause and think about being more intentional in the way we treat others and develop ourselves. Many people will recognize themselves somewhere in this book The reader's view of themselves and the way they invest the most important resource in life—their time—will not be the same. Have fun finding small things you can do that will make a big difference in your Bank of Life."

**—Spencer Holt, PhD, co-founder & Chief Learning Officer, Global Leader
Group; award-winning educator and podcaster, Philadelphia, USA**

About the Author

Dr. Katja Kruckeberg is an international executive coach, mindset architect, keynote speaker, and CEO of Global Leadership Excellence who works with top management of global organizations on the human side of organizational transformation to harness the power of human performance, intelligence, and potential. Katja has been recognized as a leading expert on mindset and business. Through her consulting, coaching, and speaking services and books, she has reached out to hundreds of thousands of senior executives and individuals in organizations ranging from Fortune 500 to start-up companies to the leading business schools in the world over the course of her career. Katja has authored and co-authored several books on leadership and transformation and holds a Doctorate in Organizational Psychology, an MBA in Business Administration, and MAs in Political Science and Sports Health Science.

As a coach Katja specializes in transition coaching for top executives (e.g., to CEO or board member) and the development of high-performing global teams using state-of-the-art insights from neuroscience, psychology, and her hands-on global business experience.

Katja lives in Germany with her family and her two children. To learn more about Katja, please visit her website:

www.kruckeberg.de

"I have never known an executive coach who taps as powerfully into the art of masterful communication as Katja does. She is knowledgeable, challenging, funny, and incredibly careful in her approach. An international executive coach and facilitator with C-suite qualities."

—Ruth McGill, Global Chief Human Resources Officer, ING Group, Multinational Banking & Financial Services Cooperation, Amsterdam, Netherlands

www.ingramcontent.com/pod-product-compliance
Lightning Source LLC
Chambersburg PA
CBHW031744200326
41597CB00039B/670